Emotional Bridges to Puerto Rico

Perspectives on a Multiracial America
  Joe R. Feagin, Texas A & M University, series editor

The racial composition of the United States is rapidly changing. Books in the series will explore various aspects of the coming multiracial society, one in which European-Americans are no longer the majority and where issues of white-on-black racism have been joined by many other challenges to white dominance.

Titles:

Melanie Bush, *Breaking the Code of Good Intentions*

Amir Mavasti and Karyn McKinney, *Unwelcome Immigrants: Middle Eastern Lives in America*

Richard Rees, *Shades of Difference: A History of Ethnicity in America*

Katheryn Russell-Brown, *Protecting Our Own: Race, Crime, and African Americans*

Elizabeth M. Aranda, *Emotional Bridges to Puerto Rico: Migration, Return Migration, and the Struggles of Incorporation*

Forthcoming titles include:

Erica Chito Childs, *Fade to Black and White*

Emotional Bridges to Puerto Rico

Migration, Return Migration, and the Struggles of Incorporation

Elizabeth M. Aranda

ROWMAN & LITTLEFIELD PUBLISHERS, INC.
Lanham • Boulder • New York • Toronto • Plymouth, UK

ROWMAN & LITTLEFIELD PUBLISHERS, INC.

Published in the United States of America
by Rowman & Littlefield Publishers, Inc.
A wholly owned subsidiary of The Rowman & Littlefield Publishing Group, Inc.
4501 Forbes Boulevard, Suite 200, Lanham, Maryland 20706
www.rowmanlittlefield.com

Estover Road
Plymouth PL6 7PY
United Kingdom

British Library Cataloguing in Publication Information Available

Library of Congress Cataloging-in-Publication Data

Aranda, Elizabeth M., 1973-
  Emotional bridges to Puerto Rico : migration, return migration, and the
struggles of incorporation / Elizabeth M. Aranda.
      p. cm.
  Includes bibliographical references and index.
  ISBN-13: 978-0-7425-4324-9 (cloth : alk. paper)
  ISBN-10: 0-7425-4324-2 (cloth : alk. paper)
  ISBN-13: 978-0-7425-4325-6 (pbk. : alk. paper)
  ISBN-10: 0-7425-4325-0 (pbk. : alk. paper)
  1. Puerto Ricans—Cultural assimilation—United States. 2. Puerto Ricans—
United States—
Psychology. 3. Puerto Ricans—United States—Social conditions. 4.
Immigrants—United
States—Social conditions. 5. Middle class—United States. 6.
Return migration—Puerto Rico. 7.
Puerto Rico—Emigration and immigration. 8. United States—Emigration
and immigration. 9.
Racism—United States. 10. United States—Race relations. I. Title.

E184.P85A73 2006
305.868'7295073—dc22   2006016966

Printed in the United States of America

♾™ The paper used in this publication meets the minimum requirements of
American National Standard for Information Sciences—Permanence of Paper
for Printed Library Materials, ANSI/NISO Z39.48-1992.

To

all the
immigrant women
in my family . . .

mi abuela,
Mary Elizabeth
immigrant to Puerto Rico

mi mamá,
Carmen
return migrant to Puerto Rico

mis hermanas,
Carmen and Mari
migrants to the mainland

my little girl,
Isabel
second generation Puerto Rican

Contents

Tables and Figures

Acknowledgments

The process of writing this book has taken on a life of its own. It began when members of my own family moved to the mainland, leaving gaps in my everyday life in Puerto Rico. Years later, my own absence from the island left gaps for those I left behind. Through my studies I searched to make sense of how centuries of history contributed to my own struggles adapting to life as an educational "migrant." One of the outcomes of this journey is found in these pages.

As I interviewed other Puerto Ricans who had their own life stories to tell about, I understood more about my own background. I thank each one of those who shared their experiences and emotional struggles with me—a perfect (Puerto Rican) stranger. They selflessly allowed me to come into their lives and get glimpses into their worldviews; for that I am sincerely thankful. Without their honesty and candor, this book would have never been written.

I owe a lot to the individuals and groups that directly and indirectly supported this research. The Sociology Department at Temple University provided seed money to pay for data analysis; Temple University's Future Faculty Fellows Program allowed me to spend two full-time years on this and other projects. The University of Miami's General Research Support Award and the James W. McLamore Summer Award also helped in completing the final stages of the manuscript. I'd also like to thank *Gender & Society* and the *American Behavioral Scientist* for allowing me to use previously published material in this book.

Mentorship from Temple University's faculty was crucial during the early stages of this project, particularly from Sherri Grasmuck, Annette

Lareau, Judy Goode, and Julie Press. Nobody believes me when I tell them that my dissertation defense was a gratifying experience. I owe this to you. I also appreciate Sherri's guidance throughout my last years of graduate school, particularly when the birth of Isabel, my daughter, shifted my plans. I appreciate her support as a mentor and fellow mother.

Several persons were crucial in helping me with the transcribing of the data. Lucy González, Jeanette Incerni, Carmen Aranda, and David Aranda were especially helpful in this stage of the project. Juan and Carmen Aranda provided their own seed money to finance the expeditious transcribing of the data. Data analysis was truly a "family affair."

As I wrote and rewrote this book over the past five years, there have been some individuals who have given selflessly to the "cause." Whether it was by providing feedback, providing moral support, or babysitting my daughter, their efforts helped me get where I am today. Thanks to Susan Eichenberger, Mayra Cordero, and Barb Zsembik and her family for their help during a very difficult time in my life. Thanks also to Tom, Rosana, and Emile de Planque; their support and assistance with Isabel freed up some time for me to write.

I also owe a lot to those who more recently supported me in the latest reincarnation of this book. I thank Silvia Pedraza, Suzanne Oboler, Rob Smith, Winnifred Poster, and Peter Kivisto for their feedback on manuscripts that contained some of the ideas in this book. Rosa Chang and Sahily Serradet, students at the University of Miami, also provided valuable research assistance. I also thank the anonymous reviewer who saw potential in the earlier draft of this manuscript. Her comments proved to be invaluable in rewriting and preparing the manuscript for publication.

I am very appreciative of Joe Feagin, who has always seen the value in my work and encouraged me to publish it. I thank him for the opportunity to contribute to this series. I also appreciate the help of Jorge Duany, who read and commented on the entire manuscript, and provided moral support on many occasions. I appreciate his mentorship and friendship. My colleagues at the University of Miami, especially Amie Nielsen, Elena Sabogal, Sallie Hughes, Joanne Kaufman, Tami Eitle, and George Wilson have read and provided valuable feedback on earlier drafts of these chapters. I am grateful for their support during this stressful time, and to all of my colleagues in the Department of Sociology for believing me when I told them that the book would be done soon. I also thank Chloé Georas for graciously allowing me to reprint her poems in this book. Her work has captured artistically many of the emotions I have felt in my fifteen years of mainland living.

My family has been a steady source of strength for me as I worked to complete this project. My mother Carmen and father Juan, along with my sisters Mari and Carmen; my brothers Juan, Robert, David, and Michael;

their spouses Suzanne, Ginnie, Chris, and Alysia; and their children Jennifer, Robert, Allie, Eva, Sarah, Maya, Kenzie, Jack, Emma, and Gracie have all contributed—whether they knew it or not—to my daughter's and my own well-being. The two Carmens, in particular, have given me the energy and support that I needed as I attempted to balance the life of a scholar with single motherhood. I know I would not be where I am today without their emotional, financial, and care-giving support. Words cannot express how I feel about them.

I owe a lot to my daughter, Isabel, and the man I will marry very soon, Ray. Both of them have sacrificed a lot as I took time from them to formulate my thoughts and put them on paper. As Isabel approaches her seventh birthday, I realize that she is as old as this project. I hope that one day she reads it, and feels proud that she was my primary source of inspiration. I also am grateful to Ray, who has believed in me and encouraged me to see this project through. His love and faith in me have proven to be the ultimate cure to writer's block. I am very grateful to him for showing me where "home" really is; I look forward to showing him now what I am like when I am not writing a book.

feet

amphibian sorcerers
shores between earth and air
unleashing bodies from places

feet
migrate from their soles
minus wheres heres and theres
fossils of an age when land existed

feet
haunted by places
unfolding across my body like horizons
anatomy of departures
a "t" lingers next to this here
my feet stray away from each other
one goes there
over there
over a there
a ghostly foot that drags me elsewhere

my tongue is there
exiled in my body
ambushed in my mouth
trance . lating me to myself
can you hear the "I" in torn?
this is not English I speak

Poem

this is not a woman you see
this is not whiteness I breath
your neighbor that

passes

but never stays beyond

lingering

Chloé S. Georas

1

~~

Where is Home?

Living Transnational Lives

R osana lives in a two-story house that her aunt owns in a suburb of San Juan, Puerto Rico. Rosana, her teenage son, and her mother occupy the bottom floor; her aunt lives on the top floor. In her forty-four years, Rosana, who was born and raised in Puerto Rico, has a long history of migration. She initially moved to the mainland to attend college in Boston. A couple of years after graduation, she moved to Brazil and met her soon-to-be husband. They got married in Puerto Rico, and planned to settle on the island. In spite of her college degree, Rosana had difficulties finding an island job. The couple decided to relocate to the mainland United States.[1] Rosana and her husband lived for some time in several different states including Texas, Florida, and then Virginia. After years of mainland living and a divorce, Rosana resettled in Puerto Rico with her son. She has lived in her aunt's house for several years. On the day I interviewed her however, Rosana was packing: she was moving to the United States for the third time. When asked how she felt about this, she responded:

> "*Me da pena* . . . I feel bad. *Me siento como una dualidad* . . . I feel like I have a duality. I feel bad leaving *Mami*, and my aunt. I am a natural care taker, but at the same time I realize that I have to find something more [economically] stable."*

Rosana's "duality" is both a cause and consequence of her many moves back and forth between the United States and Puerto Rico. Rosana's story,

---

*In most interviews, respondents spoke in Spanish. All quotes included herein have been translated into English. In some cases, however, I include parts of the original Spanish quotation to add emphasis to the ideas I illustrate.

however, is not atypical. The twentieth century saw massive emigration rates from Puerto Rico. In 2004, almost half of all Puerto Ricans lived in the mainland United States (about 3.87 million, compared to 3.9 million Puerto Ricans who lived on the island).[2] Even though the height of Puerto Rican migration (known as the Great Migration) was in the two decades following World War II, recent decades have seen migration rates equal or surpass the rates of the Great Migration. In the 1990s, almost 8 percent of island Puerto Ricans moved to the mainland.[3] Rates of return migration are also large. U.S. census data reveal that 3.2 percent of the island's population in 2000 was living outside of Puerto Rico in 1995. Moreover, of Puerto Ricans living on the island in 2000, 6.1 percent were born in the United States.[4]

The political, economic, and sociocultural links between the island and the U.S. mainland have created, as some have argued, a nation of commuters[5] who navigate through the landscapes of global capitalism by way of migration. Since Puerto Rican back-and-forth migration patterns have surfaced, social scientists have been attempting to explain the character, extent, and reasons behind the high rates of mobility.[6] As a U.S. Commonwealth, Puerto Rico's political relationship with the United States lays the groundwork for these patterns. However, much of what we know about Puerto Rican migrants has focused on mobile populations lured by manufacturing jobs whose settlement patterns in Rustbelt cities were rooted in the early labor migrations of the 1940s and 1950s. Less understood are the recent patterns of migration and settlement of broader segments of the Puerto Rican population and how these have emerged as livelihood strategies in a restructured global economy.

In this book I examine the migration experiences of the Puerto Rican middle class, a group that has been virtually absent from research on Puerto Ricans specifically and race-ethnic minority groups generally. I focus on mainland Puerto Ricans' subjective interpretations of their experiences of migration and incorporation into U.S. society, as well as the experiences of Puerto Ricans who have returned to the island following mainland settlement. In addition, I study those for whom multiple back-and-forth moves have left them in an in-between settlement condition, or as some would say, *"con un pie aquí y el otro allá . . .* with one foot here and the other there." Based on in-depth interviews with mainland Puerto Ricans and interviews with return migrants in Puerto Rico, this book examines how Puerto Ricans make sense of their social positions in the landscapes of global capitalism.

"TRYING TO DECIDE WHERE HOME IS"

"Trying to Decide Where Home Is" was a controversial subheading in an article that appeared in *The New York Times* in 2000. The article addressed the trend in which Puerto Ricans are relocating from New York to the island. Of those who returned to the island, one woman was quoted as saying, "You belong here. . . . You feel it; nobody questions it. There's no hostility. I think you don't realize how much that takes a toll." Of those who still resided in the city, one man expressed that he would never dream of returning to the island: "Why would I want to leave the vital electronic center of the world, the most interesting cultural capital of the world?" Among others who remained in New York, one woman expressed that she was only able to do so after a conscious decision "to embrace this country." She continued, "You have to make a conscious decision that you're part of this or not. . . . We're always taking the position of outsiders, outsiders that are not willing to give up the dream of going back to the island. You ask yourself, am I betraying who I am? When I answered no, then I was able to move forward. But it wasn't easy."[7]

The "in-between" status of immigrants is at the core of the research on transnational populations. Transnationalism refers to the development of "networks, activities, patterns of living, and ideologies" that span the home and host societies of immigrants, emerging out of long-standing patterns of migration and settlement.[8] In his recent book, Robert C. Smith examines what transnationalism means for the everyday lives of Mexicans in New York. In the course of analyzing how Mexicans lead transnational lives, Smith looks at the practices and relationships linking immigrants and their children to their communities in Mexico. While he includes in the study of transnationalization the meanings ascribed to cross-border exchanges, he also sees transnational life as "embodied in identities and social structures that help form the life world of immigrants and their children."[9] From this perspective, living transnationally is not contingent upon mobility, but also includes the experiences of "stay-at-homes in close relationships with travelers."[10] As such, transnationalization is part of the lived experiences of communities' members around the world, whose social fabric has been altered by patterns of mobility across generations. These patterns of living and how immigrants interpret the accompanying experiences (e.g., adapting to a new society, or adapting to life in the absence of loved ones) embody what Rosana and many of those quoted in the above article feel. While migration can improve one's life chances, it also comes at an emotional cost, even when immigrants maintain their connections to the societies they leave behind. I use Rosana's case to illustrate.

Rosana felt torn. She had to weigh the emotional and economic costs and benefits of living in the mainland versus those of island settlement. As such, she is one of the many Puerto Ricans I interviewed who were engaged in this kind of perpetual search for home. Rosana's long history of migration began when she moved to Massachusetts in 1974 to obtain her college education. After four years in college and one additional year of work in the Northeast, she decided to move to South America. Having found a job, she settled there for two years. She met her future husband there, and they both decided to move to Puerto Rico in the early 1980s to get married.

Once in Puerto Rico, Rosana had difficulties finding work. She believed that many of the road blocks she encountered on the island were due to gender inequality. As a result, she and her husband moved to Texas upon hearing of a job opportunity from one of Rosana's sisters who lived there. Rosana's husband, however, was not so lucky. Rosana explained why:

> *El sufrió mucho* . . . He suffered a lot. *Lo rechazaban precisamente porque era [de afuera]* . . . He was rejected precisely because he was a [foreigner]. He had a vision that when he got there the doors would open for him. I remember. . . . If we went to a party, people were very rude. It was hard for me. I even kissed the ground [of my new home] when I left.

Rosana believed that her husband's Brazilian background was responsible for his difficulties finding work in Texas. She even recounted one time in which her husband told her, "When they find out I am [South American], *'ahí está la puerta* . . . there's the door.'" This marginalization took its toll. Rosana's husband became so depressed that he isolated himself:

> *Ni lo consideraban. Y se hizo bien difícil la vida. Entonces él se deprimió, y entonces no quería salir de la casa.* . . . They wouldn't even consider him. And life got very hard. So, he got depressed, and so he didn't want to leave the house.

After eighteen months of living in the Southwest, Rosana's work place closed down, leaving her unemployed. Rosana and her husband decided that they wanted to leave Texas and go somewhere that was closer to both Puerto Rico and Brazil, and where there was not as much prejudice. They resettled in Florida with the hopes that their lives would improve, and they did; both Rosana and her husband found work. They also had a baby during that time. Rosana explained, however, that the experiences with prejudice continued:

> We still faced prejudice. . . . [P]eople were very nice, but they always made you feel [like], "*¿Ay, de dónde tú eres?* . . . Oh, where are you from?" Every time they would ask, where are you from? And in the end I would say, "*Yo soy de Estados Unidos.* . . . *[Y]o soy americana nacida en Puerto Rico* . . . I'm from the United States. . . . I'm American born in Puerto Rico."

Rosana is white-skinned and blue-eyed with dark blonde hair. Yet, her status as an ethnic minority relegated her to a marginalized position in which she was, nevertheless, the object of prejudice. Rosana recounted an incident when her son, who is also blonde and has blue eyes, was believed to be adopted. The person who inquired about this had overheard Rosana speaking Portuguese to her husband. This person could not believe that an "American"-looking boy—a status conferred by phenotypical characteristics—could be the biological child of "foreigners"—a status conferred by language and cultural characteristics. Rosana recalled her reaction to this experience:

> *[Me sentí] Super mal* . . . [I felt] Very badly. We were all the same color but because we were speaking another language, so they thought the baby was adopted. *Porque era rubito, [ellos asumieron que] tenía que ser Americano* . . . Because he was very blonde, [they assumed that] he had to be American.

Rosana struggled to decipher how it was that the meaning of her ethnic and cultural backgrounds were now such defining features of her experiences. Living in the U.S. mainland resulted in the emergence of an ethnic-minority identity in which she questioned whether or not she belonged in the United States. This search for belonging can be seen in Rosana's many moves throughout the mainland and Puerto Rico. They are indicative of a search for a place that feels like home. The emotional belonging she sought stemmed from her status as an outsider, or "other" in U.S. mainland society. The "other" is conceived as different, never a full member of the national collective imagination. Because of her Puerto Rican roots, and in spite of her whiteness and her U.S. citizenship, Rosana sensed and believed at some level that she would never fully belong. The emotional fallout from this realization was tied to how she interpreted the meaning of migration and her life in a new place.

Puerto Ricans' interpretations of their experiences in the United States reveal much about how they gauge the level of acceptance they get from the receiving society, and in turn, how they react regarding their own patterns of integration and settlement. In this book I explore the relationship between these subjective dimensions of incorporation experiences and how they relate to settlement decisions. I analyze how Rosana's experiences in the mainland United States and those of Puerto Ricans like her affected their likelihood of settling in mainland versus island societies. To place this issue in a broader perspective, I discuss the theories that traditionally have been used to explain international mobility and incorporation into immigrant receiving societies and how the perspective employed in this book fits within these theoretical frameworks.

THEORIES OF INTERNATIONAL MIGRATION
AND IMMIGRANT INCORPORATION

Migration Theories and Perspectives

Much has been written about the reasons why individuals and families leave their homes for a new country. On the one hand, some have argued that migration is caused by geographic differences in the supply and demand for labor. From this perspective, differential wages result in workers from low wage countries migrating to high wage countries.[11] Migration results in an investment in human capital and economic well-being in which people choose to move to where they can be most productive and maximize gain.[12] On the other hand, some have explained population movement from geopolitical and economic perspectives linking migrant flows to global capitalism and economic restructuring.[13] These theories attribute migration to the displacement that results from capitalist penetration into peripheral countries, creating mobile populations susceptible to relocation in core countries such as the United States.

These structural approaches are complemented by studies resulting in the analysis of the characteristics of migrants that make them more likely to move than nonmigrants within established migration streams. Researchers have also examined those factors that sustain migration patterns over time, even when the original reasons for migration disappear.[14] Among these factors, scholars have studied the impact of social capital and networks,[15] gender and gender oppression,[16] human capital and occupational status,[17] and race and class-based oppression[18] upon patterns of migration. In many of these studies, scholars have argued that migration decisions are not made by isolated individual actors, but by larger units of related people such as families or households.[19] These decisions reflect processes in which people act collectively not only to maximize expected income, but also to minimize risks in the labor market.

Incorporating approaches that look at various levels of analysis is part of a broader trend toward a gendered approach to understanding migration in which researchers have departed from solely envisioning migrants as male individuals, and from theorizing about migration from male-centric perspectives.[20] In these studies, researchers have moved from incorporating gender as a variable to examining how gender roles and gendered oppression affect patterns of migration and illustrating how migration is a gendered process at individual, mid-range, and macro levels.[21] In short, it was not just that women had been ignored in migration studies; the underlying assumptions of theoretical frameworks were male-centric. Only recently have women been incorporated into such frameworks, and ways of knowing about migration engendered.

Recent decades have also seen more attention paid to transnational and multinational linkages that interweave communities across borders through the exchange of information, resources, and people, further complicating the study of migration.[22] Within established transnational communities, geographic movement is increasingly part of community life. As a result, immigration scholars continue to be faced with the challenge of developing and integrating new and different theoretical perspectives to explain changing migration patterns.[23]

Theories and Perspectives on Incorporation

Just as there has been a long tradition of studies examining the reasons for migration, there has also been a plethora of research on what happens to immigrants once they arrive at their destinations and become settled. Many debates center around whether immigrants assimilate, under what conditions they assimilate, who they assimilate to, and whether they are successful once they assimilate.[24] Research reveals that there are different modes of incorporation for immigrants depending on the contexts of reception, the conditions of exit from home countries, and the kinds of capital immigrants take with them.[25]

Among the various routes to incorporation are immigrant assimilation to the dominant culture, assimilation to other segments of U.S. society excluding the dominant group,[26] or when immigrants established themselves in ethnic enclaves.[27] More specifically, Alejandro Portes and Rubén Rumbaut have written about "selective acculturation," in which second-generation youth combine aspects of their parents' home society culture with elements of the host society culture into bicultural, hybrid identities.[28]

With the increase in studies illustrating the transnational linkages binding sending and receiving communities, studies on immigrant incorporation now emphasize the ties new immigrants maintain with their home societies. Transnational immigrants are said to have multiple homes as communities around the world are increasingly interwoven into transnational social fields.[29] These social fields serve as the contexts in which "immigrants forge and sustain simultaneous multistranded social relations that link together their societies of origin and settlement."[30]

Recently, scholars have examined the relationship between transnational activities and patterns of assimilation and incorporation.[31] Initially, the concept of transnationalism seemed to challenge assimilation models given that transnational activities were interpreted as an inability to assimilate, or a rejection of assimilation.[32] Assimilation and transnationalism, however, have come to be viewed as concurrent processes.[33] Peggy Levitt and Nina Glick Schiller argue that through the concept of simultaneity we can understand the nature of the dual lives led by transnationals, both those who move and those left behind.[34] Grounded in Pierre Bourdieu's work and building on the work of Linda Basch and her colleagues,[35] Levitt and Glick Schiller elaborate on the concept of a "social field" to mean a "a set of multiple interlocking networks of social relationships through which ideas, practices, and resources are exchanged, organized, and transformed."[36] They argue that identifiable boundaries (such as local and national economies) "should not be understood as necessarily contiguous with the boundaries of social fields." They continue:

> The concept of a social field also calls into question the neat divisions of connection into local, national, transnational, and global. In one sense, all are local in that near and distant connections penetrate the daily lives of individuals living within a locale. But within this locale, a person may participate in personal networks, or receive ideas and information that connect them to others in a nation-state, across the borders of a nation-state, or globally, without ever having migrated. By conceptualizing transnational social fields as crossing the boundaries of nation-states, we also note that individuals within these fields are, through their everyday activities and relationships, influenced by multiple sets of laws and institutions. Their daily rhythms and activities respond not only to more than one state simultaneously but also to social institutions, such as religious groups, that exist within many states and across their borders.[37]

The concept of simultaneity enables an understanding of how transnationalization allows for acculturation and assimilation (economic, residential, and political integration into the receiving society) while still enabling participation in the sending society, thereby facilitating the retention of ethnic identities. In the case of political activism, for example, Luis Guarnizo and his colleagues believe that although U.S. citizenship should act as a "natural barrier" to political transnationalism, the length of residence in the United States increases political participation in the home country among the immigrants they studied. Higher levels of education increase this political participation.[38] Moreover, Levitt argues that many professionals choose to live transnational lives because they have the money and knowledge to capitalize on the economic and political opportunities in both places. She reiterates, however, that this is not always a choice for some who may wish to do so, but cannot due to economic constraints.[39]

In light of these scholarly advances regarding the conditions under which immigrants' lives span borders, it is important to note that research on transnational activities continues to exalt economic activities and exchanges as those that qualify as truly transnational.[40] These narrow definitions exclude the "invisible" work members of kinship networks and communities engage in that support the cross border activities of transnational migrants. They also ignore the reasons that originally were responsible for migrants pursuing activities that lead them to actively engage in cross-border living (e.g., affective ties to the homeland). Some have written about these affective motivations. Peter Kivisto, for example, has stated that remittances are based on "an emotional attachment to those left behind. It is a tie predicated on emotions related to longing, the sorrow of absence, and the desire to remain bonded to one's family."[41] Levitt and Glick Schiller acknowledge these attachments as well:

> Individuals may have some sort of connection to a way of belonging, through memory, nostalgia or imagination, which enables them to enter the social field. When a transnational social field is both created and named, it becomes a transnational social space. These connections, near and far, mean that daily practices, as well as ideas may be shaped by forces not confined to the nation-state. Therefore, some forms of *ways of being* and *ways of belonging* are transnational.[42]

There are still gaps however, regarding *how* these "ways of being" and "ways of belonging" relate to assimilation and incorporation, and how immigrants negotiate the contours of their simultaneous participation in host and home societies. Moreover, with a few exceptions, the subjectivity and emotions that underlie these processes have been under-explored in most dominant accounts of immigrant well-being.[43] With this book I attempt to fill this gap.

Bringing Subjectivity into Perspectives on Immigrant Incorporation

There are "unperceived realities"—gaps between "what is and what is seen"[44]—that characterize the lives of immigrants who live in one location, yet have multiple places they call "home." The subjectivity involved in the process of migration, and at a broader level from living embedded in transnational social fields, is often overlooked in research that for decades has been influenced heavily by rational choice approaches.[45] Whether or not immigrants *feel* like they belong in their new setting is often tangential to understanding immigrant outcomes. This could be because of the notion that the immigrant experience is, by definition, one of dislocation and alienation. How might the context of increasing globalization, however, affect the immigrant experience, particularly when immigrants have the resources to attempt to curtail dislocations? Moreover, within the context of an increasingly diverse and multicultural society, what are the struggles that characterize the immigrants' experiences of incorporation?

Recent studies on transnational migration and the lives of second-generation youth have begun to fill this void in the literature by focusing on the question, "What is home?"[46] Examining the immigrant experience of incorporation from a perspective of subjectivity means that a question such as "What is home" is more than a question; it is an expression of ambiguity and perhaps even loss. Answers to this question are glimpses into the internal states of migrants who might feel conflicting loyalties and are searching for meaning as they come to terms with their own location in the landscapes of global capitalism. The title of an edited volume by Peggy Levitt and Mary Waters, *The Changing Face of Home,* reflects the trend toward increasing research on this subject. The studies included in this volume seek to understand how transnational patterns of living affect assimilation among the children of immigrants. Among the research documented in this book is Diane Wolf's work on emotional transnationalism, which captures the subjectivity implied in being "embedded" in a transnational social field.

Wolf's work contextualizes the struggles of the second generation.[47] Though not immigrants themselves, Wolf contends that emotional transnationalism situates them "between different generational and locational points of reference—their parents', sometimes also their grandparents', and their own—both the real and the imagined."[48] She concludes that pressure from parents to succeed, coping with racism, and other transnational struggles such as the dual nature of "home" result in emotional dislocation among those in her sample and increasing mental health risks (e.g., depression and suicidal thoughts). Many of the other studies documented in this volume describe how members of the second generation interpret their immigrant backgrounds, and how these in turn affect their feelings toward the United States as well as the country of their parents; these chapters examine how these processes shape identity transformations and transnational activities throughout the life course.[49] Absent from this body of research is information about the struggles related to defining "What is home" among members of the immigrant generation itself. Perhaps this gap exists because it is assumed that the immigrant generation never really overcomes the dislocations of the migration experience.

In contrast, Rhacel Parreñas' work on Filipina domestic workers in Rome and Los Angeles focuses on the institutional processes related to incorporation that result in dislocations, which she defines as "the positions into which external forces in society constitute the subject of migrant Filipina domestic workers."[50] Approaching the study of immigrants from the "level of the subject,"[51] Parreñas argues that the experience of migration is embodied in dislocations, or "narratives of displacement."[52] In spite of the differing context of reception in terms of government reception and labor market incorporation that Filipinas encounter in both Rome and Los Angeles, they nevertheless share the experience of similar dislocations that include: partial citizenship in both countries; family separation; contradictory class mobility; and feelings of social exclusion. These dislocations result in ethnic identities that transcend borders and cross national allegiances as well as membership in a global imagined community, all of which are rooted in the positioning of Filipinas in the global capitalist system. Moreover, these identities are based on subjectivities, particularly how systems of inequality affect how immigrants see themselves and interpret their own experiences. In studying these dislocations, or narratives of displacement, Parreñas examines not just how they are formed, but also how they are contested.

I use Parreñas' work as a point of departure in the examination of Puerto Ricans' subjective experiences of incorporation. I seek to understand the dislocations they may or may not experience as colonial migrants, albeit from privileged economic and citizenship backgrounds. One would expect that the struggles inherent in migration and settlement in a new place would be curtailed because of my samples' privileged social positioning. Their status as ethnoracial minorities, however, may result in dislocations akin to Parreñas' subjects.

By focusing on Puerto Ricans' interpretations of their experiences living in the mainland, I attempt to broaden our understanding of the structural constraining factors affecting immigrant incorporation and how they are experienced at the "level of the subject." These internal states are gauged through migrants' retelling of their own migration experiences, revealing the meaning subjects ascribe to their experiences. Even though the interviews I conducted with Puerto Ricans in this study were "removed from actual 'raw' experience",[53] my attempt here is to shrink "the distance between the experiencing subjects and their accounts of lived experience."[54] As Carolyn Ellis and Michael Flaherty have argued,

> Grounding our interpretations in lived experience connects the internal with the social and is in accord with the goal of formulating an understanding of subjectivity from within (Denzin 1989), that is, on its own terms, and not merely as epiphenomenal to other levels of analysis.[55]

Until recently, the subjective dimensions of transnationalism were not systematically incorporated in empirical work, nor were there efforts to link it to other perspectives on migration.[56] This approach however, is crucial to painting a holistic portrait of immigrants and, in the words of Jorge Duany, to "go beyond the narrow view of migrants as simply demographic numbers or passive victims of historical and economic processes, to begin to see them as people of flesh and blood."[57] In theoretical terms, as Wolf has argued, incorporating the emotional dimensions of transnational migration into a theory of migration might help us better understand the context of migration decisions, both at the individual and group levels:

> A transnational approach acknowledges multiple locations of "home" which may exist geographically but also ideologically and emotionally, in addition to a plurality of cultural codes and symbols that go beyond the nation-state. The concept of transnationalism avoids the assumption of linearity in immigrants' thinking, decision making, and changes in practices, interjecting a more complex sense of processes that involve multiple, interacting and perhaps conflicting layers.[58]

Introduced earlier, Rosana's story is worthy of further examination given that her case illustrates the importance of analyzing subjectivities and emotions to better achieve an understanding of the complexities of migration experiences. Rosana's struggles as they related to integrating into mainland life did not end upon her relocation to Florida. After her son was born in the mainland, Rosana separated from her husband, eventually divorcing him. She subsequently moved to Virginia to "start a new life." In the process of looking for a job, Rosana struggled economically and emotionally. She interviewed for several positions in the area. She recounted this experience to me in our interview:

> In one of the job interviews, David [her son] and Mami [mother] . . . she had gone with me to this interview and she had stayed in the "lobby," and I had gone to the interview and practically had the job. And suddenly someone comes in, and the person who was interviewing me said, "*Mira nosotros te íbamos a dar el trabajo pero tú trajiste a tu mamá y a tu hijo abajo y no te podemos dar el trabajo* . . . Look, we were going to offer you the job but you brought your mother and your son downstairs and we cannot give you the job."

Rosana believed they were turning her away because, as her interviewers explained, "*No se podía mezclar familia con trabajo* . . . You couldn't mix family and work." Rosana was devastated at the realization that it would be very difficult for her as a single mother with no social support to pursue a career and be the kind of mother she envisioned for her son. Even though her own mother was with her at this job interview, she was only visiting. This experience was an important turning point in her life:

> *Ahí yo dije: "Ay no, este sitio no es para familias y yo realmente quiero criar este nene bien"* . . . That's where I said, "Oh no, this place is not for families and I really want to raise this child well." That's when I started to get disillusioned. And

although I got the job [a different job]. . . . I told them, "Look, I have decided to return to Puerto Rico to raise my son." . . . *Me dió un "down" horrible* . . . I was terribly down.

The cumulative effect of Rosana's experiences in the United States—those with racial prejudice, gender bias, and the struggles of single motherhood—were that she became very depressed. She did not want her son to be a casualty of her own mainland struggles. Rosana's ideological and emotional conflicts stemmed from the structural constraints rooted in her social position as a Puerto Rican single mother. Although she eventually did find a job, she decided to return to Puerto Rico and raise her son within the context of her extended kinship network. The multiple layers of constraints that emotionally tugged at her in both directions—toward settlement in the island and U.S. mainland—reached a critical mass given life-cycle events such as her divorce, and structural sources of inequality seen in the barriers to combine work and family as a single parent. Her migration status ruptured her embeddedness in any kind of emotional or kinship network (she was not settled in an immigrant community, which typically acts as a form of social support and/or social capital for immigrants);[59] this had the effect of tipping the balance toward settlement on the island where Rosana knew she could count on her mother and other relatives for help.

On another level, Rosana's decision to move back to the island reflected her feelings of disenchantment with the United States—a society she had grown to perceive as hostile. Years of marginalization resulted in feelings of alienation. To minimize these dislocating feelings, she returned "home." Her story is like many other Puerto Ricans whose lives are "stretched across borders."[60] This duality has emotional manifestations, yet the emotions that surface as a consequence of migration, and at a broader level from living transnationally, are dimensions of the immigrant experience often overlooked; they are among the "unperceived realities" that characterize the lives of immigrants who live in one location, yet have multiple places they call "home."

Feelings embody ways in which humans gain knowledge and understanding; they are central to interpretive processes.[61] Yet, successful immigrant incorporation has mostly been measured through objective indicators (e.g., income, occupation, education, and language acquisition). Whether immigrants *feel* like they belong is usually considered tangential. My intent on focusing on Puerto Ricans' lived experiences is to approach the study of incorporation and settlement as social processes in which emotions and cognitions merge into subjective interpretations of where immigrants feel most comfortable; I argue that these feelings determine their levels of emotional embeddedness into a particular society—an alternative assessment of incorporation, albeit a subjective one.

This book examines how subjectivity affects incorporation and settlement. Among the questions I seek to answer are: Among those who live embedded in transnational spaces, under what conditions do they decide to settle permanently in the receiving country versus returning to the sending country, or circulate between both? How are these decisions related to assimilation and incorporation processes? My approach in asking these questions is in line with emotionalist research that emphasizes transcending "the increasingly rationalized analytic languages for investigating everyday life."[62] In short, I analyze the subjectivity of migration, incorporation, and settlement to better understand the motivational infrastructures that contribute to transnational "ways of being" and "ways of belonging."[63] This approach is particularly useful to study the case of Puerto Rico, an island that has exported close to half of its population to the U.S. mainland over the past century.

WHY PUERTO RICAN MIGRATION?

Puerto Ricans have been migrating between the island and mainland for over a century. The New York City metropolitan area alone has more Puerto Ricans than the San Juan area or the island metropolitan areas of Arecibo, Ponce, and Mayaguez combined.[64] Migration has become such an integral part of Puerto Rican life that the thoughts, feelings, and the emotional negotiations required to come to terms with transnational patterns of living (through the absence of loved ones, one's own absence from "home," or feeling caught in between multiple places one considers home) can be profound. This emotion work has become so common that it forms part of the "unperceived realities" of many Puerto Ricans, and immigrants generally. These realities are captured in the following quote of a Puerto Rican author:

> What is "home" for the migrant? . . . Is there a "home" to return to after migration? Is it that easy to believe that "There is no place like home" and to just shake your heels like Dorothy and just be there? Where is "home" after you migrate? Are we all migrant aliens like E.T., always saying "E.T. phone home" and racing out to get a round-trip ticket in order to touch a national identity? Or is "home" portable . . . and all we have to do is to carry it within us whether we are *acá* [here] or *allá* [there], or in midair?[65]

Important to consider in the case of Puerto Rican migration is that certain factors that impact other migration flows, such as political restrictions, are absent. This lack of restriction serves as an internal control that renders the option to migrate more readily available. Puerto Rico's status as a U.S. commonwealth and the U.S. citizenship afforded to islanders early in the twentieth century means that their legal status is not jeopardized by leaving the United States. Puerto Ricans' political status can either result in very low levels of emotional struggles or dislocations (given Puerto Ricans' abilities to go back and forth as they please), or predispose them to high levels of emotional dislocation given the complexity of migration circuits, their vulnerability to the ups and downs of the U.S. economy, and the potential for disruptions resulting from "commuter" lifestyles. When considering that multiple generations within households experience migration, return migration, adaptation to mainland society and culture, and readaptation to island society at different points throughout the life cycle, the need for more research on these complex processes becomes evident, particularly since these patterns of migration have shown no signs of declining. Because Puerto Ricans' quests to maintain their livelihoods often involve mobility, they comprise a group especially suited to explore the emotional realms of cross border experiences and how these are structured by social and cultural transnational hierarchies. Vital to understanding these processes, however, is having a clear understanding of the history of Puerto Rican migration. The following section examines this history.

HISTORICAL BACKGROUND

Puerto Rican migration under U.S. rule dates back to the early twentieth century. After U.S. colonization of the island, labor migrants were exported to other U.S. colonies—including Hawaii and the U.S. Virgin Islands—with many of them making their way back to the island years later.[66] Emigration and return migration continued through the remainder of the century.

World War I, for example, saw thousands of Puerto Ricans exported as labor to U.S. army camps and war industries.[67] Many also served in the Panama Canal Zone. Moreover, the granting of U.S. citizenship in 1917 boosted migration to the mainland as it facilitated the flow of labor. During this time, conditions on the island were "subhuman. . . . Puerto Rico had been turned into little more than a plantation."[68] U.S sugar companies were making huge profits, displacing local landowners, and creating a mass of unemployed workers. Moreover, the Great Depression of the early 1930s greatly affected island conditions, turning the island into a "social inferno."[69] Additionally, Puerto Ricans had little say in their own affairs,[70] in that American sugar companies largely determined U.S.

policy toward the island.[71] During this decade and the one to follow, Puerto Rico would be considered the "Poorhouse of the Caribbean."[72] So dire was island poverty that the U.S. government agreed to provide assistance to the needy; by 1934, 35 percent of the population was receiving some type of aid.[73]

The Great Migration

In the 1940s, per capita income on the island was still as low as it had been forty years earlier when the United States occupied Puerto Rico.[74] During this time, World War II shut down the European labor supply to the United States, resulting in increasing efforts at Latin American labor recruitment. The flow of migrants during this time is also linked to the widespread changes being experienced on the island.[75] Focus on Puerto Rico's economic plight led to the industrialization of the island, which resulted in rapid social and economic changes.

In 1947, Operation Bootstrap was implemented. This program attempted to bring about industrialization to the island by attracting private U.S. capital lured by low wages and a tax-free environment.[76] This resulted, however, in a massive displacement of agricultural workers and heavy urbanization. Additionally, the attractiveness of industrial jobs over agricultural ones, and the inability of island industries to absorb surplus labor, led to large-scale emigration.[77] In other words, for Operation Bootstrap to be effective, the architects of the new economy, particularly after World War II, relied on the emigration of surplus labor believing that the large labor reserve on the island, in addition to overpopulation and poverty, would drain the island's resources. Island government policies, backed by American labor recruitment practices, led to the exportation of surplus labor from the island's abundant reservoir to ease the effects of poverty and unemployment.[78] Thus, large-scale emigration quelled reservations regarding the success of this model of development in Puerto Rico.[79] In short, U.S. imperialism manifested itself not just politically and economically on the island; it also contributed to a massive displacement of the Puerto Rican population, in stark contrast to what had been experienced in prior years. For example, while the 1940s net migration number stood at 145,000, it peaked at 447,000 in the 1950s.[80] This period (1945–1965) is known as the Great Migration.

The Great Migration also has been linked to the booming U.S. economy. Economic "push and pulls" are said to be at the core of Puerto Rican streams of mobility, as island migrants are vulnerable to U.S. economic cycles. The ups and downs of the U.S. economy disproportionately affect the island economy, often magnifying and prolonging the effects of similar recessionary cycles on the mainland. This vulnerability leads Puerto Ricans to seek employment where there is a greater likelihood of finding it, as studies show that their movement is significantly linked to changes in wages and unemployment, both recently and historically.[81] Moreover, in 1952, Puerto Rico acquired the status of a free political entity, associated with the United States.[82] As a U.S. commonwealth, Puerto Ricans were further usurped into the political economy of the United States. These links determine their positions in the landscape of global capitalism. The Great Migration—a period that lasted until the mid-1960s—resulted from the combination of these massive political, economic, and social changes.

Within a few decades, the "Poorhouse of the Caribbean" became the showcase of the Caribbean. The island during the 1950s had the highest average income in Latin America, and was among the most robust democracies in the Caribbean.[83] In fact, U.S. intervention and its economic and political policies toward the island were marketed as the ideal approaches to achieving democracy in a free market economy. Showcasing the case of Puerto Rico also served as a political weapon against Communism during the Cold War era.[84] Throughout this period, migration served as an escape valve: in the late 1950s, 10 percent of the island's population was engaged in external geographic mobility.[85] Much of it continued to be in the form of government-supervised contracts which resulted in the massive transfer of workers over the next two decades. Additionally, in the period between 1955 and 1960, one-third of those living on the island had some direct experience of U.S. life,[86] indicating the emergence of return flows to the island. While three-fourths of the Great Migration remained on the mainland, one fourth of this flow is estimated to have returned to Puerto Rico.[87]

In effect, Puerto Rican streams of migration have been part of larger flows of capital and commodities that are encompassed in the political and economic ties between the island and the mainland. These links were established when the United States occupied the island, and they were further institutionalized when the island government endorsed and encouraged the exportation of its productive and reproductive workers. Migration flows since this time have responded to these links.[88]

Beyond the Great Migration

Puerto Rican net migration decreased dramatically in the 1960s and 1970s relative to previous decades. Scholars attribute this to the fact that in-migration to the island (consisting of return migrants and other immigrants) was low prior to this decade.[89] As such, the 1960s mark the beginning of substantial return flows as well as growing numbers of foreign-born immigrants. Figure 1.1 illustrates the number of island residents

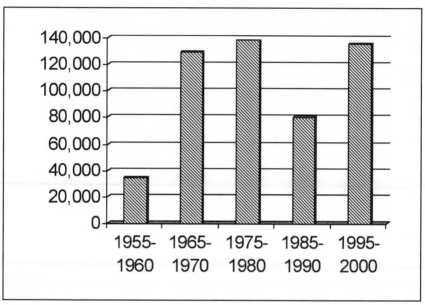

Figure 1.1. Return Migration to Puerto Rico for Persons Five Years of Age or Older, 1960–2000

Source: U.S. Census of Population and Housing in Rivera-Batiz and Santiago 1996, 55; U.S. Census Bureau, Census 2000 Summary File 3.

who in each Decennial Census since 1960 indicated that they were living outside of the island five years prior.

During the late 1960s and 1970s, however, signs emerged that Puerto Rico's model of economic development was failing. In spite of federal and local tax incentives offered to U.S. businesses,

> [p]olicy-makers learned to their dismay that Puerto Rico was no longer competing solely with decaying regions in the mainland, but with the newly industrializing economies. As a result, the traditional firms, which were losing their competitive advantage, evacuated Puerto Rico with alarming frequency.[90]

In response to these trends, government policy shifted by responding to the investment needs of new industries such as pharmaceuticals and electronics, subsidiaries of multinational corporations. In addition, the late 1970s saw changes in the tax exemption policy for U.S. firms with branches in Puerto Rico. As a result, generous federal tax credits attracted "capital-rich, highly mobile, and technologically sophisticated firms."[91] However, the weak employment-absorption capacity of these industries has been reflected in high unemployment rates and low labor force participation rates in Puerto Rico, which peaked during the 1980s. James Dietz argues that migration has been the result:

> It is precisely this dynamic insufficiency of labor demand which leads workers and their families to enter the migratory flow, as they are pushed from the local economic structure in search of employment in the United States, and the dynamic insufficiency of investment is a logical outcome of the workings of the Operation Bootstrap model.[92]

Although return migration continued in the 1980s, the number of in-migrants to the island in this decade was lower than in previous ones.[93] The main reason for this was the boom in the U.S. economy in 1983, and the fact that economic growth on the mainland was not matched on the island.[94] Despite this drop-off, of those entering during this time, 50 percent were Puerto Rican-born return migrants, and one-third were U.S.-born Puerto Ricans who came to reside on the island. In all, one in ten Puerto Ricans residing on the island in 1990 had moved from the U.S. mainland to Puerto Rico since 1980.[95] Moreover, the complex circuits of back and forth migration continued, as 12.3 percent of the Puerto Rican population that had resided on the island in 1980 was no longer living there in 1990.[96] It is important to keep in mind that these data are based on census statistics that tend to be more conservative in their estimates than data from the Puerto Rican Planning Board, which counts air traffic passengers in and out of the island.[97]

When circular migration is taken into account, it is estimated that the number of circular migrants in the 1980s approached that of return migrants for the same decade—130,335 and 158,175 respectively.[98] It is also estimated that 46 percent of circular migrants resided on the mainland for a period of six months to two years, and it appears that the length of their stay was getting shorter over time. Also, evidence suggests that circular migration patterns might follow bimodal patterns "within which some CM [circular migrants] are low on the socioeconomic ladder and others conform to a more 'upscale' image, i.e., middle class, professionally educated migrants, who migrate often, for schooling, business, or other purposes."[99]

In the 1990s, net migration declined to 325,875 from its peak the previous decade,[100] and return migration continued. The percentage of the island's population in 2000 that was living outside of Puerto Rico in 1995 was 3.2 percent.[101] In addition, 6.1 percent of Puerto Ricans living on the island in 2000 were born on the mainland.[102]

It is likely that Puerto Rican migration to the United States will increase in years to come. Economic restructuring, deindustrialization, and the presence of capital intensive industries on the island have all displaced low-skill industrial workers. The phasing out of federal tax incentives and the recent government shutdown are accelerating these processes. In addition, the worsening economic indicators for mainland Puerto Ricans in the early 1990s, and the recent recession engulfing the U.S. economy could lead to an increase in circular migration. Given the high levels of social inequality on the island that propel so many Puerto Ricans on their journeys to the United States, and the trend in which many of these Puerto Ricans make their way back to the island, I argue that the case of Puerto Rican migration can best be understood using a transnational perspective.

HAS PUERTO RICAN SOCIETY BECOME TRANSNATIONALIZED?

There has been some debate in academic circles regarding the use of a transnational perspective to understand Puerto Rican patterns of mobility. How can transnational migration exist when one of the points of reference is not a sovereign nation? Those who ask this question also are likely to argue that the case of Puerto Ricans is most comparable to other streams of migration within the United States, such as the migration of Southern blacks to northeastern cities in the 1930s.

In spite of the island's lack of sovereignty, Puerto Ricans' collective sense of peoplehood has challenged scholars to reconsider the nation in nonterritorial terms. Jorge Duany argues that Puerto Rico is a nation that extends itself across cultural borders (as opposed to political boundaries). Specifically, he argues that the geographical dispersion of the population through migration suggests that the national be decoupled from the political, as diasporic communities renegotiate shifts in their identities from territorially bounded ones to affective, cultural ones.[103] Gina Pérez has also illustrated how Puerto Ricans in Chicago and in San Sebastián lead transnational lives. Her approach to examining Puerto Rican transnational communities focuses on the links that merge these communities into one social field, as Levitt and Glick Schiller would argue. Pérez argues that mobility is not necessary for one to feel part of a transnational community. In fact, those in her study were oriented toward places in which they did not reside, while remaining firmly rooted in the places where they lived and carried out their everyday lives. Overall, these scholars argue that, although Puerto Ricans do not cross international borders when they travel to the United States, they do cross geopolitical, social, and cultural ones, and that Puerto Ricans themselves envision themselves on either side of these borders. Dual frames of reference that juxtapose social, cultural, economic, and political life strengthen the argument that the case of Puerto Rican migration might be better understood if studied from a transnational perspective. I take this approach as well for several reasons.

Some might disagree about the characterization of Puerto Rican migration as transnational given that Puerto Ricans have U.S. citizenship and are, by legal standards, Americans. This logic, however, contradicts the many transnational studies that have emphasized the power of social actors to transcend international borders in their constructions of communities and social relations. Work on how immigrants live and exist in transnational social spaces, referred to as "transnationalism from below"[104] or transnationalization,[105] emphasize the importance of technology and communications in facilitating relationships and community embeddedness, bypassing to the extent possible the controls imposed by nation-states through their political and economic policies. This stands in contrast to "transnationalism from above,"[106] in which states regulate (or do not regulate) the cross-border exchanges of capital, goods, and people. In spite of the emergence of transnational communities, nation-states still play key roles in the structuration of transnational from below. It is in this spirit that I consider the case of Puerto Rican migration to be transnational. That is, while technically U.S. citizens, the waves of migration that have endured throughout the twentieth century have been informed by geopolitics and global capitalism (from above), affected the dispersion and racialization of Puerto Ricans, and resulted in the transnationalization of families and communities.

The relationship between the island of Puerto Rico and the United States is one in which there are "permanent links" to the United States: "common defense, common market, common currency, and the irrevocable link of a common citizenship."[107] However, from "below"—from the perspectives of its people—Puerto Ricans consider themselves a distinct cultural nation,[108] as Duany has argued. Their colonial status reinforces these distinctions, relegating them to the position of outsiders in the U.S. body politic.[109] Although Puerto Ricans are indeed U.S. citizens, Puerto Rico has also been referred to as the "oldest colony in the modern world."[110] The fact that the U.S. Congress has not allowed the island's population to resolve the political status question further reinforces cultural nationalism and perceived distinctions between "Puerto Ricans" and "Americans." The difference lies, in the words of Juan González, in "belonging to the United States but not being a part of it."[111]

It is certainly the case that the political relationship between Puerto Rico and the United States has facilitated the annexation of the island—its economy, its culture, and its people—into that of the United States, in spite of the efforts on behalf of Puerto Ricans toward maintaining their cultural autonomy. This, however, is *also* the case with many other Latin American countries that have been penetrated by either direct or indirect U.S. military and/or economic intervention, especially in recent decades as the United States has sought free trade agreements across the hemisphere. These political-economic relationships increasingly contribute to the global links that result in population movements.

In the case of Puerto Rico, Ramón Grosfoguel and Chloé Georas (2000) have argued that because of global relations of inequality, similar to other colonial migrations, Puerto Ricans are incorporated to the United States as colonial racial subjects. Juan González's examination of U.S. policies toward the island confirm this mode of entry as he illustrates that the island's colonial status is maintained through policies (e.g., regarding shipping, trade, the courts, federal programs, and the military) that sustain subjugation. As such, the political-economic policies that the United States has enacted toward the island are quite distinct from those applied to state governments. Many of these colonial policies affect migration patterns, whether directly or indirectly. With island median household incomes on average much lower than mainland household incomes ($14,412 versus $41,994), and island poverty rates hovering around 50 percent (compared to the mainland U.S. poverty rate of 12.4 percent in 2000),[112] many move to the mainland for economic survival and seeking to improve their lives. These realities are direct results of Puerto Rico's location in the global coloniality of power.[113]

Given how massive Puerto Rican migration is and the political-economic dynamics underlying migration patterns, it would be overly simplistic to equate these structural dynamics with those lying at the root of internal migration patterns with the mainland United States. The migration policies of the Puerto Rican government toward its people resemble those of other countries with similar colonial pasts. For example, as several scholars have shown, the Puerto Rican government, in the interest of reducing overpopulation and labor surpluses on the island at the height of industrialization, actively promoted emigration from the island. Pérez has documented how the island government's Migration Division office has recognized migration's role in Operation Boostrap: "[I]t [Migration Division] also made clear that Puerto Rican migration and displacement was indeed a state-sponsored phenomena involving multiple sites and institutional actors working transnationally."[114] These policies were also gendered, as migration was part of a multipronged strategy toward population control that was combined with state-sponsored birth control and sterilization programs.[115] Encouraging the migrations of women in particular as domestic workers and low-wage factory workers ensured that U.S. labor demands were met while controlling fertility by backing the departures of Puerto Rican women. These programs also fully acknowledge the benefits of migration for the island's economy through the remittances they expected migrants to send back.[116] The exportation of low wage workers, in particular domestic workers, resembles patterns that have been documented in migration streams from other countries such as Mexico and the Philippines,[117] with one of the few differences being the freedom with which Puerto Ricans can move back and forth. Thus, the structural foundations at the root of this colonial migration stream render the Puerto Rican experience different from that of internal migrants but similar to other "colonized" peoples such as Native Americans, Hawaiians, and Mexican Americans.

While a unique case, approaching the study of Puerto Rican migration through the lens of transnationalism provides a potentially useful comparison. They are a group whose cross-border linkages can be more easily sustained in the absence of legal restrictions of migration in an era of increasing regulation of immigration, and deregulation of capital. When compared to the struggles of other immigrant groups, issues related to lack of documentation can be controlled for, thus increasing what we can learn from all cases by studying the exception. The case of Puerto Ricans fits well into the body of recent work on transnationalism because it involves mass migration in the absence of formal government controls, but within unequal contexts, structuring all migrant experiences, even if to varying extents. In this vein, the study of Puerto Ricans is strategic; the lack of legal barriers to mobility removes the possibility that their struggles are impacted by their legal status, as it might for undocumented immigrants.[118] At the same time, Puerto Ricans face similar transitions upon migration regarding cultural and linguistic barriers as well as racialization.[119]

Conceptualizing such a thing as Puerto Rican transnationalism serves as a recognition of their second-class citizenship on the island. This institutionalized marginality is real in its consequences and too often overlooked when Puerto Ricans are referred to as "internal migrants." Acknowledging Puerto Rican transnationalism gives this group intellectual representation within a body of literature that seeks to understand the everyday lives of individuals, families, and communities marginalized by the intersections of global politics, power, and race. This is important because it is Puerto Ricans' "uniqueness" that often results in its falling through the intellectual cracks of social science research. In an area of study where the role of the state in defining social relations is changing, to exclude a case because it does not fit according to conventional standards of statehood ignores the history of conquest and colonialism that has defined many Puerto Ricans' identities and lives.[120] In what remains of this chapter, I discuss the study logistics, beginning with the specific issue of why I have chosen to research the Puerto Rican middle class.

RESEARCH DESIGN

This study explores the particular case of Puerto Rican migration through interviews with women and men from middle-class backgrounds. Its findings are not meant to be generalized statistically, yet they are most applicable to the experiences of colonial migrants[121] particularly, and transnational populations generally. To a lesser extent, this study can also be used to interpret the subjective experiences of anyone that must depart from his or her daily realities through migration to secure economic and emotional livelihoods.

Why the Middle Class?

Much of the data on Puerto Ricans has been gathered from census statistics that have helped construct portraits of mainland communities. There are also some recent ethnographies that have facilitated the understanding of Puerto Ricans' experiences in mainland communities.[122] This study adds to this existing body of research, except it focuses on the often neglected experiences of the Puerto Rican middle class. As Silvia Pedraza has argued, one of the "unpaved roads" in the research on immigration is the need for more studies of educated, middle-class professionals.[123] This is one of the reasons I focus on middle-class Puerto Ricans.

Middle-class Puerto Ricans were chosen for other reasons as well. First, as already discussed, their political status removes the possibility that emotional struggles are affected by the process of becoming legal. Regarding the impact of social class status, research has illustrated that poverty compromises the emotional health of Puerto Ricans as well as other groups.[124] Interviewing migrants who are financially stable lessens the possibility that migrants' struggles are byproducts of economic hardships. Additionally, some have argued that transnational involvement is more common among those who have relatively high levels of education.[125]

A high level of education among study participants, however, also introduces potential biases into the interviews. For example, highly educated Puerto Ricans might have distinct political views that alter their perceptions of incorporation into U.S. society. They are also more likely to have jobs that lead them to settle outside of mainland Puerto Rican communities which might affect their modes of adaptation. Recent flows to the mainland, however, particularly after 1980, have been more representative of all social classes on the island and include new settlements in communities outside of New York City.[126] This is an important point considering that much of what we know about the relationship between migration and socio-economic status is from studies focusing mainly on Puerto Ricans from low socio-economic backgrounds. Little is known about the experiences of the growing Puerto Rican middle class in the United States; these gaps in the literature call for further examination of this underresearched segment of Puerto Rican society.

Data and Methods

In this study I examine life and migration histories of migrants from Puerto Rico currently living in the mainland, and return migrants for a total of forty in-depth interviews with women and men. I go beyond examining accounts of individual decision making, however, by including questions about how household considerations impacted migration decisions. A participant's social construction of his or her migration experience can tell us how that person sees him- or herself in relation to the social phenomenon that he or she is a part of. Such interpretations are key to understanding motivations for subsequent mobility. At a broader level, the value of a life history approach is that it captures a well-rounded history of the individual and how migration enters the individual's life and forms part of her or his personal experience, including the struggles that are shaped by social structures (particularly gender, class, and racial hierarchies) across borders. These are considerations that a narrow migration history would miss.

Even though recent trends indicate that the Puerto Rican population is dispersing throughout the country, the Northeast is still the primary destination for Puerto Ricans. Cities such as Newark, Philadelphia, Boston, and Bridgeport, as well as New York City, have some of the largest Puerto Rican communities in the country.[127] The mainland participants of this study resided in Philadelphia and its surrounding suburban areas.[128] Although it is a low immigrant-receiving mid-Atlantic city, Philadelphia has historically received many Puerto Ricans. Island participants resided in various parts of Puerto Rico at the time they were interviewed. These participants, however, had lived previously throughout the U.S. mainland, including cities in Florida, Georgia, Texas, Louisiana, New York, and Pennsylvania.

The target population on the mainland consisted of first generation migrants who moved to the United States after 1980[129] and who were at least fifteen years old at the time of migration (or who had a good recollection of the migration experience and the process of adaptation).[130] Participants were also required to be at least twenty-one years of age at the time of the interview. Only participants who had lived in the United States for a minimum of two years were interviewed. If a participant migrated to the United States to pursue an undergraduate college education and returned immediately upon graduation, that person was not interviewed given the likelihood that their experiences on the mainland were limited to the range of experiences of a student. Only if that person remained on the mainland after the completion of his or her education, and acquired at least one year of work experience, was that person included in the sample. In cases in which graduate education was combined with work, participants were included in the sample.

The target population in Puerto Rico (return migrants) consisted of Puerto Rican-raised migrants to the mainland who moved there after 1980, and returned to the island after at least two years of living in the United States. Similar to the U.S. sample, all participants were required to be at least fifteen years of age at the time they migrated to the mainland, and at least twenty-one years of age at the time of the interview. Likewise, participants who migrated as students or who were currently pursuing their education were only interviewed if they had at least one year of full-time work experience in the United States, or if they were working at the same time they pursued their graduate degree (see table 1.1).

Participants for both samples were recruited through purposeful, snowball sampling techniques. Networks of Puerto Ricans (occupational, religious, and friendship networks) were accessed through personal contacts. Multiple informants facilitated access to a diversity of networks dispersed throughout the Philadelphia and San Juan metropolitan areas. In addition, several interviews were conducted in the northwestern and western parts of the island.[131]

In-depth interviews consisted of open-ended questions to capture comprehensive life histories. I also asked questions about adaptation, specifically the positive and negative aspects of mainland and island societies, and how these related to their feelings regarding settlement. One question involved a statement in which participants were asked to explain whether and how it applied to them. This statement was: "The statement that 'Puerto Ricans have one foot on the island and one in the U.S.' has been used to describe Puerto Ricans who move between the United States and the island. Do you feel that way now, have you ever felt this way, or would you say that this statement does not apply to you? Why?" This question was significant because it was an indicator of how sample members interpreted their status and assessed the nature of their experiences with adaptation. Participants were usually candid about whether they believed this was true of their situation.

For those living in the United States, I explored whether or not they desired to return to the island. In the case of return migrants I explored this decision as it related to adaptation to mainland life. Because the interviews were semistructured, they allowed participants some flexibility to

Table 1.1. Demographic Characteristics by Sample and Gender (N = 40)

	U.S. Sample n = 20	P.R. Sample n = 20	U.S. Women n = 10	U.S. Men n = 10	P.R. Women n = 10	P.R. Men n = 10
Mean Age	38	37	37	39	40	34
Age Range	23–56	27–49	23–46	23–56	28–49	27–40
Education						
2-yr. degree	4	0	1	3	0	0
4-yr. degree	4	5	2	2	2	3
Graduate work	12	15	7	5	8	7
Marital Status						
Single	2	2	1	1	1	1
Married	8	15*	3	5	6*	9
Remarried	5	0	4	1	0	0
Divorced	5	3	2	3	3	0
No. with Children	16	14	9	7	7	7
Avg. # of children	2.2	2.0	2.1	2.5	1.6	2.4
Age range	1–26	1–26	1–20	5–26	3–26	1–16
Household Income						
Mean	$79,000	$79,000	$80,000	$78,000	$75,000	$84,000
Median	$70,000	$60,000	$60,000	$75,000	$60,00	$79,000
Migration Circuits**						
Mean	1.6	1.5	1.6	1.6	1.4	1.6
Median	1	1	1	1	1	2

*Includes participants who are separated from their spouses.
**One full circuit is defined as out migration to the mainland and return migration to Puerto Rico.

bring up whatever life experience they felt the need to discuss. Interviews mostly resembled a dialogue. I tried to establish a nonhierarchical interviewing relationship in which respondents felt free to ask me some of the same personal questions I asked them. These conversations often took place after the interview so as not to insert my own interpretations of migration into their narratives. Ultimately, being a Puerto Rican migrant myself established a level of trust and comfort that facilitated the collection of personal information that I might have not otherwise obtained.

Participants were given the option of conducting the interview in either Spanish or English. All of the U.S. participants chose to be interviewed in Spanish, and all but two of the Puerto Rican participants were interviewed in Spanish. Additionally, it was common for "Spanglish," a mixture of English and Spanish, to be used throughout the interview. Since most of the interviews were in Spanish, the transcripts were analyzed in the language that the interview took place. Only quotes that appear in this book were translated to English for publication. In presenting the quotes, however, I weave in fragments of the Spanish interview into the English translation of the quote.

Interviews lasted between two to three hours, in some cases more than three hours; few interviews lasted less than two hours.[132] Data collection occurred in phases. Most of the U.S. sample was interviewed during the span of two nonconsecutive months, June and September of 2000. The rest of this sample was interviewed as the participants were recruited in subsequent months. The Puerto Rican sample was interviewed over the course of five weeks in July and August of 2000. All of the data were collected by December of 2000, spanning the course of six months.

This research places the emotions of Puerto Rican migrants at the center of a sociological analysis of migration. Employing a grounded, textured analysis using life and migration histories facilitated an understanding of the theoretical linkages between emotional issues related to migration and the structural barriers (gender, race, and class) in home and host societies that impacted motivations for migration.[133] It is through this approach that this research has allowed for the complex case of Puerto Ricans, a group with strategic significance, to be better understood.

ORGANIZATION OF THE BOOK

The migrations of middle-class Puerto Ricans to the mainland result in positive gains in terms of money and the investment in education and careers. In chapter 2, I illustrate the modes of incorporation of Puerto Ricans into mainland society. I examine the samples' social origins and to what extent the intergenerational transmission of class contributed to social mobility. I also examine how Puerto Ricans' citizenship status impacts their educational and occupational opportunities in the mainland and the island, and how migration shapes their pathways into the Puerto Rican transnational work force.

In chapter 3, I examine the transnationalization of Puerto Rican families, including the struggles resulting from ruptured kinship networks. I analyze how Puerto Ricans' interpretations of these losses affected their assessments of their own well-being. This chapter also examines how gender and class status mediated subjectivity and Puerto Ricans' gauges of where they felt like they belonged. At the same time, I examine how gendered sources of constraint affected the ways in which dislocations are often contested (e.g., return migration).

Chapter 4 addresses how issues related to being an ethno-racial minority in the mainland impacted Puerto Ricans' experiences of integration. I examine the roots of these struggles and how they are manifestations of the new racism. Moreover, I illustrate how settlement in urban ethnic communities versus suburban communities can result in varying levels of dislocation. I examine how feelings of marginalization affect future settlement decisions.

In chapter 5, I examine the various patterns of attachment that Puerto Ricans develop to mainland and island societies. I pay specific attention to how life course events and sources of inequalities shape emotional attachments to place. I examine how Puerto Ricans weigh their settlement options given their own understandings of where they feel most comfortable and where they feel they could best enhance their emotional well-being. I conclude this chapter with a discussion of the implications of alternating periods of settlement between the island and mainland for the identities of the children of the Puerto Ricans in my study.

Lastly, in chapter 6, I discuss how Puerto Ricans' subjective assessments of incorporation challenge the dominant paradigms of what constitutes successful immigrant incorporation, especially given that this segment of the Puerto Rican population can be considered to be structurally integrated into the U.S. mainstream. I discuss the implications of these findings for research on Puerto Ricans specifically, and transnational populations generally.

NOTES

1. Even though Puerto Rico is part of the United States, in this book, all references to the U.S. imply the mainland United States.

2. U.S. Census Bureau 2004. American Community Survey and U.S. Census Bureau, Population Estimates Program.

3. Duany 2004.

4. U.S. Census Bureau 2000.

5. See Torre et al. 1994.

6. Clara Rodríguez defines circular migration as two or more back and forth circuits of migration (Rodríguez, 1993).

7. Navarro, *New York Times*, 28 February 2000.

8. Basch, Glick-Schiller, and Szanton-Blanc 1994.

9. Smith 2005, 6.

10. Smith 2005, 7.

11. Massey et al. 1993, 433.

12. Massey et al. 1997, 434.

13. Bonilla and Campos 1981; Grosfoguel 1997; Sassen 1998.

14. Grasmuck and Pessar 1991; Massey and Espinosa 1997.

15. Alicea 1997; Hondagneu-Sotelo 1994; Menjívar 2000; Portes and Sensenbrenner 1993.

16. Alicea 1997; Grasmuck and Pessar 1991; Hondagneu-Sotelo 1994; Pérez 2004.

17. Meléndez 1994; Portes and Rumbaut 1996.

18. Basch et al. 1994; Levitt 2001; Pérez 2004.

19. Ellis et al. 1996; Grasmuck and Pessar 1991.

20. Grasmuck and Pessar 1991; Hondagneu-Sotelo 1994; Mahler 1996.

21. Hondagneu-Sotelo 1994; Pérez 2004.

22. Basch, Glick Shiller, and Szanton Blanc 1994; Levitt 2001; Sorensen and Olwig 2001; Vélez-Ibáñez and Sampaio 2002.

23. Gans 1999; Massey and Espinosa 1997; Portes, Guarnizo and Landolt 1999.

24. Alba and Nee 1997; Gans 1999; Portes and Rumbaut 2001; Portes and Zhou 1993; Rumbaut 1999.

25. Hamilton and Chinchilla 2001; Levitt 2001; Menjívar 2000; Portes and Rumbaut 1996; Waters 1999.

26. Portes and Zhou 1993; Waters 1999; Zhou 1999.

27. Portes and Jensen 1989; Portes and Stepick 1993; Stepick et al. 2003.

28. Portes and Rumbaut 1996; 2001.

29. Basch et al. 1994; Levitt 2001; Parreñas 2001.

30. Glick Schiller, Basch and Szanton Blanc 1999, 73.

31. Guarnizo, Portes and Haller 2003; Kivisto 2001; Pedraza 1999.

32. Basch et al. 1994.

33. Levitt and Glick Schiller 2003; Guarnizo, Portes and Haller 2003; Smith 2005.

34. Levitt and Glick Schiller 2003.

35. Basch et al. 1994.

36. Levitt and Glick Schiller 2003, 7.

37. Levitt and Glick Schiller 2003, 7-8.

38. Guarnizo et al. 2003.

39. Levitt 2004.

40. Guarnizo 2003.

41. Kivisto, 2001, 567–68.
42. Levitt and Glick Schiller 2003, 8.
43. Studies of immigrant well-being have often focused on mental health (Canabal and Quiles 1995; Vega, Warheit, and Meinhard 1985), revealing that immigration acts as a source of stress for individuals (Cervantes, Salgado, and Padilla 1989). For example, there is a positive relationship between immigrant status and mental health indicators such as depressive symptoms (Vega, Warheit, and Meinhard 1985). Others argue that rather than immigrant status and level of acculturation, factors such as conditions of exit, contexts of reception, and variables such as social class, gender, and the availability of networks upon arrival (Canabal and Quiles 1995; Portes and Rumbaut 1996) affect immigrant mental health. These studies though, assess immigrant adaptation and well being once the process of migration is complete. They subsume emotions into the realm of mental illness, ignoring the study of emotional fluctuations that accompany immigrant incorporation and settlement over the life cycle.
44. Rodríguez 1991, 158.
45. See Massey et al. 1999 for a review of these approaches.
46. Levitt and Waters 2002.
47. Wolf 1997; 2002.
48. Wolf 1997, 459.
49. Kibria 2002; Levitt 2002; Smith 2002.
50. Parreñas 2001, 3.
51. Parreñas 2001, 250.
52. Hall, in Parreñas, 2001, 12.
53. Denzin 1991 quoted in Ellis and Flaherty 1992, 4.
54. Ellis and Flaherty 1992, 4.
55. Ellis and Flaherty 1992, 6.
56. For exceptions, see Levitt and Glick Schiller 2003; Parreñas 2001; and work on second generation transnationalism in Levitt and Waters 2002.
57. Duany 1994–1995, 73.
58. Wolf 1997, 459.
59. Portes and Rumbaut 1996.
60. Basch et al. 1994, 4.
61. Gould 2004.
62. Gubrium and Holstein 1997, 58–59.
63. Levitt and Glick Schiller 2003, 8.
64. U.S. Census Bureau 2000.
65. Sandoval Sánchez 1997, 201.
66. Bonilla and Colón Jordan 1979.
67. Bonilla and Colón Jordan 1979.
68. Trías Monge 1997, 86.
69. González 2000, 84.
70. Trías Monge 1997.
71. González 2000.
72. González 2000, 83.
73. Trías Monge 1997, 96.
74. Trías Monge 1997, 99.

75. Bonilla and Campos 1981.

76. Dietz 1986.

77. Pérez 2004.

78. Hernández Cruz 1985; Pérez 2004.

79. Bonilla and Colón Jordan 1979.

80. U.S. Commission on Civil Rights 1976, and Junta de Planificación 1978–1989, quoted in Duany 2003, 432.

81. Santiago and Basu 1993, in Rivera-Batiz and Santiago 1996, 47.

82. Torre et al. 1994.

83. Trías Monge 1997, 120.

84. González 2000.

85. Bonilla and Colón Jordan 1979.

86. Hernández Álvarez 1967, in Bonilla and Colón Jordan 1979.

87. Bonilla and Colón Jordan 1979.

88. Centro 1979; Hernández Cruz 1985; Pérez 2004.

89. Rivera-Batiz and Santiago 1996, 54.

90. Cabán 1993, 28.

91. Cabán 1993, 28.

92. Dietz 1994, 155.

93. U.S. Census in Rivera-Batiz and Santiago 1996, 46.

94. Rivera-Batiz and Santiago 1996, 47.

95. Rivera-Batiz and Santiago 1996, 19.

96. Rivera-Batiz and Santiago 1996.

97. A flaw in census data is that the number of circular migrants is not well documented given that if they resided on the island in 1980, emigrated to the mainland, and returned before 1990, they are not counted as return migrants in census statistics. A flaw in the Puerto Rican Planning Board data, which consists of data on air travelers going in and out of Puerto Rico is that it does not distinguish between tourists and Puerto Ricans, or among travelers and migrants (Rodríguez 1993).

98. Rivera-Batiz and Santiago 1996, 59.

99. Rodríguez 1993, 110.

100. Puerto Rican Planning Board, cited in Duany 2003, 432.

101. U.S. Census Bureau 2000.

102. While these numbers give us a broad picture of Puerto Rican migration patterns throughout the century, it is nevertheless difficult to estimate the number of migrants, return migrants, and circular migrants given the lack of official, reliable statistics.

103. Duany 2002.

104. Smith and Guarnizo 1998.

105. Robert C. Smith (2002) defines transnationalization and transnational life as "that sphere of life that flows out of the regular contact between sending and receiving societies, a social field of relations that, in the second generation especially, has a character akin to associational life and is particularly strong in particular phases of life" (Smith 2002, 148).

106. Smith and Guarnizo 1998.

107. Rodríguez Vecchini 1994, 37.

108. Duany 2002.
109. Grosfoguel and Georas 2000.
110. Trías Monge, 1997.
111. González 2000, 247.
112. U.S. Census Bureau 2000 Summary File 3.
113. Quijano in Grosfoguel and Georas 2000.
114. Pérez 2004, 71.
115. Pérez 2004.
116. Pérez 2004.
117. Hondagneu-Sotelo 2001; Parreñas 2001.
118. Chávez 1992; Menjívar 2000.
119. One last point to consider in this debate of whether the Puerto Rican case should or should not be considered transnational is that the politics of research often act as metaphors for broader issues of inequality. The discourse on transnational activities and identities in the work of Basch et al. (1994) and others has been posited as counter-hegemonic—mechanisms to resist global inequality and oppression. As such, transnational practices have come to be seen as symbolic. To some they represent a statement of how poorly some groups of immigrants are received and "incorporated" into the United States—manifestations of racist nativism that renders Emma Lazarus' writings (e.g., "Give me your poor, huddled masses") outdated. Transnational practices also represent the agency of the "subjects" of global capitalism and their efforts at resisting inequalities. Emphasizing that the nature of the linkages between the island and mainland are transnational makes space for the possibility that Puerto Rican migration is counter-hegemonic, and that Puerto Ricans are not passive victims, as some have argued in the past (Chávez 1991).
120. At an intellectual level, it reinforces the exclusion of Puerto Ricans from areas of research that have grown because of the increasing representation of marginalized groups in the academy generally, and in fields of study connected to their own biographies. As a Puerto Rican scholar, these issues undergird my own motivations for taking on this particular project.
121. Grosfoguel 1997.
122. Pérez 2004; Dávila 2004.
123. Pedraza 1998.
124. Canabal and Quiles 1995.
125. Guarnizo, Portes and Haller 2003.
126. Grosfoguel 2003.
127. U.S. Census Bureau 2000.
128. Because of confidentiality issues, other demographic information presented throughout this book has been changed to protect the identities of those Puerto Ricans I interviewed.
129. The year 1980 is chosen as a cut-off point for a number of reasons. First, recent migrants were chosen rather than those who had migrated before the 1980s so that the experience of migration was fresh in participants' memories. Secondly, compared to previous waves of migration, it was in the 1980s and 1990s that population movement to the mainland reflected social class diversity. Therefore migrants from these two decades were targeted. This decision was somewhat problematic

though, placing more limitations on the targeted sample, which made participants more difficult to find. Because of this, in a few cases, participants who had migrated in 1979 were accepted into the study. Lastly, although there have been studies on Puerto Rican migration that have demonstrated the presence of circular migration patterns in Puerto Rican communities (Hernández Álvarez 1967; Ashton 1980; Hernández Cruz 1985), there are few (for exception, see Rodríguez 1993; Ortiz 1994; Pérez 2004) that explore whether circular migration is a pattern that has persisted into the 1990s and 2000s.

130. In both target populations, a person's previous migration history was not taken into consideration when determining eligibility for the study. In other words, if a return migrant in Puerto Rico had gone to the United States in 1986, returned to the island in 1989, but also had migrated in the 1970s and returned, that person was considered for the study. Consequently, although not a conceptual category in the study design, interviews were conducted with people who had engaged in various circuits of migration, as long as the latest circuit occurred after 1980.

131. I made initial contact with participants by telephone and described to them the project and how I obtained their name. Once they agreed to be interviewed, we met at a mutually agreed upon location. Interviews were conducted either in the home of the participant or his or her office. Only in a few instances were interviews conducted in a public place such as a restaurant. I conducted all of the interviews with members of both samples.

132. All interviews were audiotape-recorded and transcribed verbatim. Each transcript and set of field notes was combed for the main themes as they related to the principle research questions.

133. During the process of interviewing and coding, a database was constructed that contained all of the demographic information about each participant and their information regarding various analytic and conceptual categories (e.g., gender and sample). Once this database was complete, different data matrices were constructed to analyze the data along conceptual categories. The data matrices were useful in that they minimized the tendency to report only on select cases, facilitating the examination of interviews both individually and in juxtaposition to others. The analysis presented in this book emerged from the data matrices.

2

~~

Pathways into the Puerto Rican Middle Class

Natalia is a thirty-six-year-old Puerto Rican woman who works as a case manager for a mental health agency in Pennsylvania. A single mother, she moved to the mainland in the mid-1990s with her two children (ages ten and eleven at the time of migration) in search of better economic opportunities. Even though Natalia had her bachelor's degree, her job on the island only paid her minimum wage. Because her husband divorced her when her youngest child was two, Natalia and her children had to move in with her parents so that she could have someone to watch them while she worked. This was the arrangement they had up until the time Natalia left the island.

Natalia has a history of low-paying jobs in the service industry; the prospects of finding a better job and ever making a better living on the island seemed dim. She worked as a secretary, in an insurance agency, and even at McDonald's mopping floors. Natalia worked at a credit agency as a cashier processing loans when she decided to try her luck in the United States. In the following quote, she described to me how the idea of moving to the mainland initially arose:

> Well, one day I made a comment to a sister-in-law of mine. I said, "*Ay, yo volaría, yo me iría lejos* . . . Ay, I would fly, I would go far away." So then she told me, "*Mira, ¿te gustaría irte para Estados Unidos?* . . . Look, would you like to go to the United States?" And I told her, "I don't know, because of the language issue." And she said, "That is the least [worry], you can go and take English classes. I have a daughter that went two years ago and look, she has an apartment, she has her car, she has all of that."

Natalia entertained the idea and decided to go. Her sister-in-law's daughter, who lived in Connecticut, agreed to help her get an apartment and to take her to the welfare office to get financial help until she could establish herself. Natalia explained her decision as a financial move, emphasizing that as a professional, she could never really move up in Puerto Rico earning the kind of wages she was earning:

> What I earned was $317 bi-weekly . . . and I was a professional. Do you understand? *Trescientos diez y siete dolares quincenal, y todavía yo estaba viviendo en casa de mis papás porque yo no podía pagar por una casita.* Three hundred and seventeen bi-weekly, and I was still living at my parents' house because I could not pay for a house. I could not pay for my own rent, and I gave half of my money to my mother and the rest, well, was used for gas, lunch, and I did not have the opportunity to buy myself a car. Understand? You get home tired, and then sometimes my car would break down and you'd be on foot for months . . . so I decided [to leave].

Natalia's situation is not unusual.[1] Faced with a bleak economic outlook, Natalia decided to move to Connecticut. She resigned from her job only to find out that her contact was no longer willing to help her relocate. Now jobless, Natalia decided to move anyway. At her mother's insistence, she contacted a half-brother in Pennsylvania and within two weeks she had relocated to the mainland and sent for her children.

In contrast to Natalia, Ana's U.S. job opportunity came to her when she was living in Puerto Rico. Ana is an environmental engineer who up until the date she left Puerto Rico, had lived there her entire life, completing her college education there as well. In the following quote, she explained how it was that she came to leave the island:

> When I finished . . . I was in my last year at the University of Puerto Rico. The Environmental Protection Agency came, the EPA from the different regions of the United States. They conducted some interviews and made me an offer. Since I studied civil engineering, it was the environmental aspect that I wanted to specialize in. So obviously my options were to go get my master's in environmental [engineering] or work with the EPA. They made me that offer, so I did not think twice about it. . . . As soon as I graduated, two months later, I left.

Ana was engaged to be married at the time she left the island. She was well aware, however, that there were very few job opportunities in Puerto Rico in the field in which she was trained. She realized that gaining work experience in the United States would be pivotal if she ever wanted to find employment in Puerto Rico in the future. Her engagement did not survive the separation.

Although all who participated in this study could be grouped within the middle-class rubric because of their socioeconomic status at the time they were interviewed, they comprise a heterogeneous group regarding class origins and the role of migration as a means to achieve social mobility. Although their reasons for migration are similar, the contexts surrounding migration decisions reflected variations in class backgrounds and family structures, as Natalia's and Ana's cases illustrate. For some, migration was a way to climb the socio-economic ladder from the bottom up. For others, migration served as a means to attain increased levels of education or job experience that would some day allow them to join the ranks of the middle class if they were not already part of it—whether in Puerto Rico or in the mainland. Joining the transnational professional workforce facilitated participation and incorporation into either society as Puerto Ricans had more options regarding job opportunities across borders, thereby increasing their long-term settlement options.

In this chapter, I examine the diverse class origins of the professionals in this study and how this diversity relates to their modes of incorporation into mainland society, and reincorporation into island society. I examine how Puerto Ricans' family class backgrounds structure their entry into this group and how, in turn, migration trajectories and experiences reflect these backgrounds. I also examine the resources and strategies Puerto Ricans employ to maneuver through island and mainland labor markets to achieve social mobility. In particular, I discuss the trend in which pursuing U.S. educational opportunities allows for the expansion of credentials and experiences that facilitate Puerto Ricans joining the transnational professional workforce, and the political resources and social networks that enhance these incorporation experiences. I conclude with an analysis of how incorporation into mainland labor markets affects patterns of reincorporation into Puerto Rico's labor markets.

CLASS ORIGINS AND MODES OF INCORPORATION

Alejandro Portes and Rubén Rumbaut have researched extensively how the fate of immigrants depends on the context in which they are received.[2] In response to arguments that focused exclusively on the individual characteristics of immigrants, they argue that contextual variables such as the nature of government reception, labor market opportunities, the likelihood of discrimination, and the character of the ethnic community into which immigrants arrive affect patterns of incorporation. Both Natalia and Ana's experiences illustrate the importance of the receiving context, but also of the economic conditions under which they left the island. Further analysis of these two cases illustrates these points.

Natalia moved to the mainland with $1,500 that she had accrued in unused vacation days and company stock. With this money, she found an apartment in Philadelphia. She paid $400 as a deposit and another $400 for the first month's rent. Natalia got some old furniture from her half-brother, and used several hundred dollars to fly her children up to Philadelphia. She spent the rest of her money on groceries and a television.

Because of her U.S. citizenship, Natalia was able to apply immediately for welfare benefits. She also linked up with a nonprofit organization that offered free English classes. Natalia explained that with the money she got from welfare and the money she was receiving from unemployment compensation from Puerto Rico, she made more than she was earning while working on the island. Given the recent passage of the Welfare Reform bill of 1996, as a condition of receiving these benefits, Natalia had to find a job. This meant that her two children remained home alone after school.

Within weeks of looking, Natalia found work. She explained her exhuberance when finding out about her new salary:

When the lady told me, "Look Natalia, we are offering you $17,500 starting salary. . . ." *Para mí eso era un mundo porque yo me estaba ganando en Puerto Rico, nueve mil, que el costo de vida es más caro que acá* . . . For me that was a world because I was earning $9,000 in Puerto Rico and the cost of living was higher than here [United States]. For me, I was like, "Well but, I don't know much English, you know, so that if you have to pay me a bit less," I said. *Pero es que me querían.* . . . But they wanted me, what they were offering me (*sic*) that bunch of money, you understand? And that's not much here, you understand, $17,500 is very little.

Even though Natalia doubled her income in comparison with what she made on the island, she acknowledged that by U.S. standards, her salary was still low. Nevertheless, Natalia took the job. She ended up only collecting two months of welfare.

The ensuing years in the mainland were filled with many struggles. Natalia worked all day, took English classes at night, and watched English language television until the wee hours of the morning to sharpen her language skills. Her hard work paid off. Within a few years, Natalia had found a better job that made much more than what she had started at: $29,000 a year. She also took a part-time job teaching English at a local organization that provided social services to Asian immigrants. Natalia's success, however, did not come without a cost. Even though she believed her children were mature enough to remain alone for the four hours after school, Natalia did not factor in external influences. On one afternoon when Natalia was working, her daughter was sexually assaulted by a neighbor.[3]

In spite of the tragedy that occurred in Natalia's family, her access to social services and the financial safety net she found in the United States allowed her to economically move up in a relatively short period of time. As Natalia herself indicated:

> Look, in July I'll have been here four years, and girl, there have been many people who have been living here twenty years. *Quisieran tener, tú sabes, la suerte que yo he tenido* . . . They wish they had, you know, the luck that I have had. There are still people who live in basements, who have lived here a lot, and live a life. Well, in the homes that I visit with many children (*sic*), *viven bien mal, sin embargo mira yo* . . . they do not live well (*sic*), but look at me.

What Natalia calls luck are actually the benefits that she has received due to her U.S. citizenship. Ramón Grosfoguel has argued that in addition to the receiving context, other factors must also be taken into account when theorizing about immigrant outcomes such as the political mode of incorporation, or the relationship between the sending and receiving countries.[4] In the case of Puerto Ricans, the fact that they are U.S. citizens by birth means that they have not only free access to migration but also access to services that are increasingly denied to other immigrants. For example, the same changes in welfare policies that tied benefits to paid work requirements denied benefits to other immigrants, even if they were legally in the United States. As such, being U.S. citizens results in the availability of benefits to Puerto Ricans who live in the United States that are unavailable to other immigrants.

There are other benefits as well that accrue to Puerto Ricans because of their political mode of incorporation into the United States. For instance, that the EPA recruited Ana in Puerto Rico illustrates how island college students benefit from U.S. affirmative action policies and recruitment efforts that are not hampered by immigration-related legal issues. Further examination of Ana's case illustrates this situation.

Once Ana moved to Georgia, her adjustment to mainland living went relatively smooth. Ana attributed this to the fact that the EPA recruited seven other students from her university to work in their southern headquarters. Ana ended up getting an apartment with her former university roommate who also accepted a job offer with this federal agency. Additionally, her roommate had family living in that area of the United States who therefore picked up Ana and her roommate when they arrived at the airport, and even rented them an apartment. The graduates began working two days after they arrived. In Ana's words, *"Se nos hizo bien fácil . . .* It was made very easy for us." She continued,

> *No llegamos a aventurar. Llegamos y ya teníamos el apartamento; ya nos lo habían alquilado.* We didn't get here to go on adventures. We arrived and we already had an apartment; they had already rented us one. And our belongings arrived the next day. Everything arrived quickly. And obviously we had some of her [roomate's] family members that in the beginning took us to buy

everything. In addition, later on a car and well, since there were seven of us there were already people, Puerto Ricans who worked at the EPA. *Pues, tienes tu grupito de puertorriqueños que lo hace siempre más fácil* . . . So, you have your group of Puerto Ricans that always makes it much easier.

Ana had an instant ethnic support group at her job. While they did not settle in an area in which there was a significant Puerto Rican presence, because they were recruited jointly they could rely on each other for help. Moreover, even though Ana knew English well, she said that she struggled with her accent. As such, this group served as a source of support in which she could speak Spanish and feel comfortable.

Ana characterized her experiences in the U.S. mainland as very positive, especially in terms of her career. She was always challenged in her work and experienced high levels of professional socialization, fulfillment, and social mobility. It was difficult, however, to maintain her relationship with her fiancé. At one point after she left the island, she tried to find work in Puerto Rico. Her fiancé also tried to find work in the United States, in the hopes that they could reunite. Their respective job searches, however, were unproductive. Eventually, the relationship ended. In spite of this, her level of satisfaction in the United States was such that, even though when she initially left the island she thought that five years would be enough time to gain experience to take back to Puerto Rico, once those five years passed, she decided to stay for a longer period of time.

> *[Ir a Estados Unidos] me fascinó y se lo recomiendo a cualquier persona* . . . I loved it [going to the United States] and I recommend it to anyone. The experience of going to the United States is super enriching. And it was very educational regarding the culture, the language, and in terms of systems of government and quality of life, and everything. . . . *La vida allá es bien buena* . . . Life there is very good. Like the working conditions, and respect among people. It has been a very, very positive experience for me in every regard.

The conditions surrounding Ana and Natalia's departures illustrate the importance of class origins in shaping modes of incorporation and adaptation experiences. Ana and Natalia came from different socio-economic backgrounds. Natalia lived in a small town about thirty minutes west of San Juan. Natalia grew up living in poverty. The high school she attended was in a poor area, where more than half of the student body was eligible to receive free or reduced-price school lunches.[5] Natalia managed to attend a small local college to get her degree, even though, as she stated, *"En mi casa no había nada* . . . There was nothing in my house." Even after she attained her degree she lived in poverty; her struggles as a single mother in a low-paying job led to her migration decision. Her educational background, however, did pay off in the mainland.

In contrast, Ana grew up in a home where, as she states, there were never any "struggles" and in which she was able to *"Lograr mis sueños . . .* Accomplish my dreams." With her parents' financial support, she attended a private Catholic high school in a city about twenty-five minutes southeast of San Juan. She also attended the most prestigious university on the island. More than the differing conditions of exit, their class origins, particularly having an economic safety net in the form of parental resources, shaped their quality of life and well-being prior to migration. This, in turn, shaped the contexts in which migration decisions were made. As such, class origins had ramifications for Natalia's and Ana's contrasting modes of incorporation into mainland society. The ways in which social class affected how these processes unfolded can be captured when we compare Ana's assessments of mainland living as a "super enriching" experience, with Natalia's. When Natalia was asked this same question, she responded:

> *Estados Unidos no es color de rosa como la gente piensa* . . . The United States is not all the color pink like people think. I would go [return] to Puerto Rico (*sic*). The problem is that, this country has given me the opportunities that mine did not provide. But I am not happy, I don't like this, this country is ugly. At least this region here. And, the quality of people is bad. But unfortunately, I came here in a moment of desperation, looking for something better. And yes, I have progressed, I can't complain about not progressing. . . . This is a country to come to work and make money. I don't like it to raise children. . . . *Y, yo estoy bien defraudada. A mí no me gusta. Como sociedad, esto no sirve* . . . And I feel very let down. I don't like it. As a society, this is no good. *Yo, mi país. Mi país, u otro país hispanoparlante* . . . For me, my country. My country, or another Spanish-speaking one. But not to raise children. I don't recommend it to anyone. Well look, look at what happened to me. You come with good intentions, and you don't get involved with anyone. But people come and ruin your life.

Natalia's pessimistic assessment of the United States is a product of various experiences. Since Natalia settled in the mainland, she and her children have been witnesses to much violence. Her daughter was raped, and has struggled with many emotional issues since this happened. She even ran away for weeks with a man she barely knew. Natalia, who got remarried to a Peruvian man she met a few years after she moved to the mainland, experienced another tragedy as well. Her husband was carjacked and assaulted, to the point that he suffered brain damage. Natalia and her family have witnessed much violence and heartache in the course of their mainland settlement.

What proved to be valuable in both Ana's and Natalia's cases were their educational backgrounds and the resources available to them through their citizenship status. Even for Natalia, who was disadvantaged in many ways, her college degree and the opportunities she had access to because she was a U.S. citizen proved to be invaluable in the process of incorporation, particularly regarding improving her standard of living. Thus, when we consider the varying routes to incorporation and the impact of the context of reception, we must also consider the resources and opportunities available to Puerto Ricans when they embark on their migration journeys. I turn to these issues in the next sections.

"FORMS OF CAPITAL" AND INCORPORATION: EXAMINING CLASS ORIGINS AND OPPORTUNITY STRUCTURES

Most immigration scholars acknowledge that in addition to the context of reception, the varying forms of capital immigrants bring with them factor into explaining variations in social outcomes and incorporation.[6] Not only is financial capital important in determining these outcomes, but also human capital (education and job training) and social capital (opportunities accessed through social networks) facilitate immigrants' experiences adapting to a new society and integrating into its socio-economic fabric.

Victor Nee and Jimy Sanders argue that immigrants who come to the United States with low levels of financial and human-cultural capital are more likely to find employment in an ethnic economy, while those who have larger amounts of these forms of capital will find placement in the mainstream economy.[7] While data on the precise amount of financial capital Puerto Ricans had access to upon their mainland arrivals are unavailable, thus far I have illustrated how their social class backgrounds have facilitated in some cases, and hindered in others, their migration and settlement experiences. Many Puerto Ricans come to the mainland after having secured educational opportunities or jobs, and to build upon what capital they have. And still others come to join family members, in the hopes of doing better for themselves. Given their U.S. citizenship, all had the option to come if they could gather the resources, which in itself was related to their social class backgrounds. Given that the opportunities available to Puerto Ricans were influenced by their class backgrounds, I hesitate to use the discourse of capital for it overlooks the structural inequalities that lead to the intergenerational transmission of class status (the pattern in which class status is transferred from one generation to another). Instead, I illustrate the impact of social structural factors, particularly class orgins, on educational attainment and, subsequently, labor market outcomes.

Class Background and Educational Opportunities

To determine the class background of participants when they were growing up, I examined whether each person attended a public or private secondary school in Puerto Rico. Public versus private schooling is often used as an indicator of class origins in that families must have sufficient income to afford a private school education.[8] To determine the extent to which those attending public schools grew up in economically disadvantaged communities, I examine the demographic information of each school's student population, in particular, whether or not each school attended is a Title I school (indicating that these schools were targeted for financial assistance given their large populations of low-income children) and the percentage of students eligible to receive free or reduced price lunches. The latter data are often used as indicators of the socioeconomic status of the community in which the school is embedded.[9] According to these indicators, I determine whether each respondent comes from a middle/upper middle-class background or a working class/poor background. Table 2.1 illustrates the class origins of both samples.

Of those Puerto Ricans living in the mainland at the time of the interview, all but three completed their high school educations in Puerto Rico. The three who completed high school in the United States came as teenagers and attended public schools (two of them in poor school districts near the city's Puerto Rican community). Two of these three were young men who were sent to live with relatives in the mainland to complete high school; the third was a young woman who migrated with her family in search of better opportunities. Of those who completed their secondary education on the island, four attended private schools and thirteen attended public schools.

Of the sixteen who went to public school either on the mainland or island, twelve were enrolled in Title I schools. Moreover, of the fourteen public schools for which information was available, eleven had a student population in which half or more of the students were eligible to receive free or reduced-price lunches. Given this information, in the U.S. sample,

Table 2.1. Class Origins by Sample

Class Origins	U.S. Sample	Puerto Rico Sample	Total
Working-Class/Poor Background	12	3	15
Middle/Upper Middle-Class Background	5	16	21
Other	3	1	4
Total	20	20	40

twelve of twenty participants were identified as coming from working class/poor backgrounds and five of twenty were from middle/
upper-middle class backgrounds. The remaining three in the sample attended public schools; however, data regarding Title 1 status and percent
of students eligible for reduced price or free lunch were not available.

Among both the mainland and island samples of Puerto Ricans, fur-
thering their educations was instrumental to incorporation into mainstream labor markets in the United States. Class origins, however, structured the educational opportunities available. Table 2.2 illustrates how
these class backgrounds relate to migration, educational attainment, and
labor market outcomes. I include information on the role of migration in
expanding educational credentials. For those who have embarked on
multiple migration journeys and periods of U.S. settlement, the reason for
each migration is listed. In terms of labor market incorporation, I use Nee
and Sanders' occupational categories (self employment; government; professional, managerial, technical; low semi-skilled factory service) to assess
the character of incorporation. For those in "professional" jobs, I further
disaggregate this category given the substantial number of Puerto Ricans
who worked as professionals in social service agencies. These jobs tend to
pay less than other occupations in the primary labor market in which a
high level of specialization is required. These jobs also tend to have a
larger proportion of women working in them.

Regarding their reasons for migration, middle/upper middle-class-
background Puerto Ricans were more likely to embark on their first migration experience to get a college degree (three of four who migrated for
education) while those from poorer backgrounds were more likely to attend graduate school if they migrated for education related reasons (four
of five). Regarding migrating for occupational and economic opportunities, job opportunities refers to those migration decisions made once a job
on the mainland was secured (or if job duties involved migration),
whereas migrating for economic opportunities involved individuals who
left seeking greater opportunities without having secured them yet. In the
former category, we find four migration decisions made on behalf of
Puerto Ricans from working class/poor backgrounds and one migration
decision from a participant from a middle/upper middle-class background; in the latter category of economic opportunity, we find six migration decisions made by those from disadvantaged class backgrounds
whereas none of those from middle-class backgrounds migrated for these
reasons. While not generalizable, these data do suggest that those from
disadvantaged class origins do not have a solid foothold in the island's
middle class in that they are more likely to migrate with no job opportunity in place. Moreover, half of those moving for economic opportunities
did so with the help of social networks in the United States.

Table 2.2. Class Origins (Educational Background), Reason for Migration, Educational Attainment, and Occupation by Labor Market Incorporation: U.S. Sample

U.S. Labor Market Incorporation	Class Origins (Educational Background)[1]	Reason for U.S. migration for each migration journey[2]	Degree Attained and Location of Educational Institution	Occupation in United States
Self Employed				
Diana	Middle/Upper-Middle Class Private School	1. Husband's educational opportunity 2. Job opportunity[2]	B.A. (P.R.) J.D. (U.S.)	Attorney—Mainstream Economy
Lourdes	Middle/Upper-Middle Class Private School	Undergraduate Education	B.A. (U.S.) Some Ph.D. courses (U.S.)	Owner Small Business—Mainstream Economy
Charlie	Working Class/Poor Public School in P.R.: Title 1 60% in U.S. Title 1 86%	High School Education[2]	Some college (U.S.)	Small business owner—Ethnic Economy
Professional				
Noel	Working Class/Poor Public Title 1 47%	Graduate Education[2]	B.S. (P.R.) Ph.D. (U.S.)	Administrator
José	n/a Public School[+]	1. Undergraduate Education 2. Graduate Education	B.S. (U.S.) DMD, MBA, MGA (U.S.)	Dentist
Myrna	Working Class/Poor Public Title 1 44%	1. Graduate Education 2. Husband's job opportunity	B.A. (P.R.) M.A. (U.S.)	Adjunct Professor
Juan	n/a Public School[+]	1. Graduate Education 2. Airforce duty 3. Job opportunity	B.S. (P.R.) Ph.D. (U.S.)	College Professor
Miguel	Working Class/Poor Public Title 1 94%	1. Job opportunity	A.A. (P.R.)	Consultant

(continued)

Table 2.2. *(continued)*

U.S. Labor Market Incorporation	Class Origins (Educational Background)[1]	Reason for U.S. migration for each migration journey[2]	Degree Attained and Location of Educational Institution	Occupation in United States
Professional—Social Services				
Natalia	Working Class/Poor Public Title 1 87%	Economic opportunities[2]	B.A .(P.R.)	Case Manager
Ella	Working Class/Poor Public Title 1 86% in U.S.	Family migrated in search of economic opportunities[2]	A.A. (U.S.) B.A. (in progress in U.S.)	Student and Program Assistant
Raquel	Middle/Upper-Middle Class Private School	Undergraduate Education	B.A. (U.S.) MA (U.S.)	Communications/Public Relations for nonprofit org.
Marisol	n/a Public School[+]	Family migrated due to political persecution	B.S. (P.R.) MDiv. (U.S.)	Community Outreach
Antonio	Working Class/Poor Public Title 1 67%	Girlfriend's educational opportunity	A.A. (P.R.) B.S .(U.S.)	Counselor
Alejandro	Working Class/Poor Public Title 1 54%	1. Graduate Education 2. Economic opportunities 3. Economic opportunities	B.A. (P.R.) Some graduate courses*	Former: Ultrasound Tech. Housing Counselor
Managerial				
Guillermo	Working Class/Poor Public Title 1 76%	Job opportunity[2]	A.A. (2): (P.R.)	Manager Credit Association—Ethnic Economy

Government

Name	Class/School	Reason	Education	Occupation
Emma	Working Class/Poor Public Title 1 93%	1. Joined Army to pursue graduate education 2. Economic opportunities[2]	B.A. (P.R.) R.N. (U.S.) M.A. in progress (U.S.)	Legislator
Orlando	Middle/Upper-Middle Class Private in P.R. Public in U.S. 5%	Finish high school education[2]	B.A. (U.S.) M.B.A .(U.S.)	Subdirector Government Office
Pedro	Working Class/Poor Public Title 1 76%	1. Economic opportunities 2. Economic opportunities	B.A. (P.R.) M.A. (U.S.) Ph.D. (in progress)	Civic Affairs Specialist

Not Employed

Name	Class/School	Reason	Education	Occupation
Cuqui	Middle/Upper-Middle Class Private School	Undergraduate Education	B.S. (U.S)	Homemaker; Former Pharmacist
Vilma	Working Class/Poor Public Title 1 74%	1. Graduate Education 2. Job transfer 3. Job training 4. Marriage	B.S. (P.R.) M.S. (U.S.)	Homemaker; Former Pharmaceutical Exec.

[1]Class origin is measured by whether or not respondents attended private or public secondary school in Puerto Rico. Private school attendance is used as a proxy for middle/upper middle-class status in that families must have sufficient disposable income to afford private school tuition. For public schools, information is given regarding whether or not it is a Title 1 school and the percentage of the student population eligible to receive free and reduced price school lunches. This information is used as a proxy for a disadvantaged class status given that it indicates whether or not the school was located in an impoverished community.
[2]Indicates that there was a social network available to facilitate migration and integration.
† Information not available
Sources: Project data (2001) and National Center for Education Statistics, 2005 website http://nces.ed.gov/globallocator/

Regarding educational attainment, among those from working-class/ poor backgrounds, five of twelve obtained their graduate degrees (four of these had moved for this precise reason), three obtained their undergraduate degrees, three got their associates degree, and one had some college experience. Among those from a middle/upper middle-class background, all had a college degree or higher (three of five had obtained graduate degrees).

Regarding their occupations and labor market incorporation: three were self-employed; one was from a working-class/poor background and had an associate's degree and owned a business in the city's Puerto Rican ethnic economy; the other two were women from middle-class backgrounds with advanced graduate degrees who were self-employed in the mainstream labor market. A total of five participants were in professional occupations (four of these were men and four had graduate degrees; all had attended public school in Puerto Rico). Six were employed as professionals in the social service sector (four of these were women, most came from poor backgrounds, and two out of the five had graduate degrees). One man who came from a disadvantaged class background on the island was a manager in the ethnic economy; and, three were in government positions (two from poor backgrounds and one from a middle-class background; all three had master's degrees). Lastly, two in this sample—both women—were not employed at the time of the interview (one came from a poor background and one from a middle-class background). Previously in the workforce and with their degrees in hand, both women had decided to exit the labor force to take care of their children.

My analysis reveals that in terms of labor market incorporation, class origins matter. These findings also highlight the role of gender in labor market outcomes. With the exception of the two self-employed women and the two women who were homemakers, most of the remaining women in my sample, although professionals, were in lower paid, gender stereotyped occupations geared toward providing services to vulnerable populations. This finding signals the need to examine gender and occupational sex segregation's role in immigrant labor market incorporation, and precisely *how* Puerto Rican women and men are incorporated.

When looking at the secondary educational backgrounds of participants, whether they attended public or private school is indicative of the material advantages with which they grew up. It also determined how stable their class status was and the likelihood that they could remain in this status. Class stability was partly a product of what Oliver and Shapiro have called the intergenerational transmission of class, or a family's ability to pass on their wealth and other resources to the next generation. This process can take a variety of forms, such as having the money to finance a prestigious education or being able to provide one's children with a down payment for a home.[10] It can also take the form of access to certain social networks and cultural practices that distinguish members of one class from another. For many whose parents were integrated in the island's professional labor market or who were self-employed, the pursuit of high levels of education was a family expectation as seen in the following examples.

Cuqui wanted to leave her small town in the center of the island to study in San Juan in one of the local colleges. Her parents, however, had something else in mind for her:

> When it came time to decide where, well I thought that I would study in San Juan, *pero mis papás fueron los que me orientaron que viniera a Estados Unidos* . . . but my parents were the ones that oriented me to come to the United Status. And they, they were the ones who pushed, they were the [sic] I applied, and they accepted me, and they accepted me in Puerto Rico. *Pero ellos fueron los que decidieron* . . . But they were the ones who decided. . . . *Ellos pensaban que la educación acá iba a ser mejor* . . . They thought that an education here [United States] would be better. That a person who graduates from a prestigious American university would find better jobs, better job opportunities, salaries. It was more a decision, well, thinking of the future, and I decided the place.

Cuqui dreamed of leaving her small town for San Juan. In her mind, people in San Juan were more cosmopolitan—they did "bigger and better" things compared to those who lived in her town, which she described as "closed-minded." Her parents had bigger plans for her. They pushed her to go to the mainland because they believed she would get a better education. Cuqui's parents' decision making embodied concerted efforts to enhance Cuqui's opportunities in the future; more importantly, her parents—small business owners on the island—had the resources to finance her move to the United States.

Daniel also pursued a mainland education. In the following quote he explained the circumstances under which he came to study at a prestigious university in Indiana.

> After studying in high school, I went to Indiana and it was mostly because I *quería estudiar afuera* . . . I wanted to study abroad . . . and the experience of going abroad I think . . . has a lot of value and that's why I went. . . . I know that the education over there is better and also, *mis papás querían que fuera para afuera, o sea todos mis hermanos estudiaron afuera, casi todos* . . . my parents wanted me to go abroad, I mean all of my siblings studied abroad, almost all of them. . . . *Así que fue "just a natural choice" de ir para fuera* . . . So it was "just a natural choice" to go abroad. I applied to about five universities, and then Indiana, I knew it had a good football team, but in truth I did not know it was

that good of a university until I applied there and went there, you know, "then you learn." *Uno está más pendiente al "ranking" y eso, pero el motivo original era para ir para afuera* . . . One is paying more attention to the ranking and such, but the original motivation was to go abroad.

Pursuing an undergraduate education in the mainland was a pattern already established in Daniel's family, as is common among middle- and upper-class families on the island. It was a "natural choice" because it was a privilege conferred in part by his parents' solid middle-class position. This also was the case with many others in this study. For example, Rosana, discussed in chapter 1, had a grandfather who was a university professor. She attended college in the same U.S. city in which her sister lived. Liesl, too, attended the same university to which her mother had gone. Liesl's parents encouraged all of her siblings to go abroad for their college educations. This was ingrained in them from an early age:

> *Bueno, básicamente cuando nosotros nos íbamos criando ya mamá y papá nos habían dejado saber que nosotros no íbamos simplemente a terminar la escuela superior.* Well, basically when we were growing up my mother and father let us know that we would not simply just finish high school. For me it was a continuation of my education, I was not going to have nor did I consider an option of whether or not to study in college. For me, I did not think that. I went abroad because I had the opportunity, *porque mis papás obviamente los dos estudiaron afuera* . . . because obviously my parents both studied abroad. My aunt also studied abroad and she's very (*sic*) about people going abroad, *y mis hermanos también se fueron para afuera, yo era la tercera* . . . and my siblings also went abroad, I was the third. My older sister had broken away, and I was next, so *me fui para afuera sin pensarlo* . . . I went abroad without thinking about it. I applied, my parents took me to look at which college I liked the most, which one to pick. We went with some of my friends too. I mean, it was a continuation, in reality, for me, it was not like something that would not happen. *Ir a universidad era oficial* . . . Going to college was expected.

Liesl's mother still knew some of the teachers and administrators at the university she attended. As such, sending Liesl there provided an added measure of reassurance of her well-being given this level of familiarity. Additionally, Leisl had a cousin attending that college which played into the decision as well.

A mainland education was also viewed as better by some of the Puerto Ricans I interviewed, given the social status a U.S. degree conveys to future employers, whether on the island or mainland. This prestige was a component of the college decision-making process. For example, in the following quote, Teresa, a return migrant to Puerto Rico, explained that she made the decision to go to a mainland university in the South because of the status and prestige it conferred:

[I went there] because of its name, I mean it was a combination of name and it was a school that everybody knows of. . . . If I didn't go to a well known school, then I would go to Mayagüez [a university campus in P.R.], but it had to be a well known school. . . . *Yo no iba a ir a los Estados Unidos si no era una escuela que se conociera realmente* . . . I was not going to go to the United Status if it was not a school that was really known.

The importance placed on going to a prestigious university is a manifestation of the absorption of U.S. culture and its standards of success. It is so common, that some (particularly those who could afford to) pursued this kind of education just to satisfy their curiousity. Teresa discussed how this also motivated her to study abroad:

Well, curiousity, *yo siempre he sido una persona sumamente curiosa* . . . I've always been a highly curious person. *Siempre veía televisión, y . . . quería ver otra gente, otra manera de vivir, conocer a gente de muchas partes del mundo, siempre me gustó eso* . . . I always would watch television, and . . . I wanted to see other people, another way of living, and to meet people from all parts of the world, I always liked that. And I actually achieved that goal. I have friends from all parts of Europe, India, China, all parts of the world. France, well, everywhere, and I've always liked that. I have always been very curious and so I was able to meet a lot of people like that and I would never have done so in Puerto Rico.

Parental socio-economic status shaped the routes to a college education among those I interviewed. In a global, restructured economy, a college education is increasingly fundamental to achieving a middle-class lifestyle. Parents who encourage their children to study abroad are aware of this reality; at the same time, sending one's children to a mainland university is a status marker on the island, exemplified by the many high-end cars on island roads with bumper stickers bearing the brands of U.S. universities. Like Cuqui, Daniel, Liesl, and Teresa, many others decided to pursue a U.S. college education with the backing of their parents. They benefited from the intergenerational transmission of class status and wealth.

This path to getting a mainland education reflects one perspective on the class divisions that are reproduced with each generation on the island and mainland. For these Puerto Ricans' children, college attendance was a family expectation. Contrary to those Puerto Ricans who joined the middle class after overcoming backgrounds of economic hardship, those in this group were born into this privileged class. Their educational options regarding college and postgraduate studies were more than just "natural choices" as Daniel stated, they were structurally enhanced resources. For those who did not have access to resources or a financial safety net that

would facilitate a U.S. education and migration, U.S. citizenship conferred by the island's political status proved to be a crucial factor in ac-
cessing educational institutions and other opportunities for social mobility. I discuss the impact of the island's political status on educational
opportunities later in this chapter.

Social class advantages that would enhance educational outcomes were
transmitted in other ways. In the following excerpt from Liesl's interview,
she described how her adjustment to mainland living was made easy by
her prior in-depth knowledge of English:

> E: And when you arrived there [United States], how did it go?
>
> L: It went well. Because, *gracias a Dios era bilingüe* . . . thank God I was bilin-
> gual.
>
> E: So you already knew English when you arrived?
>
> L: Yes, I knew English. Dad and Mom . . . *nosotros estuvimos expuestos,* we
> were exposed. We went to camps there, it was only one year but it was
> enough to expose you. We also traveled to the United States a lot and to other
> parts of the world and so you're not fearful. In reality it was an adventrure.
> So in my case it was an adventure, and, of course in the beginning you feel
> homesick and you get, down. [You say] "I miss my home," and all those
> things but at the same time you are having a world of fun.

Part of parents' efforts at preparing students for a mainland education
involved steering them to learn English as part of their education. In
Liesl's case, she had received her primary and secondary education at a
bilingual private school in the San Juan metropolitan area. Like Liesl,
many in my study knew English well before moving abroad. This may be
part of a larger trend in which the use of English on the island has been
increasing.[11] According to 2000 Census Bureau statistics, 14.2 percent of
the island's population over the age of five spoke *only* English at home; of
those who spoke Spanish at home, 34 percent reported knowing English
well or very well. In all, 61 percent of islanders say they speak English,
and 42.9 percent of the island's population over the age of five speak English well or very well.[12]

Liesl's bilingual fluency is a result of her parents' concerted efforts at
ensuring that she master both languages. Just as important, however,
were her parents' resources, allowing them to provide opportunities that
would enhance these skills, such as trips to the mainland and attending
summer camp abroad. In this case, parental resources undergird the experiences that contributed to Liesl's fluency in both languages.

At the time of the interviews, all participants in this sample had overcome English language barriers. In fact, all respondents in the U.S. sample reported that they spoke, understood, read, and wrote in English ei-

ther well or very well.[13] For some, however, achieving this level of competency in English was more difficult than it was for others, particularly when the first time they were faced with speaking English on a regular basis was when they arrived in the mainland.

In the case of Lourdes, her English was good enough to get her admitted into an Ivy League university. However, her first year of school did not reflect her knowledge, jeopardizing her scholarship. She described how she struggled to improve her language skills in the effort to continue her studies abroad:

> My English was not very good. *So, me tomaba una hora leerme diez páginas.* So it would take me one hour to read ten pages. And I had to read after every class, one hundred or so pages every day. There were never enough hours for me to read all those pages. *Y de los que me leía, la comprensión no era suficiente.* And of those I read, I did not entirely comprehend. I thought that having had such high grades in English all my life was equivalent. "Of course I can study in English." Well, no, it is simply not the same thing. They gave me free tutoring because I was on financial aid, but I was too proud to accept tutoring. So . . . at the end of the year, [I got a] 1.8 GPA. If you were under a 2.0, your scholarship would be in danger. So, *me fui a Puerto Rico y me pasé el verano entero, en hamaca, leyendo libros, ocho horas al día. Y eso es lo que hice el verano entero.* So I went to Puerto Rico and I spent the whole summer in a hammock reading books, eight hours a day. Cable TV at night, and books during the day. . . . Fiction so that it would be more entertaining, but to practice, practice, and practice. And the next semester I arrived, *estudié como una loca,* I studied like crazy, and [I got a] 3.5.

Similarly, Natalia spent many hours at night watching cable television to learn the language. Natalia's struggles with the language were intense given her limited proficiency. She was taking English classes at night at a nonprofit agency, given that her new job, even though it was working with Latino students in two schools, still required knowledge of English, which she did not have. The quote below illustrates how deeply Natalia's struggles with learning English impacted her experiences regarding adaptation to mainland living:

> When I began to visit the schools . . . when I had to [give a talk] for the first time, *¡Ay mija!* . . . *Yo pues lo decía y todo el mundo se miraba y, y torcían las caras como que; "¿Qué estará diciendo ésta?"* Oh girl! I would talk and everyone would look at each other and, they would turn their heads as if, "What is she saying?" And the children were laughing, and I said, *"Ay Dios mío, o salgo corriendo o ¿qué hago? . . .* Oh my God, I either run away or, what do I do?" *Y yo lloraba.* And I would cry. You know, I would arrive home in the afternoons and cry for a good long while, and I would kneel and ask God. I would tell him, *"Dios mío, abre mi mente . . . ya que me diste esta oportunidad Señor . . ."*

"My God, open my mind . . . since you gave me this opportunity Lord." So I
would go to bed every day at three in the morning watching television in
English. And so, I continued to go to the [English] classes and did all of my
homework. I would go to class at night.

Some participants struggled with the language and this impacted the
kinds of jobs that were available to them when they first arrived. Additionally, level of competence in English was important; those who knew
English well did not express as much anxiety about language issues when
discussing their experiences with adaptation. In one case, difficulties with
the language kept one woman out of the labor force altogether. While I
was interviewing Miguel, his wife, Olga, interested in the topic, joined
our conversation. She described how her own language limitations kept
her from working outside of the home. Even though Miguel's salary was
enough to support their family, the isolation she felt at home all day by
herself, while her husband and children were creating new lives for themselves, contributed to feelings of depression. Miguel's job opportunity led
them to settle in an area with few Latinos. As such, Olga had not met anybody who spoke Spanish. Learning English for her represented a way to
connect with others in her new neighborhood.

While not necessarily a big issue if one were to incorporate into an ethnic enclave, weak English skills meant a sharp reduction in job opportunities, status, and, in turn, overall well-being when one incorporates into
the mainstream labor force. This is common among immigrants whose
educational credentials and skills do not adequately transfer upon migration to a new country.[14] In these kinds of cases, citizenship allows Puerto
Ricans to access services to help with migration transitions more rapidly
than would be the case with other immigrant groups. I elaborate on this
in the next section.

Citizenship-Based Opportunities and Resources

Puerto Rico's status as part of the United States confers opportunities and
resources to migrants. Like formal education, citizenship can be used as a
resource for social mobility as I illustrated at the outset of this chapter
with Natalia's and Ana's migration experiences. When Puerto Ricans did
not have parental economic resources at their disposal, opportunities bestowed by citizenship facilitated educational attainment on the island, as
well as migration and educational attainment in the mainland, both of
which, in turn, impacted labor market incorporation.

As I have illustrated, the pursuit of a university degree was a strategy
used to increase one's chances of successful labor market integration,
whether on the mainland or the island. At a broader level, high levels of

education facilitated entry into the transnational professional workforce, thereby increasing cross-border settlement options. While having the resources to finance an island or mainland college education is an important factor in explaining the conditions under which Puerto Rican teenagers decide, or their parents decide for them, to continue their undergraduate studies on the island or whether to go "abroad" for school, having access to educational institutions because of federal loans or scholarships was important as well, particularly among those Puerto Ricans who came from working-class or poor backgrounds. Puerto Ricans are eligible for college loans regardless of whether they decide to attend an island or mainland university. Regarding migration for educational purposes specifically, affirmative action policies make mainland institutions more accessible to island Puerto Ricans regardless of class background. While these sources of aid helped all Puerto Ricans to different extents, they were most crucial for those with limited resources. Two cases in particular illustrate how the island's political status as a U.S. commonwealth facilitated educational attainment for those from disadvantaged socio-economic backgrounds.

Lourdes, discussed earlier, moved to a Pennsylvania city when she was eighteen years old to attend college. Currently a thirty-four-year-old entrepreneur, she has lived there since. She and her husband, also an immigrant, recently opened their own business, a store in the city that specializes in Latin food products. Lourdes has an Ivy League education and has been quite successful economically. This, however, was not always the case.

Lourdes had a difficult childhood. Her parents divorced when she was thirteen; her younger siblings were five and one at that time. After the divorce, Lourdes' mother supported the family working as a secretary. She managed to put Lourdes through private school, even though they lived in one of the metropolitan area's housing projects for a brief period of time. Lourdes' mother was the only breadwinner in the family. As such, Lourdes took on a large share of the household work. She acknowledged that this played a part in her fervent desire to leave the island to pursue her college education abroad:

> I was the oldest, and I had a lot of responsibilities at home. Taking care of my siblings, my cousin, and cleaning and cooking. *Encargada de todo* . . . In charge of everything. So, for me, it was, "*Me voy para la primera [universidad] que me coja* . . . I'm going to the first one [school] that takes me." And so for mom, it was difficult because, "*Se va mi mano derecha* . . . My right hand is leaving."

Lourdes' mother was not supportive of her decision to go abroad for school because she could not afford to pay for a U.S. education. Moreover, her mother felt that Lourdes was taking a big risk by not including a Puerto Rican school among those to which she applied. Lourdes recalled her words: "'How do you know this is going to work, that you're going to have a place to go, and that you'll be able to pay for things?' [I said], 'No,' *no es una alternativa* . . . 'No,' is not an option." Lourdes was also seeking to leave the island to get away from her uncle's sexual molestation. Studying abroad solved this problem. Lourdes was offered a full scholarship to pursue her education on the mainland, which she took.

In Lourdes' as well as other cases, a mainland education was a vehicle to escape from gender oppression. When analyzing the context in which migration decisions are made, even if they were for educational-related purposes, they reveal much about how island structures of inequality shape migration decisions. Vilma's experiences represent another example of how multiple inequalities shape Puerto Ricans' life chances.

Vilma grew up in a poor family in a suburb of San Juan. Both of her parents were orphans. As orphans, Vilma's parents grew up in extreme poverty. In his book, *Harvest of Empire*, Juan González discusses how the levels of absolute poverty on the island during the Great Depression led to the abandonment of children who could not be taken cared of. Some of these children ended up in the care of relatives or godparents.[15] In short, it is not uncommon to hear of cases like Vilma's parents.

As an adult, Vilma's father served in the U.S. Army in Korea and worked as an office worker upon returning. He took night courses and tried to get his college degree, but was unable to finish. Her mother was raised in an orphanage and went to the ninth grade as an adult, where she learned to read and write. For twenty-five years, she worked as a school cafeteria worker and a janitor. Vilma and her two brothers would help their mother with her work after school.

Vilma believed that her parents valued education, but that their lack of resources undermined their attempts to educate themselves and to extend this opportunity to their children. She stated:

[My father] wasn't able to finish [college]. He was always a very frustrated person because of that, a brilliant poor person and so was my mother, brilliant and intellectually awake, *pero no tuvieron oportunidades en la vida de estudiar* . . . but they did not have the opportunities in life to study. *Lo que tuvieron fueron malos ratos, dolor, pobreza. Y nosotros pues, ellos siempre nos decían: "Estudien, estudien"* . . . What they had were hard times, pain, poverty. And we, they always would tell us, "study, study." They wouldn't tell us how nor would they facilitate it but they would encourage us and that's so ingrained in your head that you do it. And not for ambition but for the hunger of learning.

As a woman, Vilma experienced another dimension of constraint. Vilma was interested in science, but she had to keep her ambitions a secret because of her father's attitudes regarding gender roles and what he considered to be appropriate work for women:

> It was still the time when my father especially thought that women would either stay at home or become secretaries. And in high school my dad would tell me to take the commercial course to be a secretary and I enrolled in this course in high school. But I don't know if it's genetic or something, but there was an affinity in my family for science. And I, *yo pasaba por el laboratorio de química y se me salían las babas* . . . I would pass by the chemistry laboratory and would drool, but I had to take typing classes. And I switched the second year, myself, as they say out of my own will, without asking anybody, I switched. As a matter of fact I graduated from high school in two years, that's why I entered college at fifteen *y no le dije a nadie* . . . I didn't tell anybody. I told my mom and nobody else.

Going against her father's wishes, Vilma switched tracks in high school. Had she let herself go by what was expected of her because of her gender, her life would be very different today. Even though her parents could not help her financially, with the economic assistance she obtained through a federal scholarship geared to low-income students, she began to study science at a local university in Puerto Rico. When Vilma's father found out, he did not stand in her way; he did not, however, help her either, quite different from the approach taken with her male siblings:

> The oldest went to school because my father's dream was to be an engineer, so he pushed him all the time. *A mí me dejaron quieta. A mí nadie me preguntó, nadie me dijo* . . . They left me alone. Nobody asked me, nobody informed me, I made my own decisions.

Vilma's education was the object of benign neglect due to her gender, and was afforded virtually no help from her family to pursue her education. Federal aid in the form of scholarships and loans, however, facilitated the accomplishment of her goals. After finishing her college degree and gaining teaching experience at the local university, she secured another scholarship to pursue graduate studies in the United States. She moved to the Midwest in 1981 to pursue her doctoral degree. Vilma was able to complete her master's degree but could go no farther because the federal funding for her scholarship was cut. Unlike others who relied on their parents' economic resources to pursue undergraduate and graduate studies, Vilma did not have this financial safety net. As such, she cut short her educational plans. In spite of this, she had a successful career as a pharmaceutical executive.

Just because the Puerto Ricans who are included in this study can be classified as middle- or upper middle-class because of their educational attainment and current occupations, as I have illustrated, this does not mean they have never known poverty or economic hardship. Even among those who pursued a university degree in the mainland, economic survival was not always easy. Thus, the different paths to pursuing an education and where this education would be sought reflect the different socio-economic backgrounds of Puerto Ricans' families of origin and the importance of citizenship. Vilma's pursuit of a mainland education, facilitated by her legal status that rendered her eligible for a U.S. scholarship, allowed her to achieve upward mobility in her adult life. Important to note, however, is that while she completed her graduate education in the U.S. mainland, she attained her undergraduate degree in Puerto Rico, as many others from working-class/poor backgrounds did. This reflects the outcomes of commonwealth public policies that have emphasized the expansion of island educational institutions in the past fifty years, making higher education more accessible to all Puerto Ricans.[16]

Puerto Ricans who came from modest socio-economic backgrounds found other ways to pursue their educations that relied on their legal status as U.S. citizens. Bryan, Carmen, Robin, and Franco, for example, joined the U.S. Armed Forces and were able to further their educational training in the process of fulfilling their military duties. Carmen, for example, grew up and completed her bachelor's degree in Puerto Rico. Her father encouraged her to further her education. Interested in going to law school, Carmen heard that she could continue her education if she went into the army. Under the assumption that they would finance her schooling, Carmen enlisted:

> I left Puerto Rico because, once I completed my bachelor's, well, it's a bit more difficult to try to, to continue. And the expenses of a master's degree are greater. . . . *Me dijeron que tenía buenas oportunidades si ingresaba al ejército de los Estados Unidos porque me ayudaban con los estudios, me daban unas becas, me daban dinero* . . . I was told that I would have better opportunities if I entered the U.S. Army because they would help me with my studies, they would give me scholarships, and money. . . . So I went in search of financial help to continue with my graduate studies.

The U.S. Army traditionally has been an avenue for social mobility for members of minority groups, especially African-American and Mexican-American men.[17] Those who were enlisted at some point in their lives were also among the Puerto Ricans who had moved between the island and the mainland the most. Although Carmen did not get her law degree, she did pursue training as a registered nurse. When I interviewed her, however, she was living in Pennsylvania and working as a social worker, a job she combined with her elected position as a state legislator. Bryan,

Robin, and Franco, who also entered the army, eventually settled on the island, and were economically secure because of the educational opportunities they received. Bryan worked for a U.S. company in sales, Robin was a successful attorney, and Franco had recently opened his own veterinary clinic. In all, Puerto Ricans' political mode of incorporation[18] often facilitated social mobility among many participants in both mainland and island samples.

In sum, these were some of the conditions under which Puerto Ricans ended up pursuing educational opportunities in the United States. College recruiting practices among mainland universities often tap into Puerto Ricans' middle class high schools to diversify their own student populations. Although many of these universities rely on students' privileged financial backgrounds to pay their own way through school, for those without the means to pay for a mainland education, U.S. scholarships and grants were available to them provided that they met the eligibility requirements. Thus, Puerto Rico's political relationship to the United States has facilitated the social mobility of many of its island residents who otherwise might not have been able to access institutions of higher education, either mainland or island ones, because they lacked the means to pay for it.

One last point to consider regarding a mainland college education is that while many viewed pursuing this as a better choice in terms of quality of schools, not all ascribed to the ideology that a U.S. education was always better than an island-based education. This very point caused friction in some families. Sometimes there was resentment towards those who left to pursue their studies abroad. For example, Lourdes' mother interpreted Lourdes' desire to leave Puerto Rico negatively, as a statement of how Lourdes viewed her mother, and Puerto Rico generally. This caused tension between them:

> In a certain way . . . my mother [thought] "Well, and what is wrong? I went to UPR [University of Puerto Rico]. *¿Por qué tú no crees que sea educada suficiente? ¿O que no me ha servido? Los he mantenido siempre.* Do you not believe that I'm sufficiently educated? Or that it has not been of use to me? I've always supported you." Blah blah. And it's like, [I would say], "Mami, it is not a statement about you, or about what you did. Simply, I just consider that for me, in fact, *sería mejor irme a estudiar a una universidad de mejor calibre* . . . it would be better if I go study at a university of a higher caliber." [Mother would say], "UPR is great . . ." and this and that. And I [would say], "Well, perhaps it was great for you, but it is not great for me." And in a certain way, every time, the whole time I was studying here [United States], there was that friction in the sense that, [she felt like] *"¿Por qué crees que lo de afuera es tan mejor que lo de adentro?* . . . Why do you think that everything from abroad is better than what is in here?"

This kind of clash reflects the backlash to the ideology that U.S. products, services, and ways of living are superior to island opportunities, practices, and lifestyles. While some clearly valued a U.S. education and U.S. quality of life over that experienced in Puerto Rico, others demonstrated pride in living in Puerto Rico for the number of years that they did, and missed it. As Marta said to me in her interview, she was very proud to be a product of the University of Puerto Rico.

Just as a high level of educational attainment reflects advantages of class and legal status, having a family history involving migration leads to other intangible assets that are manifested in ties with mainland communities. Ties to social networks embody another resource that resulted in advantages regarding incorporation. I turn to this in the next section.

Social Networks

Currently, about half of Puerto Ricans reside on the mainland. According to scholars such as Doug Massey, as more people migrate, network expansion increases so that "each act of migration creates a social infrastructure capable of promoting additional movement."[19] Known as the theory of cumulative causation, part of this social infrastructure involves social capital, or having access to social networks in the mainland. Pierre Bourdieu defines social capital as "the sum of the resources, actual or virtual, that accrue to an individual or a group by virtue of possessing a durable network of more or less institutionalized relationships of mutual acquaintance and recognition."[20] Thus, having a friend or relative in the area of destination helps with adapting to a new society, thereby increasing the likelihood of migration.

A study by Jorge Duany of 650 households in four Puerto Rican communities indicated that multiple linkages connected these island communities to certain cities in the United States. Among those who circulated within these communities, recurrent migration was associated with close kinship networks in the United States. Duany argues that these ties helped migrants secure opportunities in both the mainland and island, including financial support, jobs, housing, and emotional support.[21] His findings highlight the importance of access to social networks in facilitating immigrant incorporation.

Among those interested in moving to the mainland but who had not secured formal employment or education prior to moving, social networks opened up the option of migration and influenced decisions regarding where to settle. We saw this at the outset of this chapter with Natalia. Even though her half-brother helped her initially, he remained uninvolved after she moved. As such, not all networks resulted in social capital. As Cecilia Menjívar's study of Salvadoran networks in the United States reveals, poverty and undocumented legal status greatly hindered the ability to activate social capital within immigrant networks.[22] While legal status does not hinder networks in the case of Puerto Ricans, it is possible that class background does. My data show that in most cases, networks facilitated positive migration experiences and determined the areas of the country in which Puerto Ricans, particularly those from working-class/poor backgrounds, decided to settle. Given that all of those whom I interviewed had attained a middle-class lifestyle, they did not face to the same extent the structural constraints that affected those in Menjívar's sample. The lack of legal restrictions to migration also meant that the ties binding mainland and island networks were easier to sustain.

For example, Antonio, discussed earlier, visited the mainland as a child because members of his extended family lived in New York. Even though he grew up in Puerto Rico, he spent his summers in New York:

> It turns out that on my mother's side, my mother, and one of her sisters . . . *todo el mundo se vino p'acá* . . . everyone came here [United States]. I had from my mother's side, my grandmother and all of my uncles here [United States]. And then (*sic*) my grandfather, who also ended up here after he was old, and an aunt. So my mom always sent me up to visit my grandmother. She would send us in the summers, and I spent many summers in New York. With my grandmother and my cousins . . . *pa' que, no perdiera el contacto* . . . so I wouldn't lose contact. But when my grandmother died, and I was eleven or twelve, well, my mom stopped sending us because my grandmother wasn't there. But I always spent my summers in New York.

As Antonio's explanation of his extended family's settlement illustrates, having social networks abroad influenced his worldview and the options he perceived available to him. By partaking, even if occasionally (i.e., summers), in other family members' lives abroad, Puerto Ricans witnessed firsthand that migration was an option as a livelihood strategy, opening avenues that otherwise would be outside of one's realm of possibility. As networks expand, so do life chances, both real and perceived. Many Puerto Ricans on the island became socialized into these possibilities. In Juan's case, his opportunities expanded once he decided to follow in his brother's footsteps by getting his undergraduate degree *afuera* (abroad).

Juan grew up in the San Juan metropolitan area, in a neighborhood infamous for its poverty and crime. One of seven children, he decided to go to college in the mainland because his role model—his older brother—embarked on a similar path. Juan also credits his oldest brother for his own successes as well; Juan's oldest brother dropped out of college to work and help put the rest of the children through school when their father became ill. Juan explains:

> My older brother, the oldest, he wanted to study engineering, but he couldn't study engineering because for a time my dad was sick. He left, he left his first year in college, he left college and began to work, and he really ran the family for a time, my older brother. *Así que en cierto modo se sacrificó por el bienestar del resto de la familia . . .* So in a way he sacrificed himself for the well-being of the rest of the family. My second brother, the second in the family, finished his bachelor's and studied engineering at Cornell, New York. He got his master's and started working at a paint company in Puerto Rico, and eventually established a paint factory in the Dominican Republic. *Y mi inspiración fundamentalmente fue ese hermano Armando.* Fundamentally, my brother Armando was my inspiration. Armando was very focused, he was a real intellectual guy . . . the truth is that he was a great *role model.* . . . I had a great affinity for his friends, I mean the people with whom he socialized. He had a. . . . We have a *casi hermano de crianza* . . . quasi brother we were raised with . . . also a guy very inclined toward intellectual things. He finished a doctorate in sociology and is now a professor. And that guy also helped me focus on these things.

Juan credits his successes to members of his network of family members and close friends who paved the way for him to have certain opportunities and experiences. Connections to social networks, however, did not always have positive results—not because of the particular network, but because of Puerto Ricans' general social positioning near the bottom of mainland occupational queues. As such, the activation of social capital is structurally constrained, as seen in the following example.

Pedro migrated to New Jersey twice, first in 1983 and then again in 1988. In his first trip he stayed for only a year and returned to Puerto Rico. He had an uncle living in New Jersey, and he aspired to do better for himself than what he was doing in his small town in Puerto Rico. His uncle, however, steered him toward the only work he perceived was available to Puerto Ricans in that area—he encouraged him to work in the fields picking mushrooms:

> *Ellos me querían poner a trabajar en el campo . . .* They wanted to put me to work in the fields, and I didn't think that I had prepared myself to go to the fields . . . *recogiendo "piches"* . . . picking mushrooms. My uncle told me that this was the work that was available.

Disillusioned with this option, Pedro looked for work elsewhere. Within one year, however, he ended up returning to Puerto Rico, in part due to feelings of loneliness when his aunt and uncle decided to relocate elsewhere in the Northeast. Pedro's network played a role in his own mode of incorporation into the bottom rung of the occupational hierarchy. Despite this, his relatives did help him adjust once he arrived.

This was also the case with Rosana and Guillermo, except they were steered to better jobs compared to Pedro. Rosana's network in Texas proved fruitful; her sister was able to secure her a well-paying job in a bank. Likewise, when Guillermo moved to New Jersey because he was frustrated with the occupational stagnation he experienced on the island, he stayed with his sister and within one month he found a job, also at a bank. In sum, for families that had a history of migration to the mainland, previous experiences of migration increased the likelihood that there would be supportive kin in the mainland. As such, their choices in terms of the location of settlement were more likely dictated by whether they knew someone there.

This kind of support, however, was not typically found among mainland Puerto Rican professionals, particularly those from middle/upper middle-class backgrounds given that they often settled in locations determined by their jobs or educational institutions and not necessarily their social networks. Unless there was an established migration stream of Puerto Ricans into the particular area of settlement (or in the case of Puerto Ricans who are jointly recruited to one company such as in Ana's case), those whose mode of incorporation led them into the professional labor market were least likely to benefit from the help and support ethnic networks provide given that they settled in areas with no preexisting ties, as Olga's and Miguel's cases indicate. As I illustrate in the next chapter, separation from support networks has consequences for the well-being of mainland Puerto Ricans. Among return migrants, most professionals resettled in Puerto Rico to reconnect with their families and kinship networks. Their abilities to do this, however, depended on their modes of reincorporation into island labor markets.

THE TRANSNATIONALIZATION OF THE PUERTO RICAN MIDDLE CLASS: MODES OF [RE]INCORPORATION

The resources that Puerto Ricans have access to by way of the intergenerational transmission of wealth, class-based educational outcomes, citizenship status, and mainland social networks directly and indirectly affect their trajectories of incorporation into U.S. labor markets. I argue that these factors also impact modes of reincorporation into island labor markets upon return migration. Unlike the approaches of assimilation scholars who view integration into the dominant group in the *receiving* society as the manifestation of successful incorporation, my data suggest that Puerto Ricans' modes of incorporation involve periodic settlement experiences in both sending and receiving societies fostering assimilation into a transnational professional workforce. Similar to those who have argued that circular migration usually improves the occupational status of Puerto Ricans,[23] I argue that circular migration enhances transnational labor market incorporation. Among return migrants to Puerto Rico in particular, educational attainment and job experiences in the United States often are associated with entry into the professional sector of the island's occupational structure. More generally, these opportunities and resources are built upon to enhance socio-economic opportunities in the mainland *and* island, thereby producing a transnational middle class in which migration as a strategy to build up formal and informal education serve as the main modes of entry.

The same information provided for the U.S. sample in table 2.2 is illustrated for return migrants in the Puerto Rico sample in table 2.3. In addition to providing information on class backgrounds, migration circuits, reasons for U.S. migration, degrees attained, and labor market incorporation while living in the United States; I also include information about reincorporation into island labor markets. I organize this data according to the following occupational mobility categories: upward occupational mobility; lateral occupational mobility; downward occupational mobility; and "other." Within each occupational mobility category, I specifically illustrate the labor market transitions that return migrants undergo upon their latest island resettlement.

Recalling table 2.2, contrary to the U.S. sample, more people in the sample of return migrants to Puerto Rico had attended private school on the island (sixteen) than public school (four) and as such, were from middle/upper middle-class backgrounds. Of the four who went to public school in Puerto Rico, three attended Title I schools (there is no information available for the fourth public school). As such, only three participants in this sample are considered to be from working-class/poor backgrounds. This differs considerably from the U.S. sample in which twelve share this class background. When comparing the educational backgrounds of both samples to the general population in Puerto Rico, census data from the year 2000 reveal that 82.4 percent of all children enrolled in grades one through eight and 82.7 percent of all adolescents enrolled in grades nine through twelve attended public schools.[24] Thus, the mainland sample more closely reflects the educational experiences of Puerto Ricans raised on the island than the Puerto Rico (return migrant) sample does.[25]

In terms of the reasons for U.S. migration, twelve of the twenty-three migration decisions made on behalf of those from middle/upper middle-class backgrounds were for educational related purposes (nine to pursue undergraduate degrees). Moreover, seven of the migration decisions

Table 2.3. Class Origins (Educational Background), Reason for Migration, Educational Attainment, and Occupation by Labor Market Incorporation and Reincorporation: P.R. Sample

Labor Market Mobility: U.S. and P.R.	Class Origins (Educational Background)[1]	Reason for U.S. Migration for each Migration Journey[2]	Degree Attained and Location of Educational Institution	Occupation in the U.S.	Occupation in Puerto Rico upon Return Migration
Upward Occupational Mobility: Professional in U.S.; Self-Employed in Puerto Rico					
Edgardo	Middle/Upper Middle-Class Private School	1. Medical Training/Job 2. Medical Training/Job	B.S. (P.R.) M.D. (P.R.) M.D. Specialization (U.S.)	M.D. Training	Doctor-Private Practice
Ivonne	Middle/Upper Middle-Class Private School	Medical Training/Job	B.S. (P.R.) M.D. (P.R.) M.D. Specialization U.S.)	M.D. Training	Doctor-Private Practice
Ricardo	Middle/Upper Middle-Class Private School	1. Undergraduate Education 2. Job opportunity	B.S. (U.S.) M.B.A. (U.S.)	Business Executive	Small Business Owner
Liesl	Middle/Upper Middle-Class Private School	Undergraduate Education[2]	B.A. (U.S.) M.S. and Ph.D. courses (U.S.)	Engineer; Graduate Student	Graduate Student, Bookkeeper for family business, Homemaker
Rosana	Middle/Upper Middle-Class Private School	1. Undergraduate Education 2. Job opportunity[2] 3. Job opportunity[2]	B.A. (U.S.) Some M.A. courses (degree not completed) (P.R.)	Banking	Translator
Upward Occupational Mobility: Government in U.S.; Self-Employed in P.R.					
Franco	Middle/Upper Middle-Class Private	1. Undergraduate Education 2. Army Duties (paid for education)	B.A. (U.S.) Ph.D. (U.S.)	Army Veterinarian	Veterinarian Private Practice

(continued)

Table 2.3. *(continued)*

Labor Market Mobility: U.S. and P.R.	Class Origins (Educational Background)[1]	Reason for U.S. Migration for each Migration Journey[2]	Degree Attained and Location of Educational Institution	Occupation in the U.S.	Occupation in Puerto Rico upon Return Migration
Upward Occupational Mobility: Government in U.S.; Professional in P.R.					
Robin	Middle/Upper Middle-Class Private School Middle/Upper Middle-Class Private School	1. Educational Exchange 2. Army Duties (paid for education)	B.S. (P.R.) J.D. (P.R.)	Army	Lawyer
Upward Occupational Mobility: Low Wage Service in U.S.; Professional in P.R.					
Taína	Middle/Upper Middle-Class Private School	Undergraduate Education	B.A. (U.S.)	Hotel Hostess	Paralegal
Lateral Occupational Mobility: Professional in U.S.; Professional in P.R.					
Bryan	Working-Class/Poor Public Title 1 95%	1. Army Duties (paid for undergraduate education) 2. Economic opportunities[2]	B.S. (P.R.)	Consulting	Consulting
Marta	Middle/Upper Middle-Class Private School	Job opportunity	B.A. (P.R.) M.A. (P.R.)	Teacher	Teacher
Cristina	Working-Class/Poor Public Title 1 46%	Graduate Education[2]	B.S. (P.R.) M.A. (U.S.) Ph.D. (U.S.	Psychologist	Psychologist
Teresa	Middle/Upper Middle-Class Private School	Undergraduate Education	B.S. (U.S.) M.S. (U.S.)	Engineer	Engineer
Dana	Middle/Upper Middle-Class Private School	Husband's Medical Training	B.S. (P.R.) Ph.D. (P.R.) Post Doc: (U.S.)	Post Doctoral Researcher	Researcher

Name	Background	Reasons	Education	Occupation	Occupation
Eliud	Middle/Upper Middle-Class Private School	Medical care for daugher and Medical Training/Job[2]	B.S. (P.R.) M.D. (P.R.) Residency (P.R.) Fellowship: (U.S.)	Medical Doctor	Medical Doctor
Jaime	Middle/Upper Middle-Class Private School	Undergraduate Education[2]	B.S. (U.S.)	Scientist	Scientist
Lateral Occupational Mobility: Managerial in U.S.; Managerial in P.R.					
Pablo	Middle/Upper Middle-Class Private School	Undergraduate Education	B.A. (U.S.) M.A. (P.R.)	Manager	Manager
Lateral Occupational Mobility: Government in U.S.; Government in P.R.					
Ana	Middle/Upper Middle-Class Private School	Job opportunity	B.S. (P.R.)	Engineer	Engineer
Downward Occupational Mobility: Professional in U.S.; Low-Wage Service in P.R.					
Paloma	Working-Class/Poor Public Title 1†	1. Ex-husband's job transfer 2. Job opportunity	B.A. (P.R.) Some graduate courses (U.S.)	Teacher—worked at a Community Agency	Customer Service Representative
Other: Professional in U.S.; Not Employed in P.R.					
Javier	Middle/Upper Middle-Class Private School	1. Pilot Training 2. Job opportunity	B.S. (P.R.)	UPS—Former Editor	Unemployed, considering job offer in publishing company in U.S.

(continued)

Table 2.3. (*continued*)

Labor Market Mobility: U.S. and P.R.	Class Origins (Educational Background)[1]	Reason for U.S. Migration for each Migration Journey[2]	Degree Attained and Location of Educational Institution	Occupation in the U.S.	Occupation in Puerto Rico upon Return Migration
Other: Not Employed in the U.S.; Self-employed in P.R.					
Daniel	n/a Public School†	1. Undergraduate Education 2. Graduate Education	B.S. (U.S.) M.B.A. (U.S.)	Business student	Small Business Owner

[1]Class origin is measured by whether or not respondents attended private or public secondary school. Private school attendance is used as a proxy for middle/upper middle-class status, in that families must have sufficient disposable income to afford private school tuition. For public schools, information is given regarding whether or not it is a Title 1 school and the percentage of the student population eligible to receive free and reduced price school lunches. This information is used as a proxy for a disadvantaged class status given that it indicates whether or not the school was located in an impoverished community.

[2]Indicates that there was a social network available to facilitate migration and integration.

†Information not available.

Sources: Project data (2001) and National Center for Education Statistics, 2005, http://nces.ed.gov/globallocator/.

among this group involved occupational reasons, in particular, specific job opportunities. Given that the working-class/poor group has only three participants (five migration circuits), it is difficult to compare these groups. One can note, however, that only one of these migration decisions was for educational-related reasons (pursuit of a graduate degree), one was for a job opportunity, and one of them was in search of economic opportunities, while none of the middle/upper middle-class group migrated for economic opportunities—they were more likely to have a job in place before migration. Lastly, both groups had participants who migrated to join the armed forces.

In terms of returnees' educational attainment, all had at least a college degree. One of the three participants who came from a working-class/poor background had a graduate degree; eleven of the sixteen from middle/upper middle-class backgrounds had graduate degrees.

These high levels of education are reflected in patterns of U.S. labor market incorporation and reincorporation. Table 2.3 illustrates the patterns of occupational mobility across labor markets—the mainland and the island's. When examining the most recent job held when they were living in the United States, fourteen Puerto Ricans were integrated into the professional labor market, three were in the government sector, one worked as a manager, one worked in a low-wage job (in spite of her college degree), and one was a full-time graduate student. At the time they were interviewed in Puerto Rico (postmainland settlement), nine worked in the professional labor market, one worked in the government sector, seven were self-employed, one worked as a manager, one was in the low-wage sector, and one was unemployed but contemplating a job offer back on the mainland.

In terms of transnational occupational mobility, three patterns of labor market mobility emerged from the data. One pattern involved upward mobility in which participants in this sample moved from being professionals in the U.S. sector to self-employment in Puerto Rico, employment in the government sector in the United States to self-employment and the professional sector on the island, and from low-wage employment in the mainland to employment in the island's professional sector. The second pattern of occupational mobility involved lateral mobility seen in participants in the professional, managerial, and government sectors. Two of the three participants from working-class/poor backgrounds experienced lateral mobility upon island relocation. The third pattern was of downward occupational mobility seen in a professional from a working-class/poor background who integrated into the low-wage sector in Puerto Rico upon return migration.

Further examination of transnational mobility patterns reveals several trends. The increase in return migrants who transitioned into self-employment reflects the payoffs of the accumulation of formal education

in the United States. It also reflects the trend in which a U.S. graduate education is the means by which Puerto Ricans achieve higher levels of
specialization within their fields, allowing them to set up their own businesses in Puerto Rico. This is seen in the few examples of Puerto Ricans
who were in the medical profession, and the process by which their
training abroad facilitated the establishment of their private practices on
the island.

Another trend that emerges is regarding the educational payoffs of en-
listing in the armed forces (important to note that these data were collected before the Iraq war and the war on terrorism). For example, two
who worked in the government sector in the United States who experienced occupational upward mobility were in the armed forces before they
returned to the island; one integrated into the professional sector and the
other set up his own veterinary medicine practice.

None of the three participants from working-class/poor backgrounds
falls in the category of upward occupational mobility. Two of them,
however, fall within the category of lateral occupational mobility, con-
tinuing as professionals upon island resettlement. The other seven from
middle/upper middle-class backgrounds held onto their placement as
professionals (five), one continued to work as a manager, and one
continued to work in the government sector. Interestingly, Ana, who
worked as an engineer for the EPA, moved back to Puerto Rico to be
with her ailing father, but continued to hold her U.S. job. Her employers
at the EPA allowed her to telecommute from Puerto Rico and continue
to carry out her occupational responsibilities. Others who experienced
this pattern often were able to remain in the same occupational field,
even if their employment changed.

The last trend to emerge involves one of the participants who experienced downward occupational mobility upon relocation to Puerto Rico.
Paloma had worked at a community agency coordinating social services
in the mainland, and returned to live in Puerto Rico because her mother
became ill. She was only able to find work as a customer service representative, her wages declining in turn. Having attained her undergraduate degree in Puerto Rico, she had taken graduate level courses while she
lived in the mainland. Her family emergency, however, cut short her education plans.

Gender impacts transnational occupational mobility patterns in the
sense that women often had a tenuous foothold in the island's middle
class due to lower paying jobs and changing family structures and responsibilities. For example, the fourth category of upward occupational
mobility involves one woman who moved from the low-wage service sector in the United States to the professional sector in Puerto Rico. Even
though she had a college education, she was not able to find work in her

area of expertise during the time that she lived in California. Once in Puerto Rico, she found work as a paralegal, an occupation that allowed her to modestly support her family. In comparison to other professionals with similar degrees of education, her placement in the Puerto Rican middle class was not as stable given that her job paid lower wages in comparison to other primary sector jobs. Additionally, as a single parent she only had one income to support her household.

It is important to examine the context in which transnational occupational mobility occurs as in the case I just discussed. The opportunities and constraints that are rooted in class backgrounds help to explain the trends in transnational labor market mobility, particularly reincorporation into island labor markets. The economic and occupational opportunities in sending countries shape the conditions of exit and the intended goals of migration. Similarly, the contexts in which return migration decisions were made are important to explaining patterns of reincorporation as seen in Paloma's case.

Among those who moved to the United States to pursue their educations, migration was often a concerted decision undertaken to improve their labor market status upon graduation, particularly when forshadowing the likelihood of successful reincorporation upon island resettlement. For example, Dana and Carlos, now living in Puerto Rico, were married years ago and moved to Florida the day after their island wedding. Carlos was going to pursue his medical specialization in Florida even though prior to this he had been planning on completing his training in Puerto Rico. The island hospital where he was supposed to train lost its accreditation. Because he had selected a mainland hospital as a second choice, he had to change his plans. Dana, who already had a Ph.D., decided to apply for a postdoctoral position in the same city. Within a couple of weeks after moving, both Dana and Carlos were busy working in their respective positions. Years later, as I interviewed Dana in Puerto Rico on her lunch break from her job as a researcher, she shared with me that, "*Siempre teníamos como meta volver a Puerto Rico* . . . We always had as a goal to return to Puerto Rico":

> That was there from our original plans, to return to Puerto Rico. First because all of our family is here [Puerto Rico] and it was just us two alone over there [United States] and so family pulls you a lot. And we always said, "*Pues vamos a Estados Unidos, nos entrenamos en algo distinto, cogemos la experiencia, nos perfeccionamos en el inglés con planes de eventualmente volver* . . . Well, let's go to the United States, we'll get training in something different, we'll get experience, we'll perfect our English, with plans to eventually return."

Dana and Carlos knew it was in their best occupational and financial interests to go abroad to build up their qualifications in the hopes of

returning in a better position to secure professional and economic opportunities on the island. As such, migration was not just one of many stages
in their life course as a newly married couple, it was a strategic investment in an island-based middle-class lifestyle. These investments paid
off; Carlos and Dana were more marketable in their respective fields,
opening up various opportunities which allowed them to relocate to
Puerto Rico years later. Nevertheless, their years in the United States were
challenging, as the next chapter will illustrate. In spite of these challenges,
their time in the United States allowed for reincorporation into island professional jobs and indirectly gave them more flexibility to cultivate their
familial relationships in Puerto Rico upon return migration:

> Fue una experiencia preciosa . . . It was a valuable experience, I would say, per-
> sonally, in the sense that my husband got some distance from his family,
> he would be alone with me. And I would do the same. And professionally
> because, we perfected our English, [and] nos desenvolvimos independiente . . .
> we developed our independence.

This kind of concerted decision making in which Puerto Ricans thought
about what it would take for a successful career on the island structured
their pathways into the transnational professional workforce. Teresa is another one who took this into consideration when she was in the process of
deciding on where to go to college. She knew from the beginning that she
wanted to settle in Puerto Rico down the line:

> Basically, I always wanted to return. . . . Two reasons if you divide them. . . .
> El lado professional . . . The professional aspect is that my dad has his own
> business and it's a business that I've always considered to have a lot of po-
> tential. So, on the professional side there has always been a lot of opportuni-
> ties. En el lado personal . . . On the personal side, well, I have my whole fam-
> ily here [Puerto Rico]; my mother and my father are here, my grandparents
> are here, my brother is here, [although] he recently moved to Miami. And my
> sister is still here. Así que básicamente ése es mi núcleo familiar y decidí regre-
> sarme. So basically, that is my family nucleus and I decided to return.

Vilma made similar decisions regarding wanting to be closer to family
members on the island, and her graduate training and U.S. occupational
experiences in the pharmaceutical industry afforded her this option:[26]

> We went to Puerto Rico, because obviously there are many opportunities in
> the pharmaceutical industry in Puerto Rico, that's why I pursued that field,
> porque era más fácil conseguir trabajo en Puerto Rico, en ese momento, que acá . . .
> because it was easier to find work in Puerto Rico during that time than it was
> here. . . . At that moment Puerto Rico experienced a boom in the pharma-

ceutical industry that here [United States] was more stable. And of course here [United States] you have to relocate to another state, move there, here, and well in Puerto Rico, you were just there.

Migration was a strategy for many Puerto Rican middle-class members to attain greater credentials and to achieve or maintain their position within the transnational professional workforce. Along the way, however, many became accustomed to U.S. patterns of living. The efficiency and emphasis on convenience that characterizes American society resulted in a more positive quality of life for many in my study. These were the aspects of American society Puerto Ricans missed the most upon relocation to the island. Consistently, return migrants would complain about issues related to resettlement—such as hooking up electricity, phone service, and overall customer service. Thus, although U.S. experiences increased Puerto Ricans' labor market opportunities upon island resettlement, it also complicated the process of adapting back to Puerto Rican society and its bureaucracies.

For many, however, reconnecting with island kin networks and sources of social support overshadowed these negative aspects. For these return migrants, island relocation gave them a sense of comfort and familiarity, in spite of the annoyances of daily life. And for those who had accrued wealth, they could always fix their annoyances with money, as Ricardo explained in the following quote:

> *El aspecto de calidad de vida me molesta en ocasiones* . . . Sometimes the quality of life aspect bothers me. . . . Because the people who are *por allá*, out there [United States], and return, realize and always have that ingrained in their head. . . . It bothers me that sometimes we lose water in the mornings; that we lose power; it bothers me that people do not respect human beings here, fights on the streets, and anywhere you go, traffic . . . so there are a number of things. . . . And I have to draw a balance between what I expect, my future (*sic*) and the quality of life, and that's where the balance is. And right now I have a reasonable balance. I mean, if things in my business don't go well, I'll close up and leave. Now, if things flourish like I expect them to flourish, well, like they say, "*El dinero puede ayudarte a subsanar muchas de [estas] cosas* . . . money can help to solve many of [these] things."

In sum, Puerto Ricans' modes of incorporation to mainland as well as reincorporation to island society hinged upon the opportunity structures and resources available to them, which either enhanced or constrained formal and informal educational attainment at each migration juncture. U.S. citizenship facilitated educational attainment, ultimately helping some Puerto Ricans climb into the transnational professional workforce regardless of where they settled. For those intent on returning to the island (and those who did return), these kinds of opportunities increased the likelihood of finding work in tight island labor markets. My findings also suggest that it is possible that successful reincorporation into island labor markets is contingent on a level of class stability and resources that are linked to one's social class origins. In other words, just as the intergenerational transmission of wealth allows for a financial safety net for the children of middle-class parents, so might parental resources serve as safety nets for those attempting to resettle on the island.

Among those still settled in the mainland, some did want to return, but could not necessarily afford to because of financial constraints or lack of job opportunities. For example, Natalia believed that the high cost of living in Puerto Rico was prohibitive, and she was not optimistic about the availability of good jobs. As she stated, "*No hay trabajo. No hay trabajo. Los trabajos se lo guardan pa' ellos mismos* . . . There are no jobs. There are no jobs. They [the rich] set aside the jobs for themselves." Natalia's words imply feelings of class antagonism by implying that the good jobs are reserved for those in the upper middle class. Jaime, a return migrant to Puerto Rico, also expressed this in the following quote, in which he explained how he perceived the island's social structure to be a closed system. He indicated that this was the reason why he pursued his degree in the mainland rather than at a university on the island:

> And with that structure, I said, "*Mira pa'l carajo, yo quiero estudiar bien. Yo me voy de aquí a buscar otras oportunidades en otros lugares* . . . Screw it, I want to study well. I'm leaving here to look for other opportunities in other places." Now here in Puerto Rico, after I've become a researcher and I come with a degree from the United States, well, I know that the opportunities will be greater here, you see? *Porque ya entras dentro de esa élite, dentro de esa estructura que te deja.* Because you can then enter into that elite, into a structure that allows you. In Puerto Rico I knew that when I arrived. And I proved it now that (sic) people to choose. It is easier for you to hire a researcher who studied in the United States or anywhere, than one who studied at the University of Puerto Rico. . . . *Es la estructura, es una estructura arcaica. Nosotros estábamos viviendo en un país tercer mundista que creemos que no lo somos, pero lo somos.* It is the structure, an archaic structure. We are living in a third world country but we believe that we're not, but we are.

That Jaime compared the island's class structure to that of a "third world country" is a statement against what he perceives to be the vast inequalities that prevent people from moving ahead financially and socially, as if the island resembled a caste system rather than a class system in which social mobility is possible. He left the island to study abroad to improve his chances of moving up upon resettlement. He accomplished this, but like others, still resents that the island's class structure appears to be closed. Paloma, the only returnee who experienced downward occupational mobility, had similar feelings:

> We moved to Puerto Rico and here, well it was very difficult, *bien cuesta arriba* . . . an uphill battle. We did not have jobs, and everything here is based on connections. Everything is based on *padrinos*. You can have all the credentials and the desire to work, all of the knowledge, but, *si tú no tienes, como quien dice, una conexión, olvídate* . . . if you do not have, as one would say, a connection, forget it.

There is validity behind these frustrations when one considers that 48.2 percent of the island's population lives in poverty.[27] This number is dramatically high when compared to the mainland Puerto Rican poverty rate, which is half the island's (25.1 pecent), yet two times as high as the U.S. poverty rate (12.4 percent).[28] In short, most Puerto Ricans are not members of the middle class. These data indicate that formal educational attainment is of crucial importance in a system of stratification in which upward mobility is also influenced by the class backgrounds of one's family of origin and social networks. For those with limited access to well-off networks, citizenship and migration are more likely to be invoked to break through the dividing line separating the low-wage and high-wage labor markets on the island. In this vein, pursuit of higher education is of critical importance, as are the structural mechanisms that facilitate access to higher education, such as government funded loans and scholarships and the expansion of the island's education system. Despite the fact that many in my study had entered into the transnational professional workforce, it is important to remember that this was a purposeful sample; there are still considerable transnational class disadvantages among Puerto Ricans. Moreover, island Puerto Ricans do not have access to the full range of advantages that U.S. citizenship bestows in comparison to those who migrate to the mainland or who have been raised there. For example, they cannot vote for a U.S. president and have no meaningful vote in Congress.

Recognizing the advantages and disadvantages of island resettlement, there were some in the U.S. sample that aspired to be transnational entrepreneurs. They envisioned having a job in the United States that would allow them to travel to the island, or even live half of the time in the mainland and the other half in Puerto Rico. Lourdes discussed this ambition in her interview. Although she did not visualize herself doing so for a while, Lourdes talked about the possibility of some day returning to Puerto Rico

and setting up her own business there, which would allow her to spend
part of the year in Puerto Rico and part in the United States:

> In reality, I don't know. I don't know if I'll finally decide to do my bed and
> breakfast there someday, *y que estoy mitad del año allá, y mitad acá* . . . and I'll
> spend half of the year there, and half here. I have no idea of how much time.
> I would like that the kids learn Spanish. . . . Maybe we can spend part of the
> year in both places, or maybe, if not, we can retire in the Caribbean.

Lourdes' ideas regarding having an economic tie to the island to facilitate her visits and increase the time she spends there resembles patterns
found among transnational immigrants who maintain their ties to their
home countries. Recent studies have discussed how transnational entrepreneurs are more likely to be "assimilated" in the United States, thereby
having access to capital that facilitates their transnational business ven-
tures,[29] further rooting their presence in both societies. Among those in
this sample, there are a couple of these entrepreneurs. However, most of
the ways in which Puerto Ricans are linked to each other across borders
go beyond economic exchanges and into the arena of relationships, kinship patterns, and family issues which I discuss in the next chapter.

In sum, there are several factors to consider when interpreting these
findings, particularly regarding the implications for the transnationalization of Puerto Rican life. Rather than a one-way or even two-way flow of
people, migration is indicative of larger changes that have resulted in
strategies in which Puerto Ricans integrate migration into the different
stages of their lives. As such, migration is not an event, and transnationalism involves more than sustainable cross border exchanges. Migration
and transnationalization have become part of the life course for Puerto Ricans; within this framework, individuals and families invoke migration
and settlement strategies to advance their particular goals at different
stages of their careers and lives.

Regarding its political incorporation into the United States, Puerto Ricans are under the influence of U.S. policies regardless of migration status. This can be seen in several examples, such as the island's education
system and the federal aid it receives in the form of Title 1 grants and free
and reduced-price lunches. Puerto Ricans, however, do not have access to
the full benefits of citizenship unless they migrate and settle in the United
States. Given the recent events surrounding the island government's shutdown and the thousands of public sector employees that were temporar-
ily laid off, preliminary evidence already suggests that economic instability on the island will give way to increases in U.S. migrations in coming
years.[30] Puerto Ricans are likely to continue in the tradition of back and
forth migration as a concerted way to piece together strategies for social

mobility. These strategies however, are not limited to the poor who follow economic opportunities. Members of the Puerto Rican middle class also have to strategically navigate their ways through transnational labor markets to advance in their careers and continue on paths that lead to upward social mobility. From these findings we can infer that how lives unfold across transnational social fields is very much rooted in the class structures of both sending and receiving societies and the mechanisms that reproduce inequalities.

NOTES

1. The mean per capital household income in Puerto Rico in 1999 dollars was $8,185, less than half of the U.S. mean per capita household income ($21,587), and about 60 percent of the per capital household income of Puerto Ricans living in the United States ($13,518) (U.S. Census Bureau 2000). Poverty rates on the island are high as well. In 2000, the poverty rate on the island was 48.2 percent compared to the poverty rate in the United States (12.4 percent), and the poverty rate for mainland Puerto Ricans (25.1 percent) (U.S. Census Bureau 2000), which is considered to be among the highest in the United States. Moreover, one-parent households in Puerto Rico, particularly those headed by women, are more likely to experience poverty. In 1999, while 44.6 percent of island families lived in poverty, 60.7 percent of island families with a female householder and no husband present lived in poverty (35 percent of families are headed by a female householder). When examining female-headed households with related children under five years of age, the poverty rate goes up to 76.9 percent (U.S. Census Bureau 2000).

Women's salaries on the island are generally lower than men's, especially since the female labor force has been segregated into lower paying clerical and administrative support positions (Mulero 1990; Núñez 1990 in Rivera-Batiz and Santiago 1996, 89). In 2000, the median earnings of women who worked full-time, year round were $15,698, compared to men, whose median earnings were $17,097. Even though the gender gap in wages is less than the gender gap between U.S. women and men (92 percent versus 73.4 percent), it is important to consider that only 33.7 percent of island women sixteen years of age and over are in the labor force, a much lower proportion when compared to U.S. women (U.S. Census Bureau 2000).

2. Portes and Rumbaut 1996; 2001.

3. One of the criticisms of welfare reform has been the issue of affordable childcare for recipients' children. Tying benefits to work-related activities has resulted in an increase in the number of children who are home alone. One study found that more than 15 percent of low-income parents had children between the ages of four and seven spending time alone or under the care of a sibling under the age of twelve (Alter 1998, in Seccombe 1999, 81). Seccombe's study on welfare mothers describes how prior to welfare reform, women chose to receive welfare rather than work outside the home for pay because they did not trust others to care for their children (Seccombe 1999).

4. Grosfoguel 1999.

5. U.S. Department of Education, National Center for Education Statistics, 2005, http://nces.ed.gov.

6. Nee and Sanders 2001.

7. Nee and Sanders 2001.

8. U.S. Department of Education, National Center for Education Statistics, 2005, http://nces.ed.gov.

9. U.S. Department of Education website, www.ed.gov/programs/titleiparta/index.html.

10. Oliver and Shapiro 1995.

11. Duany 2003.

12. U.S. Census Bureau 2000.

13. Respondents were asked how well they speak, understand, read, and write English. Possible answers included: (a) Does not know; (b) Does not know very well; (c) Knows well; (d) Knows very well.

14. Parreñas 2001; Sabogal 2005.

15. González 2000.

16. I thank Jorge Duany for bringing this particular point to my attention.

17. Minorities are consequently disproportionately represented among war casualties. In her book, *Puerto Ricans: Born in the U.S.A.,* Clara Rodríguez cites several studies that reveal that Puerto Ricans' participation rates in combat and casualties are high. Falcón (1984, 37) reported that in World War II, Puerto Ricans had the second largest number of wartime casualties and *Caribbean Business* (9 April 1987, 8) reported that Puerto Rican soldiers' participation in combat in Vietnam was disproportionately high (Rodríguez 1991, 21).

18. Grosfoguel 1999.

19. Massey 1999, 49.

20. Bourdieu and Wacquant 1992, 119.

21. Duany 2002.

22. Menjívar 2000.

23. Duany 2002.

24. U.S. Census Bureau 2000.

25. The variations in class origins of "stayers" versus "returners" in my sample may be due to sample biases. Given that the recruitment of participants on the island was made difficult because of the need to insure that participants met all of the criteria for this study, I relied more on personal networks to find return migrants who had settled in Puerto Rico. Given my own background of having been raised in the metropolitan area and having attended a private high school, and in spite of my efforts to diversify the networks from which I drew, the participants may be a reflection of my own social contacts.

26. As part of efforts to industrialized the island, Section 936 of the U.S. Internal Revenue Code was enacted, offering local and federal tax incentives to U.S. companies to relocate part of their manufacturing to Puerto Rico. The incentives attracted capital-intensive industries, such as pharmaceutical and petrochemicals during the 1970s. (Cabán 1993; Ríos 1993). These tax incentives, however, were phased out in the 1990s. As a result, some of these companies have since left the island.

27. U.S. Census Bureau, Summary File 1 (SF1) and Summary File 3 (SF3). Census 2000 Demographic Profile Highlights, American FactFinder.

28. U.S. Census Bureau, Summary File 2 (SF2) and Summary File 4 (SF 4). Census 2000 Demographic Profile Highlights: Selected Population Group: Puerto Rican, American FactFinder.

29. Guarnizo 2003; Guarnizo, Portes and Haller 2003.

30. Ramos, Victor Manuel. "Puerto Rican Crisis Sparks Exodus." *Orlando Sentinel*, 13 May 2006.

3

~~

The Empty Spaces of Migration

The Transnationalization of Puerto Rican Families

Myrna and José met in Puerto Rico and have been married twenty-two years. Myrna, forty-six, has a master's degree and worked at a university in Puerto Rico. José worked for an American pharmaceutical company on the island. In 1994, José was promoted to a higher position within the company. Accepting the promotion, however, meant that José and his family would have to move to New Jersey. Considering that Myrna and José recently had been carjacked twice in front of their home, and were living in *temor* (fear), they were eager to leave the island. Upon hearing of José's opportunity, Myrna, José, and their three children decided to move to the mainland.

After just one year in their new home, José's company transferred him to neighboring Pennsylvania. Myrna explained that when her husband was relocated again, the lack of social connection and the loneliness she felt began to take a toll on her:

> *Donde yo me mudé se sentía como tan solitario, me sentía bien solitaria...* Where I moved [it] felt so lonely, I felt very lonely ... even though I had neighbors and we'd get together and everything, I had this sensation of feeling so lonely ... *Yo recuerdo que yo miraba por la ventana y yo me decía a mi misma: "Allá afuera no hay ninguna persona que yo, que me conozca bien a mi, que yo conozca"* ... I remember I'd look out the window and I'd tell myself, "There is no one out there that, knows me well, whom I know." It's not like in Puerto Rico that you've lived there all your life and you know that next door lives so and so and you have a relative or something. My family was far away and in that sense it really made it difficult for me that year to adapt.

81

In this Puerto Rican family, migration meant social mobility. José was promoted within this multinational company, which meant multiple relocations. However, the economic well-being of the family came at an emotional cost to Myrna. Even though Myrna recovered from this bout with depression, she still felt a void—a void that resulted from migration and U.S. settlement.

In the course of my research, struggles resulting from ruptured social networks and the loss of face-to-face contact with family and friends proved to be the most agonizing, particularly among women. These struggles emerged as the most widely reported sources of emotional hardship, especially for those informants who lived in the United States at the time of this study since they were in the throes of these struggles. For those who had returned to the island, however, many of these hardships were in the past and resolved through resettlement; in fact, reentering kinship networks was among the main reasons for why they returned.

In this chapter, I examine the struggles resulting from the separation from island networks of family and friends. These are the empty spaces of migration that lead to feelings of emotional isolation. I examine how gender shapes the contours of these struggles, particularly regarding the transnationalization of Puerto Rican families. I also examine how the empty spaces of migration vary in intensity between single migrants versus those who come with their spouses and families. Lastly, I illustrate how gender constrains migrants' efforts to resolve these struggles.

THE STRUGGLES OF PHYSICAL SEPARATION

Social networks of family and friends often act as support systems by providing help, access to information and resources, and nurturance through emotional support. Families are the main sites for providing this kind of care.[1] But globalization and migration fracture the social and emotional infrastructures of families, a finding that has been reported in several studies on transnational family structures.[2]

Pierrette Hondagneu-Sotelo and Ernestina Ávila illustrate how the circumstances of their employment in domestic work or child care do not permit Mexican and Central American migrants to take their children with them to the United States, resulting in high emotional costs to these mothers. They show how many "transnational mothers" tried to remain active influences in their children's lives. Similarly, Rhacel Parreñas has shown how migration from the Philippines has transformed Filipino families through a process of separation and reconstitution in which children and other loved ones are often left behind in the home country, and new families sometimes emerge from patterns of union formation in the countries of settlement.[3] Family separation through globalization and migration is so widespread that Arlie Hochschild has argued that emerging patterns of care form "global care chains: a series of personal links between people across the globe based on the paid or unpaid work of caring."[4] In other words, the care that mothers would provide to children in developing countries is taken from them by way of migration (particularly the migrations of reproductive workers, i.e., nannies) for the benefit of families in developed countries—the families for whom immigrant women often end up working. Hochschild raises questions about the implications of the globalization of care for families split apart by the working of global capitalism. From this perspective, I examine how separations due to migration affect emotional well-being among those in my samples.

It was uncommon in this sample for parents to be separated from young children. This is largely because their resources allowed for the migrations of the entire household, and because there were no issues related to the legal documentation of family members that would keep them apart. That families could migrate together eased the emotional adjustment they experienced in comparison to families that were split because of chain migration patterns and constraints regarding legalization, or getting one's "papers" in order.

Nevertheless, separation from extended family networks, and in the cases of single migrants, separation from their families of origin affected their settlement struggles.[5] Migration compromised the ability to actively nurture these relationships, resulting in more conflictive experiences adapting to mainland settlement. For women in particular, these difficulties resulted in feelings of isolation and were exacerbated by the lack of communal sources of support (e.g., help with reproductive work such as taking care of children). Family support networks alleviate women's double burden of paid and unpaid work.[6] The emerging voids—the empty spaces of migration produced by the loss of active participation in networks that afford one with love and care—affect the internal struggles related to settlement in another country. When Puerto Ricans felt they did not have these ties in the receiving society, or could not recreate them or the feelings of belonging they produced, migration and settlement decisions were reexamined.

Returning to Myrna who was introduced at the beginning of this chapter: Her initial adjustment to life in New Jersey seemed to go smoothly. She attributed this to her participation in a women's group within the transnational company her husband worked for, established to help migrant women—particularly the wives of executives—adapt. But as the introductory quote in this chapter suggests, a lack of this kind of support can be detrimental to one's emotional health. Myrna explained that this was what happened when they relocated again to Pennsylvania.

Kinship ties make a great difference in Puerto Ricans' adjustment to U.S. society; more important, however, is to feel a sense of belonging that comes from feeling cared for within such a context—of feeling emotionally embedded into that context. Originally a concept used in the field of economic sociology, the notion of embeddedness implies that economic action is constrained by the structures of social relations.[7] Alejandro Portes and Julia Sensenbrenner further developed this notion in their theoretical elaboration of the concept of social capital, which they define as "collective expectations affecting individual economic behavior."[8]

Being an active part of a family or social network is instrumental in that they both act as support systems, fulfilling needs such as kinship and caregiving. In a society that is foreign, social ties can become sources of capital, particularly when relationships act as conduits to other kinds of opportunities and resources. Having sources of social capital does not mean, however, that positive emotions will be generated or that one's emotional well-being will be enhanced. This is particularly the case with professional migrants whose U.S. social capital is rooted more in occupational networks—networks that may be void of emotions of love or care. As such, I argue that relationships and the emotional support one gets from them result in more than just social capital; social interaction, companionship, and feelings of connection to a group or community increase feelings of *emotional embeddedness* that are often compromised upon migration by the rupturing of active network participation. My use of the concept of embeddedness in this book moves it beyond its economic sense to mean how an individual's emotional well-being is affected by social relations that are contextual and structurally constrained. I argue that positive emotions, such as happiness, emerge out of feelings of *emotional embeddedness*. From this perspective, home society networks remain significant because they increase the personal satisfaction that comes from a sense of belonging to a place, however distant. They provide the support that is often relied on when struggling with issues related to migration and settlement. Migration, however, frequently strains these relationships. Additionally, not having support from a network in the receiving context can compound these struggles. Thus, many Puerto Ricans are left to cope with and reconcile their settlement decisions with their feelings of emotional isolation.

Positive feelings of belonging are conducive to greater emotional well-being, a more successful experience of incorporation, and the likelihood of a more prolonged settlement experience. This can be seen in Pedro's case. Pedro, discussed in chapter 2, moved to the United States twice. He was interviewed in the mainland during his second settlement experience. Discussing his first experience of migration in which he moved by himself, he described how he felt so alone that he returned to the island after just one year of living in the mainland: *"Estaba solo, no tenía familia . . . y decidí irme . . .* I was alone, I had no family . . . and I decided to go. . . . The second time I wasn't so alone, I was with my family, with my wife."

Migrating as part of a larger household eased the effects of losing immediate contact with island networks that included family, long-time friends, and local community. It also provided support for struggles related to immigrant adaptation such as language barriers, encountering racism, and managing conflicting cultural ideologies. In spite of leaving his network behind in Puerto Rico upon his second U.S. migration, this time Pedro came with his wife who was a source of support that insulated him from the isolation that he had experienced during his first migration.

Just as migrating and settling within a family unit had its payoffs, it was not uncommon for single migrants to feel the voids of social networks more acutely than those who brought spouses or children with them. As I will discuss shortly, migrating alone has profound consequences, particularly for women who moved to the United States to pursue job opportunities.

Transnational migration also affected Puerto Ricans' abilities to nurture extended family ties. Embeddedness in extended families is not just a way in which relationships are nurtured and maintained, but a strategy that helps families survive.[9] As seen with Puerto Ricans like Marisol, a perceived weakening of extended kinship ties was a source of struggle, for these ties represented feelings of nurturance that participation in care networks provides. Marisol, who has lived in Pennsylvania for fifteen years, discussed how this was affecting her.

> I take it personal when I see that my aunts aren't calling me with the frequency that they used to. *Y pues me siento como si estuviera perdiendo la relación* . . . And so I feel like I'm losing those relationships. . . . I haven't heard anything from her [aunt] and we usually talked at least every two or three weeks.

Migration and U.S. settlement among island professionals meant that life often took on a strong individualistic tone: some were living alone, nuclear family units were separated from extended family, and most were struggling with the loss of communal sources of care and support. The benefits accrued through embeddedness in family networks took on greater meaning after migration. Edgardo, a repetitive return migrant to Puerto Rico, explained how the two times that he migrated and the time away from the island changed the way he saw his family:

> The distance from my immediate family . . . *te afecta* . . . it affects you. . . . *Somos bastante unidos* . . . We're pretty close, we try to get together, and they

are large families. . . . You end up distancing yourself a bit. You always try through e-mail, the Internet, or by phone. *Pero, siempre quieres regresar, pa' tener algun tiempo más con tu familia* . . . But, you always want to return, to have some more time with your family. And, I think it is positive to go to the United States and to return, because you start to value a bunch of things, that, [you] take for granted.

Edgardo's experience suggests that Puerto Ricans who move and are separated from kin networks begin to value them more when faced with their absence. This quote also suggests that the desire to recapture these positive feelings and experiences could alter the course of U.S. settlement, as it did in his case.

Many participants in this study maintained their connections to friends and family on the island through phone, e-mail, and visits. For some, the emotional fallout from a lack of active network embeddedness that is nurtured through consistent face-to-face contact became more evident as they returned to the island for visits. Comparing the levels of comfort and happiness they experienced on the island as opposed to the mainland resulted in contrasting experiences of well-being. Like Edgardo, Taína, a return migrant to Puerto Rico, discussed how this void in her mainland life resulted in her return to the island.

And I told them [parents], *"Yo me siento tan sola aquí* . . . I feel so alone here." I would vacation here [Puerto Rico] and everything was so nice. . . . During my vacation that December . . . I decided to leave, and return to Puerto Rico. . . . I returned to California, sold my things, among them my apartment, and I came to Puerto Rico.

In Taína's case, she never fully adjusted to the loneliness she felt in California, so she returned to Puerto Rico to recapture the feelings of comfort that visits provided her. Even though these struggles affected both men and women alike, the empty spaces of migration are gendered, and the voids were more acutely felt among women.

GENDERED EMPTY SPACES AND LIFE CYCLE EVENTS

Women are key figures in managing and sustaining transnational households, doing most of the reproductive and caregiving work with children across transnational fields.[10] Women increasingly are also managing the demands of unpaid work in the home with work for pay outside of the home. Because of this, they desire to be in environments where the burden of these responsibilities is lessened. From past research, we know that for many women, this preferred location is usually the United States, given the availability of social services and a cultural context in which gender roles are less rigid than in home countries.[11] However, as Marixsa Alicea has argued, the isolation that emerges from one's immigrant and racial minority statuses on the mainland interact with women's experiences, so that the home country is the context in which reproductive work is done in community, even if it also represents the site of oppression.[12] This leads to contradicting perceptions of "home" among women.

I argue that migration as a process that unravels care networks— networks composed of family and friends who are both sources and objects of love and emotional support—can affect the struggles related to migration, to the point where it could lead to a reevaluation of settlement. This is particularly the case for middle-class women who rely less on mainland social services to maintain their independence and whose resettlement options are more varied because of their class status. Thus, the conditions under which women opt for return migration are not just gendered but also class-based.

For women in particular, life-cycle events often altered settlement experiences. Dana, for example, discussed in chapter 2, returned to Puerto Rico to resettle. It was not, however, until the birth of her child that being apart from her family of origin and their care became a deeply emotional experience in which the payoffs of being connected to a social and emotional network were so clear to her. Dana had a postdoctoral position at a university in the South. Her husband was also undergoing training at a local hospital. Dana and her husband were doing well financially— they were investing in their careers and they felt comfortable there. Like many others documented in the previous chapter, they were doing well economically.

Even though Dana's experiences in U.S. society were positive, the birth of her son proved to be challenging, particularly because of the absence of her family. Her mother did come to the mainland for the birth, and even stayed with her for a month after the baby was born, helping her and caring for the baby. Once her mother returned to Puerto Rico, however, Dana became severely depressed. Although postpartum depression is common for women, Dana was in a tenuous state given the physical separation from her family. In addition, she could not get the support that she needed from her husband, since he had just started a new training at a hospital forty-five minutes away from their home. Dana was left alone to cope with her depression, her new baby, and a newfound sense of isolation:

Me dio una depresión terrible . . . I was terribly depressed. . . . I [was] practically alone with the baby. . . . I would see the sun go down and come up in the morning with Miguel on my shoulder crying. . . . He never slept more than two hours in a row, and, because of his colic, I was in such a deep depression that I told my husband, *"Mira, mañana voy para Puerto Rico; cojo un avión y estoy con mami para que me ayude con Miguel porque no puedo, [no] aguanto más* . . . Look, tomorrow I'm leaving for Puerto Rico; I'm getting on a plane to be with my mom so she can help with Miguel because I can't take it anymore." And that's what we did.

Because of her U.S. settlement, Dana was now part of a transnational family. Dana's cultural background had not prepared her for this situation. Dana's vision of what a family was transcended immediate ties—her husband and her new son—and included her family of origin—her parents and sisters. Although in the initial stages of her migration Dana appeared to be adjusting well, the birth of her child led her to struggle with her own settlement decision, as she was conscious of the pain resulting from this separation. Dana felt the same duality that Rosana spoke of in chapter 1. She felt that there were two places for her, or at least that she needed elements of both places in her life to pull through a difficult transition. Dana had to reconcile the positive outcomes of U.S. settlement with her longing to be embedded in her own island care network. For her, these were the contradictions of transnational living.

Dana improved once she decided to go to Puerto Rico for a visit. Even if the visit was temporary, getting a reprieve from dealing with feelings of emotional and social isolation allowed Dana to focus on her own well-being. The time she spent with her mother seemed to have a healing effect on her, not to mention having access to the emotional benefits of care giving within a familiar context and in the presence of loved ones. The island thus represented a respite, giving meaning to Dana's return "home":

I think those two weeks that I was here in Puerto Rico, my mom took the baby, then his colic went away, [and] I was able to rest. Maybe it was also the chronic tiredness that I had. Not knowing, not being able to make a call, "Mami, come get the baby." *Por el hecho de ellos estar aquí en Puerto Rico y yo por allá* . . . Because of them being here in Puerto Rico and me being over there [U.S. mainland]. So I came here, we were together two weeks, resting. Mami took the baby, gave him his bottle with squash baby food. His colic went away. And after two weeks I returned and everything settled down.

In this context, a visit to the island represented a strategy that made life on the mainland more palatable. Temporary visits "home" allow Puerto Ricans to replenish the mental and emotional energy required to continue to endure transnational lifestyles—that is, living in one location, but considering another location to be one's home. These are the emotional and social costs of leading a transnational lifestyle. As such, these visits facilitated long-term adaptation to U.S. settlement; there was comfort in the knowledge that one could visit at any time:

> For me it was my mother's support, who raised five children and had so much experience, so at that moment it was the "support" that I needed that wasn't from my husband. . . . My sisters, who are like mothers to me, are so excellent that I had my family's support. [They said] "Give me the baby and go to sleep so you can rest." I couldn't do that in the United States, none of that. *Y fue como que un apoyo que yo necesitaba, como un respiro para no estar toda agobiada* . . . And it was the support I needed, like a respite so as to not be overwhelmed.

On a deeper level, the respite Dana spent in Puerto Rico represented an alternative lifestyle to the one she was experiencing in the United States—one surrounded by family and social networks in a familiar cultural context. It was common for participants in this study to discuss that when they got back to the United States after a visit to the island, they felt like outsiders for a period of several weeks. This emerged as a recurrent theme in the interviews; it is indicative of how a dual frame of reference (in which migrants compare their feelings of emotional well-being across borders) fuels the notion that, "Perhaps I'd be happier if I moved back to the island." In many cases, family ties and social networks contributed to migrants feeling more connected to their surroundings in Puerto Rico. Thus, when migrants perceive that they only experience high levels of emotional embeddedness on visits to the island, and they continually noticed the stark contrast once they returned to their mainland homes, migrants questioned their settlement decisions and evaluated whether they should act to recapture the feelings of emotional well-being experienced in the home society on a more permanent basis.

Although she had initially reported that she had resettled in Puerto Rico because of a job opportunity, Dana acknowledged that the main pull to return was her family, especially having their presence in her son's life on a more consistent basis:

> *Yo quería que mi hijo creciera entre su familia* . . . I wanted my son to grow up among his family and to know his grandparents and his cousins and his uncles . . . from my side and Carlos's [her husband] side so that pulled us a lot. I would say that it was the main factor, the family aspect. *Y no estar nosotros por allá . . . solitos . . .* And for us to not be over there . . . **alone** [emphasis added].

Even though her nuclear family was intact in the United States, she still considered her "family" to have been separated because of migration.

Although she was with her husband and newborn, she considered them to be *"solitos,"* alone. At a broader level, Dana's cultural ideologies conflicted with her material realities. Her desire to return to Puerto Rico on a more permanent basis became more acute and manifested itself in other realms of adjustment to U.S. society:

> *Yo honestamente quería regresar . . .* I honestly wanted to return. There were days where, I didn't want to speak English that day. Like, *"¡Ay! Hoy no quiero hablar inglés otra vez . . .* Ugh! Today I don't want to speak English again." I needed a . . . because of my family. We, I come from a very close family and, and I needed, it's like I was ready to return. No, I never visualized myself living a whole life in the United States.

Dana's statement is not just about not wanting to speak English, but about wanting to be in a familiar environment where she could be herself. The emotional embeddedness for which she longed meant being able to speak her native language, but more importantly, being in the context in which that was possible—the context in which she could also be with those with whom she had spent all of her life. These wants emerged to a new level of consciousness after Dana's child was born:

> *En realidad fue bien fuerte irme y para mi mamá fue bien fuerte también porque nunca, nadie de mi familia se había separado así . . .* In reality it was very hard to leave and it was very hard for my mother too because, nobody in our family had been separated like that. So, I longed to be able to return to Puerto Rico and say to my mother, "Mom, please stay with the baby that I'm going to . . . go to the store" or "I'm going out to x place" or "the baby wants to stay with his grandparents."

Dana's quote reveals that Dana herself wanted the option of leaving her child with her parents. While this want might be for instrumental reasons—having access to free babysitting—it also represents a desire to nurture intergenerational bonds. Dana acted on this desire and returned to the island. She found a job in her field and resettled in Puerto Rico with her newborn. Her husband remained in the mainland, and joined her after his medical training ended one year later. Dana's family in Puerto Rico helped her with the transition to island living and single-parenthood, providing her with emotional support as she dealt with relocation and the temporary separation from her husband. They also provided tangible support, such as caring for her one-year-old during the initial months of her return. Overall, having daily access to familial sources of support greatly helped in the resettlement process.[13] As Bryan, a two-time return migrant to Puerto Rico put it, "At least here [P.R.], you have everyone's help."

Wanting to recapture feelings of emotional embeddedness on a more permanent basis was a consistent theme found, felt by women and men alike but more clearly expressed by women in the sample. Having the resources to make decisions based on one's emotions is an advantage bestowed by socio-economic status and legal access to mobility. Thus, socio-economic status mediates how emotional considerations are weighed into settlement decisions. At the same time, the reevaluation of settlement decisions reveals how assimilation and incorporation are gendered processes.

GENDERED ROUTES TO INCORPORATION

Migration created unanticipated problems in fulfilling previously held ideologies and values regarding gender-based work and family socialization. These emotional dislocations varied with marital and motherhood statuses. Most women and men worked to reconcile struggles and come to terms with transnational constraints.

For women, the emotional struggles of migration and U.S. settlement often involved reconciling traditional, culturally-bound gender ideologies with the values of western capitalism absorbed through middle-class socialization in Puerto Rico. Some reconcile these conflicting ideologies by building up social networks in the receiving society and seeking out sources of emotional support. As I have illustrated, others draw on the support from island networks through visits. Others seek the avenue of island resettlement to recapture these positive emotions on a more long-term basis. My findings also reveal that island patriarchal structures and relations constrain the options of transnational actors, particularly women. Thus, while for some, mainland settlement is interrupted through return migration, mainland settlement for others is characterized by persisting emotional dislocation when competing cultural ideologies cannot be resolved through transnational strategies or return migration itself.

Recently divorced with no children, Raquel, who had lived in the mainland for eleven years, discussed how months earlier she attended a good friend's wedding on the island. This event had a profound effect on her:

> The wedding was in August. I was with my best friends from childhood, with my family, and I left Puerto Rico. . . . I even thought, "*Dios mío voy a llamar que no vuelvo* . . . My God I'm going to call [work] that I'm not returning [to United States]," because I was desperate. And it's just that my family and I are very close. Everyone seems to be there [P.R.]

Raquel struggled with her transnational status. This anguish intensified after her divorce. As a professional who was moving up in her field, Raquel was making more money than before. Yet, she seemed very sad and very lonely:

> *Que no sé por qué estoy aquí. O sea, yo digo: "¿Por qué yo estoy aquí?" Si soy la única aquí. Tengo un buen trabajo, pero, ¿qué más? ¿Qué más yo tengo aquí? (silencio)*
> . . . I don't know why I'm here [U.S]. I mean I say, "Why am I here?" I'm the only one here. I have a good job, but what else? What else do I have here? (silence)

Raquel's statement, "Why am I here? . . . I'm the only one," indicates that not being able to be an active part of her island network, and no longer having her own nuclear family unit in which to channel her energies, took meaning away from what she had attained through migration. Additionally, as women are thrust into global migration patterns, the geographic spaces separating them from their care networks limit their abilities to "do gender."

Socialization in Puerto Rican (and U.S.) society traditionally emphasizes family orientation for women and paid work for men.[14] When women and men engage in gender appropriate behaviors, they accomplish, or "do gender." Depending on the reasons, migration can compromise the ability to accomplish gender, as it leads to a dichotomizing of social life in which professional success is, in many cases, pitted against emotional fulfillment through embeddedness in island networks; for single women specifically, work and family stand in opposition to each other across borders.

While the work/family bind is typical for many women, geopolitical and cultural factors mediate this dichotomy for migrant women. Migration for men does not necessarily position them in opposition to their gender role; that providing is endemic to masculinity minimizes the potential for ideological collisions (migration status versus gender identity) resulting from migration. In fact, migration typically enhances men's ability to do gender. For women, however, particularly those who leave family and kin behind, migration precludes them from doing gender as is culturally prescribed—as caregivers and kin keepers in their families and communities. Thus, the potential for emotional dislocation resulting from colliding ideologies is much greater.

A case such as Raquel's reveals that her own assessment of how successful she has been goes beyond the economic and professional accomplishments she has attained through migration and U.S. settlement. The fact that she lives by herself, over a thousand miles away from "everyone," as she puts it, places her in a position in which her accomplishments in the mainland take on less importance. Emotionally, Raquel is not fulfilled, bringing into question her decision to live and work in the United States. In short, the conflicting emotions associated with migration and settlement are part and parcel of everyday life for immigrants. Moreover, for the participants of this study, they are also molded by the dynamics of social class and attainment ideologies, as well as transnational linkages.

"Doing Gender," Attainment Ideologies and Circular Migration

As single professionals, many of the Puerto Ricans in this study moved to the mainland to pursue educational goals and enhance their careers— aspirations that took them away from their families who remained on the island. While perhaps not evident at the time of migration, for women these decisions carried with them the potential to conflict with home society ideologies regarding gender expectations. These contradictions between middle-class attainment ideologies that invoked migration[15] and traditional gender ideologies in which family orientation represents the accomplishment of femininity resulted in feelings of dislocation for some single women. Since traveling back to the island, and at a broader level, relocating there is easier than for typical immigrants who must consider legal issues; perhaps these conflicts can never be put to rest given that the option to migrate is always available. Vilma, discussed in chapter 2, is one example.

Of the circular migrants interviewed in this study, Vilma is among those who has come and gone the most. At the time of our interview in the mainland, she was on her fourth migration circuit. Vilma worked in the pharmaceutical industry most of her adult life. Her career served as a backdrop to her journeys to and from the island.

Vilma had lived in the United States for some time when she met her first husband. Professionally speaking, she was doing well. There was, however, something missing in her life. She described her situation as follows:

> Actually in terms of work, yes, I can't complain. It was a job that required travel all over the world. I was traveling to all parts of the world for practically three years. It was a great work experience. *Pero que yo extrañaba mi familia* . . . But I missed my family. And I didn't have children either, so that's when we went to Puerto Rico.

Being away from her family began to take its toll; although Vilma had her husband, she felt alone and isolated while living abroad, even though she cultivated friendships and support networks in the United States and had social connections through her church. While these helped her combat social isolation, she stated that, *"En ese momento no era suficiente para mí . . .* at that moment it was not enough for me." In short, even though Vilma had other sources of support available to her in the United States, her growing feelings of attachment to her family in Puerto Rico overshadowed the positive side of U.S. settlement. The resulting feelings were of emotional isolation:

> [The city] was further away; the winters were colder; the winters were longer; and it wasn't as easy to travel. The trips were longer in terms of hours. So it was more, *yo me sentía más "isolated," como que estaba por allá sola* . . . I felt more "isolated," like I was over there [United States] alone.

Vilma believed that returning to Puerto Rico was the only way to cope with her struggles related to mainland living. The separation from her family of origin in Puerto Rico became increasingly difficult to tolerate as they grew in size:

> My siblings started to have children, and I had all of my nieces and nephews over there [P.R.] and *quería estar con ellos . . .* I wanted to be with them. And me not having any [children], that for me, that dream was, emotionally it was very hard. To not be able to have children.

As discussed earlier, when a woman has children and nurtures them, she accomplishes her gender.[16] Like other cultures, Puerto Rican culture hinges on these gendered expectations. Even though Vilma had rejected stereotypical feminine roles throughout her life, she nevertheless fervently desired to be a mother. Her infertility, however, was incompatible with her cultural background. To fill this void, she sought out her own family of origin, especially when her siblings began having children. Not being able to actively be a part of their lives invoked sadness and heightened her isolation. She searched for a compromise, or a way to reconcile these conflicts. Thus, after years of U.S. settlement, she confronted the possibility that she could not merge her professional aspirations with her personal goals of emotional fulfillment through children and family. She decided to redirect her personal goals and return to Puerto Rico to fill this void. The following quote reveals how she even believed that had she had children during that time, she might have remained in the United States:

> Remember that during that time I had no children. *Si yo hubiera tenido quizás mis hijos . . .* had I possibly had children and formed my own family nucleus, my life, well, then you establish roots and you get to know people from school and you go here, and to church, and the rest.

Having one's own nuclear family unit in the United States eased some of the angst women felt from being away from their families of origin. If that family, however, dissolved, or if that family was unattainable (as in Vilma's case), then the conflicting feelings resulting from incompatible goals were heightened. These gendered processes were powerful enough that they intensified the internal struggles related to adaptation. As seen with Vilma, these struggles compromise U.S. settlement when one's own migration trajectory is blamed for the inability to accomplish gender and be actively embedded in kin networks left behind.

As migration has become more and more common, Puerto Rican families are increasingly becoming transnationalized. Within transnational family structures, return migration to the island can be seen as movement inspired by the desire to reconnect with kin and care networks, as was the case with most of those who were interviewed in Puerto Rico. These decisions were motivated by the instrumental and emotional payoffs of network embeddedness and being able to have face-to-face contact with kin. As I have argued, women in particular struggled more with the loss of kin networks because they are often the ones in charge of reproductive and care work. In effect, seeking to recapture positive feelings of emotional embeddedness through return migration was a way in which conflicting ideologies rooted in socialization and culture were reconciled. At a broader level, return migration challenges conventional approaches to incorporation as predicted by much of the sociological literature. In altering the course of mainland settlement in which assimilation processes may be in motion, return migration embodies not just an expression of ethnic retention but also the manifestation of gender and cultural ideologies.

As illustrated in the previous chapter, migration and the acquisition of education lead to structural integration both in the mainland and island. Social fields that encompass island and mainland communities and institutions allow for transnational patterns of living—whether through the maintenance of a variety of cross-border linkages or through mobility itself. As such, migrants have the option of merging structural integration into a transnational professional workforce with ethnic, or hybrid, transnational identities. These identities embody livelihood strategies that seek to merge the economic and professional payoffs of U.S. experiences with emotional and cultural rewards garnered through island emotional embeddedness.

Not all Puerto Ricans, however, are able to pursue livelihood strategies that meet both their economic and emotional needs. Just as gender affected the experience of migration's empty spaces, it also affected those strategies that allowed Puerto Ricans to cope with the struggles of U.S. settlement. I turn to this issue in the next section.

Transnational Strategies, Cultural Ideologies, and Gendered Sources of Constraint

Some of the Puerto Ricans I interviewed coped with their struggles by re-creating support networks in the mainland as well as other explicit attempts to alter their social environments to improve their emotional states and that of their kin.[17] To illustrate, Pedro, who had moved for the second time to New Jersey, explained how his wife and his own involvement in a predominantly Latino (mostly Puerto Rican) church helped them create a network of friends that facilitated adaptation to mainland living:

> We befriended members of our church; we made very good friendships; we met very good friends. We'd take trips, we made plans, we formed groups, we'd go to different places . . . *ya uno no se sentía así tan solo* . . . and so then you didn't feel so alone.

For others, this strategy was itself a source of struggle. As middle-class professional migrants, many in my study settled in predominantly white, middle-class areas to which they felt loosely attached. The lack of cultural diversity in many of these neighborhoods exacerbated the loss of their own kinship networks. As such, middle-class migrants, particularly those who lived in suburban, and even gentrified urban areas where there were few Latinos, often felt removed from sources of cultural nourishment. While some Puerto Ricans like Pedro and Vilma managed to construct social networks involving other Puerto Ricans through church and work, being disconnected from areas with established Latino or Puerto Rican communities exacerbated these feelings. I will elaborate on these settlement issues in chapter 4.

As I have illustrated, return migration became a viable strategy for coping and reconciling conflicts regarding separation from kin. Because of the perceived rigidity of the island's gender system, however, some women were more apprehensive about the prospects of return migration, even if the purpose was to curb feelings of dislocation. Previous experiences with gender discrimination on the island sometimes resulted in the weighing of the negative emotions resulting from separation against the positive gender experiences in the United States regarding less rigid gender roles.

Recall the example of Raquel, who struggled with the meaning of her migration after her divorce and who felt isolated from her island kin network. A strategy such as return migration was not necessarily an option for her. Raquel was hesitant to return because of her perception of island gender norms:

Porque hay más convenciones sociales y [es] una sociedad más cerrada . . . There are more social conventions [in Puerto Rico] and [it's] a more closed society. . . . Regarding marriage, regarding male-female relationships, regarding sexual relations, female and male sexuality, many about sexuality, and the expectations if you are of one sex or another. . . . The expectations of, *una mujer sola, independiente que no tiene familia, ni hijos, ni nada* . . . a woman who is by herself, independent with no family, no children, or anything. *Pues tal vez eso me asusta, que aquí, que aquí es la norma, y allá es la diferencia* . . . Well perhaps that frightens me, that here [United States], here it is the norm, and over there it is the difference. Although over there [P.R.] people get divorced, I mean the same, 50 percent of people get divorced, but it's different.

Vilma, who experienced cultural collisions regarding wanting to have children and reconnect with her family in Puerto Rico but also wanting to maintain her levels of success in her career in the mainland, echoed these sentiments regarding apprehensions to return to the island. Contrary to Raquel, Vilma actually did move back to the island, and more than once. Her third relocation to the island, in particular, posed a different set of issues for her. Vilma divorced prior to resettling on the island. She perceived that her experience of adaptation to island society might be different this time around. In the following quote she discussed her fears about the perceptions of her divorced status, especially since her family was Catholic:

Cuando regresé pues ya era otra vida, ya era una mujer divorciada . . . When I returned it was another life, I was a divorced woman, and you know it was different. . . . In Puerto Rico you know that divorce is still, although it is so common today, it's still, my family is a Catholic family and I was one of the first to get divorced in my family, so it is still a source of stress.

Although Vilma explains that her family did support her decision to divorce by providing emotional comfort to her from a distance before she moved back, Vilma experienced a broader sense of stigmatization upon her return:

I felt the difference in terms of society. When you end up as a divorced woman . . . the wives of the other husbands and coworkers *te miran diferente,* look at you differently, *como si tú fueras a quitar,* as if you were going to take away, you understand? Because it is still a society, that in a certain sense marriage occupies an important place, same as here [United States], but it's part of our culture. *Y sí, yo sentí la diferencia* . . . And yes, I felt the difference.

With other participants in this study, the stigma against divorcees that Vilma discussed spurred migration to the United States when the divorce occurred in Puerto Rico. When women and men felt that they were break-ing these norms, this perception became the underlying motivation for their decisions to leave the island. Similarly, there were participants who, upon divorcing in the United States, delayed their return to the island for fear of this social stigma and how they would be perceived.

For women, the island also represented other elements of their gender identities that were marginalized, resulting in struggles when the out-come was resettlement. Cristina was going through this when I inter-viewed her on the island. She had lived in the United States for twenty years, and returned to the island to be with and care for her aging mother. Her relocation to the island, however, was negatively affecting her health status. The stresses associated with reintegration resulted in severe weight loss and hair loss. She explained how returning to the island made her feel:

> *Aquí [P.R.] yo me siento bien fuera de lugar* . . . Here [P.R.] I feel really out of place. . . . *Las expectativas de lo que es una mujer, o no es una mujer* . . . The ex-pectations of what a woman is, or what a woman isn't. A single woman, a woman with my academic background, or with power or status . . . to de-velop relationships with women, (*sic*) . . . whether it's appropriate or not ap-propriate; to go have a glass of wine at 11 at night alone, to one of San Juan's cafes. You (*sic*) stop (*sic*). . . . There is a constant judging, and there's a con-stant preoccupation with the "*¿qué dirán?* . . . What will they say?" And, a constant fear of these social norms, that we still do not know where they came from, but they are imposed.

As this quote indicates, Cristina was struggling with Puerto Rican soci-ety's rigid gender norms and expectations regarding sexuality and the "proper" roles of women. Cristina never openly discussed her sexual ori-entation with me; however, her interview led me to believe that she per-ceived island society as deeply homophobic, a very different experience from where she lived in California for twenty years. As a result, her strug-gles with resettlement were manifesting themselves physically in terms of her deteriorating health.

Like Cristina, Paloma resettled in Puerto Rico to take care of her mother who was suffering from Alzheimer's disease. Contrary to others who willingly relocated to care for an ailing parent, this was not an obligation Paloma happily embraced. While a source of fulfillment, care work is also a source of considerable constraint, especially for women, who are held to "higher standards of family responsibility than men."[18] While the pres-ence of women in the paid labor force has grown, the expectation of women as caregivers has not changed. Compulsory caregiving, the expectation that it was Paloma's duty to take responsibility for her parents, conflicted with her new-found independence in the United States, in which she had found a good and fulfilling job. Adhering to gendered expectations through return migration came at the expense of her professional career in the United States. This in turn, negatively affected her own well-being on the island, particularly since after sometime, Paloma's mother passed away and she took over caring for her father:

> *A mí [me] encantaba mi trabajo . . .* I loved [my] work and here [P.R.] . . . I had to take, so to speak, the first job that appeared because you have to work. And so they were very difficult changes that I think that yes, there were significant repercussions. . . . My mother's death was very hard, *adaptarme al sistema de vida nuevamente en Puerto Rico, fue bien difícil . . .* adapting to a new lifestyle again in Puerto Rico was very difficult. . . . I had left some things that for me, my work was very "rewarding". . . . At an economic level, but at a personal and professional level, it fulfilled me very much, *era como sacrificar muchas cosas . . .* so it was like sacrificing many things.

After her mother's death, Paloma's marriage ended as well. As a single mother, her job did not pay enough to make ends meet. Paloma's case illustrates the gender and class constraints that affected the experiences of single mothers in particular. Among the Puerto Ricans I interviewed, single mothers with children comprised the group that had the most constraints and the fewest options. Fulfilling gendered obligations put Paloma's economic stability at risk.

Paloma's case supports Alicea's argument regarding the oppressive effects of Puerto Rican culture on women. She argues that Puerto Rican culture is built upon patriarchy. As such, traditional gender roles result in women being treated as "emblems of cultural authenticity and purity,"[19] thereby ensuring gender inequality through expectations of subservience. The expectation of women to be family caregivers relies not only on traditional gender roles, but also on island cultural norms. Going against these norms posits Puerto Rican women against their own culture. In this regard, for women like Raquel, the island gender system acted as a barrier to reconnecting with island networks because of its patriarchal foundations. Moreover, for women like Paloma and Cristina, the island gender system negatively impacted their economic and emotional livelihoods. As Gina Pérez puts it, "Women are expected to signify cultural tradition and are the contested terrain upon which nationalist projects and ethnic identity and self-respect are constructed, resisted, and reconfigured."[20] In the empty spaces of migration, women are left to contend with their struggles regarding the pursuit of individual versus group-oriented goals. These conflictive states are rooted in cultural understandings of family.

Consequently, while family ties can fill the empty spaces of migration, they can also be sources of constraint. Just as family ties spurred most Puerto Ricans to return to the island, in the case of Ricardo and his wife, Beatriz, it was a reason for them to leave the island. During his initial migration to the mainland, Ricardo spent his last year of graduate school in the Northeast with his wife. Although they experienced difficult times economically, they bonded in such a way that they became independent from their respective families. Therefore, after a period of time resettled in Puerto Rico, his wife too,

> *estaba loca por irse* . . . was dying to go . . . so that [the decision to go for the second time] was no problem, no problem in the least. She had some problems with her mother and her grandmother because she had been with them for a long time and she was raised with them, but it wasn't a dramatic change for her, and she wanted to go.

After six years on the island, Ricardo and his wife decided that they would return to the United States for the second time. This time, they settled in Florida, remaining there for another six years.[21] Their experiences during this second migration were generally positive. Ricardo enjoyed being away from the intrusiveness of his in-laws, and felt that in the United States they were more on their own. Similar to their prior experience of migration, Ricardo's relationship with his wife grew during this second period of mainland settlement. They grew as a couple, and he even admitted to gaining more respect for his wife during this time as he saw how she became more independent when faced with having to deal with day-to-day challenges on her own, without her family's help.

While gender and family issues constrained return migration options for some, they also were related to the original motivations explaining some Puerto Ricans' departures. Like Cristina and Paloma, Lourdes also felt that the U.S. context was liberating. Prior to leaving Puerto Rico to go to college as discussed in chapter 2, Lourdes' mother was the only breadwinner in the family; therefore Lourdes took on a large share of the household work when she was growing up. She acknowledged that this role played a part in her fervent desire to leave for school abroad:

> I was the oldest, and I had a lot of responsibilities at home. . . . In charge of everything. So, for me, it was, "I'm going to the first one [school] that takes me," no? And so for mom, it was difficult because, "*se va mi mano derecha* . . . my right hand is leaving."

In spite of the many emotional struggles that Lourdes experienced in the mainland over the years, she never moved back to the island. She had lived in Pennsylvania for seventeen years. In this time she went through a divorce, many years of single parenting, and bouts with extreme loneliness. Even though at times she wished to return and reconnect with her mother and siblings, she refused to move back to the island. The distance she maintained between her family and herself was purposeful. This was because her maternal uncle sexually molested her when she was younger:

> *Años y años "of sexual molestation"* . . . Years and years of sexual molestation, so. . . . Obviously I don't want to hear from my uncle, or anything. And then, this caused much friction too. Obviously, at 17, *me quería ir corriendo* . . . I wanted to run away. So, it was like, "no, I'm not staying here. . . ." *No quiero saber nada de él* . . . I don't want to know a thing about him.

Lourdes wanted freedom from oppression; therefore she purposely remained detached from her family. She believed that some members of her family condoned her uncle's actions by maintaining an environment of silence in which discussing the matter was discouraged. As Lourdes explained this to me, something else became evident. Even though most of her interview with me was conducted in Spanish, she said to me in English, "I think I needed the distance not to be defeated." For Lourdes, Puerto Rico was the locus of gender oppression. When she discussed the oppressive elements of Puerto Rican society, she elaborated on them in English. This code-switching revealed that much of the processing she had done regarding her own gender oppression had occurred while she lived in the mainland. She associated the United States with greater levels of gender equality. For all of these reasons, Lourdes never seriously considered resettling on the island.

In some cases, in spite of perceptions that island society was more patriarchal than mainland society, the experience of U.S. settlement changed the patriarchal relations between some couples. Before migration, for example, it was important to Dana's husband that she cook a meal every night for him. After having spent several years in the mainland, and then a year apart when Dana returned to the island and her husband remained in the United States to finish his work, their roles had changed in such a way that if she chose to not cook, it did not pose a problem, although it had in the past. She noted other changes in her husband's attitudes toward gender roles as well. She attributes these changes to their time in the United States:

> For his wife to exercise alone, *pues, quizás eso antes a él le hubiera molestado* . . . well, before, that might have bothered him. But it's something that is so normal in the United States that I think that the system and the experience of having lived over there . . . he got past that a lot and now he's super, super changed. . . . He doesn't see women ironing, cooking, sweeping,

mopping. . . . He's much more open in that regard. . . . *Y yo estoy segura que el haber estado en Estados Unidos le ha ayudado a superar mucho eso* . . . And I'm sure that him being in the United States helped him get past that.

In sum, even though return migration embodied a viable strategy for some in which they could recapture feelings of emotional embeddedness, patriarchal structures and gender relations on the island were often powerful enough that they acted as barriers to resettlement for Puerto Rican women living abroad. Thus, in spite of wanting to reconnect with island care networks and achieving greater levels of emotional embeddedness, those women who perceived that rigid gender roles would negate the benefits of island embeddedness were caught in a continual struggle in which they attempted to reconcile conflicting desires rooted in gendered ideologies with the daily realities of U.S. settlement.

ENGENDERING ASSIMILATION BY LIVING TRANSNATIONALLY

The gendered issues that emerge from struggles with U.S. settlement and incorporation bring up questions regarding the gendered nature of assimilation. Revisiting the discussion in chapter 1 regarding the relationship between assimilation and transnationalism, in the process of U.S. incorporation, living transnationally may be a way in which immigrants "engender" assimilation.

Selective acculturation represents to the children of immigrants the merging of their parents' home society culture with those aspects of American culture they are exposed to everyday. Similarly, transnational living for immigrants represents a variation of selective acculturation. Important to note is that transnational activities are defined by dominant perspectives as frequent cross-border activities sustained over time. Very few Puerto Ricans in my sample fit this description. Even circular migrants spend several years in one place, and their activities were locally oriented. I argue, nevertheless, that these Puerto Ricans live transnationally, because, while their daily activities are oriented toward the location of settlement, their emotional lives transcend the boundaries of the communities in which they live. That settlement decisions are renegotiated on an occasional basis indicates that migration is always a possibility, as is the option of carrying out one's life in another part of the transnational social field in which one lives. As I have shown, particularly in the case of women, the emotional payoffs of participation in their kinship networks are significant enough that the material advantages migration bestows may take on less importance when weighed against the positive feelings that settlement within these networks engender. As such, even though the dominant discourse on transnational actors defines them as those who engage in constant cross-border activities (i.e., transnational entrepreneurs), when viewed through the lens of gender, transnational patterns of living for women involve ways in which they can remain attached to those they care for.

Transnational "ways of belonging"[22] embody gendered routes to U.S. incorporation in which the maintenance of kinship ties and the desire for positive feelings of well-being result in patterns of living—thinking, feeling, and acting—that span borders. In other words, if assimilation has been the story of male immigrants, living transnationally is how women attempt to gain independence and mobility[23] (tenets of assimilation) yet also retain their homeland identities (ethnic retention) by recreating homeland culture into hybrid, transnational identities with the intention of transforming, even coopting, their cultural backgrounds so as to redefine them, absent culture's patriarchal undercurrents. In this sense, transnational patterns of living are to women what assimilation is to men.

Since island communities are fractured by large-scale circulatory migration patterns, kinship relationships serve as proxies for emotional embeddedness. The impact of migration on family structure, however, strains these ties, giving additional credence to the argument that globalization fractures kinship patterns.[24] Advances in technology, communications, and transportation, in addition to the relative ease with which Puerto Ricans can travel back and forth, mean that they do not necessarily let go of the networks and communities they leave behind since "the idea of community is an idea about belonging among people who know one another and who care about and feel responsible to each other."[25] Given that some Puerto Ricans in my study experienced the opposite of community in their struggles with mainland prejudice, it is important to consider these experiences as well, before we examine patterns of emotional embeddedness and the factors that shifted the contours of these feelings over time. Thus, I turn to the subject of mainland prejudice in the next chapter.

NOTES

1. Cancian and Oliker 2000.
2. Hondagneu-Sotelo and Ávila 1997; Parreñas 2001.
3. Parreñas 2001.
4. Hochschild 2000, 32.
5. Vilma Ortiz (1996) has found that as single women and mothers, women use migration as a tool to achieve independence, since unmarried women were more

likely to migrate from Puerto Rico to the United States. At the same time, recently married women were more likely to migrate to and from the United States back to Puerto Rico (Ortiz 1996, 460). Given these patterns, it is important to understand how marital and motherhood statuses affect the settlement struggles of women in particular.

6. Menjívar 2000; Pérez-Herranz 1996.

7. Granovetter 1985.

8. Portes and Sensenbrenner 1993, 1326.

9. Hidalgo 1997.

10. Alicea 1997; Mahler 1998.

11. Grasmuck and Pessar 1991; Hondagneu-Sotelo 1994; Levitt 2001.

12. Alicea 1997.

13. This sheds light on research that has shown that under certain conditions, changes in family structure spur migration (Ellis et al. 1996), and that Puerto Rican women are more likely to return to the island (Conway et al. 1990).

14. Torruellas, Benmayor, and Juarbe 1996.

15. Because of the island's occupational structure, people often migrated to the United States to move up in their professions, whether because the postgraduate education they sought was not offered on the island, or because they had experienced the island glass ceiling given its position in the international division of labor.

16. West and Fenstermaker 1993.

17. Aranda 2003.

18. Badgett and Folbre 1999.

19. Alicea 2001.

20. Pérez 2004, 115.

21. Florida, particularly central Florida, has increasingly become the primary destination for Puerto Rican migrants to the mainland in recent years.

22. Levitt and Glick Schiller 2003.

23. Studies that approach migration by looking at multilevel variables and their effects on mobility argue that Puerto Rican female circular migration is a way to challenge traditional gender roles. Women see men using migration as an adaptive strategy to class struggles, and coopt it to overcome patriarchal relations (Conway et al. 1990; Ellis et al. 1996, 38).

24. Chavez 1992.

25. Cancian and Oliker, 135.

4

~~

Ethnoracial Marginalization and Cultural Alienation[1]

Noel, age forty-five, works as an administrator in one of New Jersey's many universities. He has lived in the United States for about twenty years, split among different northeastern states. Noel grew up in Puerto Rico; his parents, however, were both return migrants to the island. They had independently gone to the mainland to work in northeastern factories as part of the Great Migration in the mid-twentieth century. They met each other in the United States and resettled on the island in 1956 when Noel was one year old.

Noel got his bachelor's degree at a university in Puerto Rico. He then decided to move to the mainland to pursue his graduate education. He received his Ph.D. at a university in Pennsylvania, and later moved to New Jersey because of a job offer. Over the years, Noel did well in his career. In spite of his many successes, he felt that he had limited room for professional growth in the mainland. He shared with me an experience that heightened these feelings:

> I was looking for a higher position in public relations for which there were racial difficulties; there were difficulties with my control of the language. *Yo hablo muy bien el inglés, pero sí tengo acento . . .* I speak English very well, but I do have an accent, and there was always the perspective that perhaps I would not be good at public relations, which was false because my record in public relations is impressive. I managed [to publish] articles in the *The New York Times*, the *Washington Post*, *The Economist*, [and] the *Wall Street Journal*, something that the university had not achieved in a long time. [But] people would say, "No, *¿cómo eso que este tipo habla español, cuyo idioma principal es el*

105

español, pues sea un buen publicista? . . . No, how is it that this guy speaks Spanish, whose primary language is Spanish, could be a good publicist?"

Noel believed that because of his Puerto Rican background and the fact that his first language was Spanish (although he was fully bilingual), he had reached the glass ceiling in the field of public relations. He felt he faced opposition from people who could not get past his Spanish accent, as his cultural background was viewed as a liability rather than an asset. Noel also felt professionally marginalized because of the different perspective he brought to his field. His writing was considered by others to be "different," a bias that he believed played into his own professional marginalization:

> My approach toward advertising . . . it was an unconventional approach. *Así que yo no estoy seguro cuánto de esta [barrera] era porque la gente no estaba de acuerdo con mi acercamiento, y cuánto de esto era por cuestión de raza* . . . So I am not sure how much of this [barrier] was because some people were in disagreement with my approach, and how much of it was because of racial issues. What the facts say is that I attained more publications in the most important magazines and journals in the United States that prior to this, nobody had managed.

The outcomes of discrimination are not just that an opportunity is withheld from an individual; marginalization occurs when one's ideas and what one deems important (which might differ from the "conventional," dominant approaches) is excluded from representation. Noel's approach was not unconventional to him and it achieved results. He was published in prestigious publications and advanced the interests of the institution. Nevertheless, he reached the upper limit of the occupational ladder that was accessible to him; the rest of his moves within this institution, although challenging in certain ways, were mostly lateral.

In this chapter I discuss how marginalization, particularly Puerto Ricans' experiences with racialization and discrimination, affects their interpretations of their experiences on the mainland. I explore the multiple manifestations of racism among a group that is difficult to classify; since Puerto Ricans are racially diverse, their placement in the mainland's racial hierarchy is ambiguous. Specifically, I argue that, in addition to skin color, accents, manifestations of culture, and just being Puerto Rican can stigmatize Puerto Ricans in the eyes of mainland Americans. The resulting marginalization is rooted in ethnoracism, an ideology in which individuals are deemed inferior based on racial and ethnic backgrounds (e.g., skin color, language use, and/or cultural backgrounds). These experiences socialize Puerto Ricans into the system of U.S. race relations and, at the same time, facilitate the recognition of racism in island society as well. I examine how these experiences impact decisions to remain in the United States vis-à-vis returning to the island.

MIGRATION, ETHNICITY, AND RACE

In contemporary U.S. society, race is often conceptualized as a matter of physical difference in terms of skin color, hair texture, eye shape, or other features. These phenotype differences are used to distinguish groups from each other. In this way, race is a social construction in which we assign meaning to these distinctions. These racial constructs, however, overlap with ethnicity;[2] language use, for example, can influence the social construction of a racial group (e.g., a white person who speaks Spanish may be thought of as racially distinct from the majority, white Anglo-Saxon group). As such, ethnic factors in addition to physical characteristics influence how a person or group is racialized in the United States.

Theoretical discussions of racism and racial discrimination, however, often exclude ethnic dimensions. The ideology of racism implies that groups identified as darker in terms of skin color are discriminated against. Given that racial distinctions are social constructions, ethnicity, along with other factors such as religion, also matter when examining race and racism—they matter because they are racial in their consequences as they play into the racial formation process. As such, other markers of "race" impact outcomes such as marginalization and discrimination, even when the victims are phenotypically white.

The social construction of race also involves global-scale factors such as country of origin and the historical relationship between sending and receiving countries, and colonial powers and their political subjects.[3] In combination with language, religion, and skin color, these factors as perceived by an individual result in ethnoracism. None of these alone explains the outcomes of racism, but their totality amount to a racial matrix of domination. Similar to the matrix of domination that involves race, class, and gender as interlocking forms of oppression,[4] the social construction of race in contemporary societies consists of the interlocking effects of these ethnoracial, cultural, historical, and geopolitical factors. Within this hierarchy of racial formation, when Puerto Ricans go to the mainland, they are placed near the bottom, close to other minorities such as African Americans. This subjugation, however, is not always readily apparent to Puerto Ricans themselves. Similar to other immigrants documented in previous studies, they expect to be incorporated into mainstream American society, particularly if they were considered white in their home countries.[5] Because many of those in my samples are among the island's upper middle class, it is only after migration that some en-

counter marginalization, in particular, racialization. If they had not been
exposed to discrimination beforehand, they had difficulties comprehend-
ing the structural dynamics underlying their struggles. As such, once
Puerto Ricans settle in the mainland, the transformation of an ethnic identity and the process of racial socialization begin anew. Ethnicity, culture,
and Puerto Rico's colonial relationship with the United States, in addition
to nationality and race, stigmatized Puerto Ricans in spite of whether they
appeared to be black, brown, or white. In the next section I illustrate how
these factors alone as well as in combination with each other resulted in
racial marginalization.

MANIFESTATIONS OF ETHNORACISM: CULTURE, LANGUAGE, AND COLONIALISM

Ethnoracism has cultural manifestations. Factors such as one's native language, foreign accents, as well as other cultural forms of expression
racially mark ethnic minorities. Bonnie Urciuoli's study on Puerto Ricans'
use of Spanish and English illustrates this point. She argues that language,
in particular, the use of Spanglish or "good" English plays into the racial
formation process. In other words, Puerto Ricans are racialized through
attention to their "linguistic disorder."[6] Use of nonstandard language becomes a sign of a nonwhite race. Moreover, Spanish or a Spanish accent
serve as racial markers when racial differences are not readily apparent. A
fragment of the interview conducted with Myrna, who was introduced in
chapter 2, illustrates the racializing effects of Spanish accents:

M: I don't have a problem with English, the only thing is, I know that I will
not lose the accent. I thought that I could come to speak it and lose the accent, but I've realized . . . it's been six years and there's no way . . . (laughs).
And so as soon as I talk, people tell me I have an accent . . . and that obviously makes you feel like you are never from here. *Porque rápido que tú hablas,
por tu acento saben que no eres de aquí, no hay forma de evitar eso. Y por esa misma
razón, pues, es lo que yo siento; siempre me siento que no soy de aquí. Tengo siempre esa sensación* . . . Because as soon as you speak, because of your accent,
they know you are not from here, and there's no way to avoid that. And
that's the reason, well, it is what I feel; I always feel that I'm not from here.

E: And has anyone ever made any comments about your accent or the way
you speak?

M: Well, it's not that they've made fun of the accent, no. But yes, for example, on one occasion I went to pick up my son at his football practice, and I
couldn't find him or I didn't know where he was at that moment and I asked.
And when my son was approaching, immediately a man told him. I mean
my son was walking in my direction, but he didn't know where I was, and

so the person immediately said, "Does your mom have an accent?" And he said yes. "Oh, then she's there." *Que ya de por sí notan inmediatamente un acento que no es de aquí . . .* So as a matter of fact they immediately notice a foreign accent.

Myrna's account of this "colorless" activity—picking up her child at a football practice—lingered in her memory by the way language differentiated her when the man identified Myrna as the woman with the accent. Interestingly, this man did not single her out because of how she appeared phenotypically (Myrna identifies as *trigueña*, or wheat/brown) but because of how she sounded; her accent racialized her in that it made her feel like an outsider. Racial difference mediated and shaped this experience and created in Myrna a distinct sense of incompatibility with her surroundings; she was not "seen" for who she was as an individual, but was "seen" for what she sounded like. Not sounding white or like a native English speaker, she was singled out as different. Even though this experience did not result in discrimination per se, it touched on Myrna's perception that she did not fit in:

I don't have a problem with the accent, because I know that what's important is communication and I know I can communicate well. *Pero en ciertas situaciones me hacen sentir incómoda porque inmediatamente se dan cuenta que no soy de aquí, y eso es obvio, ¿no? . . .* But in certain situations it makes me feel uncomfortable because immediately they realize that I'm not from here, and that's obvious, isn't it? But it's like they immediately turn around, as if this person . . . calls attention because of it. And for example, when I'm with my daughters I like to speak in Spanish all of the time, and sometimes in stores, in places, restaurants, and the like, *me siento incómoda . . .* I feel uncomfortable, because people hear you speaking Spanish and quickly start to look. Maybe because of curiosity, and I [prefer] to think it's out of curiosity and not prejudice. *Pero pues te hace sentir incómoda que te estén mirando así con tanta curiosidad . . .* But it makes you feel uncomfortable that they are staring at you with so much curiosity. That's speaking Spanish, and obviously when I speak English with an accent, well they also immediately (laughs) yes, immediately you feel like they are looking at you or they are trying to listen maybe because it's different. You draw attention, let's say, in a way that I don't find pleasant.

As Myrna states, her experiences of being stared at made her feel "unpleasant." Moreover, these feelings of discomfort resulted every time she spoke—whether it was in English or Spanish:

Lo que a mí me gustaría es poder hablar como yo estoy hablando aquí contigo y no llamar la atención por eso . . . What I would like is to be able to speak like I'm speaking here to you and not attract attention because of it. *En Puerto Rico tú hablas y pues eres igual que los demás* . . . In Puerto Rico you speak and you are equal to everyone else, but then here quickly they notice that you are not from here.

The racialization of language, or using one's form of expression as an indicator of one's racial background, draws attention to group differences, particularly when they are not readily apparent. As such, it results in and continually reinforces feelings of not belonging among Puerto Ricans, reifying their colonial status as "a part of, yet apart from" U.S. society.[7] Spanish and Spanish accents not only mark minorities; through the racialization of language, a person's ability to comfortably speak is stricken when the manner in which it is done is deemed improper, inferior, and unnatural. With the recent debates regarding immigration reform, particularly the xenophobic character of public discourse over immigrants' knowledge of English, the use of Spanish in public is increasingly likely to invoke the scrutiny of native whites. Use of Spanish invokes the public's fears of "alien invasions" that could "threaten" the cultural fabric of the country (even though the fabric is a multicultural one). This leads one to wonder if the practice of racially profiling minorities will take on new dimensions (one could add "speaking in Spanish" to "driving while black," and "flying while Arab").

Stigmas related to language take other forms. Marta was born in New York City, but her family moved back to Puerto Rico when she was a child. Marta, a brown-complexioned, divorced, single parent in her late forties, moved to Florida with her daughter and got a job as a teacher. In her interview, she discussed the difficulties she had with some of her colleagues and students when she taught at an affluent boarding school. The difficulties with prejudice and discrimination that she faced as a Puerto Rican woman led to her deep dissatisfaction with work. The following quote illustrates how she felt that she was perceived by her colleagues:

> The people with whom I worked in Florida, I found some prejudice against Puerto Ricans. I had to prove myself because they kind of doubted my capability. . . . My experience over there wasn't very pleasant. There were lots of times that I had to prove myself.

Although Marta was fluently bilingual, she was among the few participants who chose to conduct their interview in English. Ironically, it was her fluency in English and the fact that she had *no* Spanish accent that revealed underlying racial assumptions. Being Puerto Rican and sounding "American" were viewed by others as an anomaly:

> Most people were surprised by the fact that I could speak the language fluently. They would ask me if I had lived in the States or if I had gone to col-

lege in the States, and I very proudly said that I was a product of the University of Puerto Rico.

Implicitly, the reaction Marta discussed was really surprise that she "sounded" white, yet was one of the "others," implying the palpable presence of stereotypes regarding Puerto Ricans. Furthermore, astonishment at the fact that a Puerto Rican could be fluent in English and have no Spanish accent reveals that the stereotypes of Puerto Ricans are built upon their juxtaposition to whiteness. Marta discussed her interpretations of how Puerto Ricans are generally perceived in the United States:

> I think that without a doubt, people in the States have a very poor opinion of Puerto Ricans. They judge us without even knowing us. The truth is that they are very ignorant in regards to Puerto Rico and Puerto Ricans. They think that we are the same people who had gone to New York, in the movie the *West Side Story*; the Jets and the Sharks. They think that we are that kind of subculture. They think that, even in the media, in the movies, in Hollywood . . . Puerto Ricans and also Mexicans are, and of course, let's say Hispanics in general, they are usually portrayed as low-life people. If it's a male, he is either a drug pusher or a drug addict; he is a criminal. If it's a woman, she is either a prostitute or a maid. And I am kind of tired of seeing that image of Puerto Ricans and Hispanics in general on T.V. and [in] the movies.

In much the same way that Spanish accents work against Puerto Ricans by marking them as alien, several other personal and cultural traits are racial markers that magnify Puerto Ricans' sense of alienation with U.S. society and, in some cases, with their own selves. These feelings of alienation erode any possible sense of emotional embeddedness to mainland society that might exist or develop. As Cuqui illustrates in the following excerpt, when a person's ethnic attributes come into question and are viewed negatively by the people around her, that person's entire self and body also come into question, making every single physical, mental, and emotional manifestation of difference seem inadequate. Similar to Myrna, Cuqui felt that the way she expressed herself marked her, making her stand out in the social circles to which she belonged:

> Where I live, the majority of the people are of, what they call WASPS. And, those people are, like, English . . . they walk a certain way, act a certain way, and they, I think that in the United States, they are the ones that form the rules . . . establish the norms. So . . . *siendo yo la única puertorriqueña aquí* . . . me being the only Puerto Rican here . . . of the people I know, well, I, moved a lot, I felt like I moved my hands a lot. . . . Nobody would move their hands and arms, and their eyes were not expressive, or anything. You know, the people talk that way. And, they don't move their mouths a lot either, nor their faces. There are many rules. *Y yo pensaba que yo hablaba muy alto, que me oía*

demasiado, y pues yo me sentía como que, que yo no tenía cultura . . . que una persona civilizada no puede actuar así . . . And I thought that I talked too loud, that I was too loud, and well I felt like, that I had no culture . . . that a civilized person did not act that way.

As seen above, the cultural differences between Cuqui and her Anglo-Saxon neighbors, latent in the very different ways in which they talk and carry themselves, led to Cuqui's sense of personal inadequacy, which to her felt like a lack of culture. Moreover, this uncultured feeling that Cuqui made reference to was a product of her becoming aware of the U.S. racial structure as manifested in her own community (i.e., "in the United States they are the ones that . . . establish the norms"). Her uncultured feeling also emerged from having internalized the implicit superiority afforded to whiteness and expressions of whiteness. As a consequence, Cuqui felt the need to change and better her "uncivilized," racialized self:

So I began to [walk] straight too; and, not laugh too loud; and, not open my mouth too much, you understand? *Son esas cosas que uno siente . . .* Those are the things you feel. And I started to change, and I got to the point where I said, *"No, pero ¿cómo eso? O sea, ¿por qué yo estoy haciendo eso? Yo me estoy convirtiendo en otra persona . . .* No, but how can this be? I mean, why am I doing this? I'm turning into someone else!"

This situation was further complicated when Cuqui compared herself to her Latino friends from independent countries. When Cuqui realized that she was becoming somebody she did not want to be—that her mannerisms, way of speech, and walk were *"bien también"* (also okay)—she still found herself alone, as a second-rate Latina:

To act like I act is also okay, *lo que pasa es que no conozco a nadie que actúe como yo . . .* the thing is that I don't know anybody who acts like me. And also, *el español de nosotros es terrible . . .* our [Puerto Rican] Spanish is terrible. And so I have friends from Chile, from Guatemala, from Ecuador, from Colombia, they all, well, pronounce Spanish beautifully. And then ours is so . . . *tan tira'o, estruja'o . . .* sloppy, creased. And, I too feel like I don't speak well. So I personally started to, to attack myself, and the way in which I did things, as if they were wrong.

Like Cuqui, many consider Puerto Rican Spanish to be a lowly dialect among Spanish-speaking populations. I argue that racialized images of Latinos due to their country of origin's position (or perceived position) in the global coloniality[8] manifested themselves in ethnic-specific terms. These ethnic-specific images stem from the "primal" characterization of their countries of origin rooted in the history of European colonial expansion. Modern-day racism is rooted in the legacy of colonialism. In effect, one's national origin is often viewed as embodying this history, particularly when such colonial subjects settle in the country that "occupied" them, revealing global dimensions to racism based on colonial legacies.[9]

Marta, introduced earlier in this chapter, had some interesting experiences reflecting this aspect of ethnoracism. While living in Florida, Marta taught English to international students and Spanish to U.S. students. Her retelling of one of her experiences illustrates the nature of life as a "colonial subject."

> That's where I had my contact with American students. I noticed that they really had no interest in learning Spanish. Their attitude was one, one of mocking the language, mocking that which was Hispanic. Because I am from Puerto Rico, when we spoke of Puerto Rico they would ask me questions. But the questions in a way I felt . . . were mocking, too. There were so many times that I heard expressions such as "Oh, we own you."

Marta's experiences reflect the dominant view of Puerto Ricans as conquered, colonized, and currently, U.S. "owned." This power relationship played out in Marta's classroom, in that her authority as an educator was undermined by her global social position as a colonial subject. This experience reflects her students' feelings of superiority associated with the role of colonial power. This example is also an instance of gendered racism, in that these young men felt that, as members of the dominant American group, they were entitled not just to own, but to subvert Marta's own authority, an expression of power that is laden with overtones of sexual exploitation by colonial "masters."

Among the Puerto Ricans I interviewed, many discussed that while they lived in the United States, they encountered widespread ignorance toward Puerto Rico. From having to show a passport when cashing a check to having to provide "history lessons" about Puerto Rico's political status, many were amazed at the ignorance of Americans about other societies, especially one that was part of the United States. Explicitly, this ignorance suggests a manifestation of ethnocentrism that some might argue plays out in any society. But, viewed against a historical structural backdrop of colonialism, implicitly the message is that some groups of Americans, in this case Puerto Ricans, are invisible and unimportant, while others, such as the Irish, Cubans, or Jews are usually considered in a more positive light.

At a structural level, American policies of benign neglect toward the island and its people and what they want regarding the island's political status amount to institutional racism, embodied in Congress and the Supreme Court position that Puerto Rico "belongs to but is not a part of the United States."[10] Puerto Ricans often internalize this status,[11] which influences the ways in which they identify (they are among the only ethnic groups to not hyphenate their identities)[12] and interpret individual acts of discrimination. As Juan González has argued, in today's anti-immigrant climate, "it is almost unthinkable that a congressional majority would be prepared to admit an entire state whose people are racially mixed and who speak Spanish as their main language."[13] Puerto Ricans' marginal status regarding their racial and cultural backgrounds is embodied in their colonial relationship with the United States.

Consequently, at both institutional and individual levels, Puerto Ricans frequently sense their positions at the fringes of American society. As Cuqui revealed in discussing the evolution of her own racial identity, "*Me dió mucho trabajo entender que yo también soy un 'outsider,' cuando yo siempre pensaba que yo estaba dentro* . . . It took a lot of work to understand that I too am an 'outsider,' when I always thought I was on the inside." One of the outcomes of colonial structures of domination is that the victims often blame themselves for their own marginality. This resembles Cuqui's actions when she was trying to act white or, as she put it, "civilized."

In short, everyday experiences with ethnoracism marginalize Puerto Ricans. One case in particular illustrates how these mechanisms of racial formation work regardless of skin color. Eliud's most memorable experience with discrimination, for example, had nothing to do with his skin color. I discuss this in the following section.

SKIN COLOR, ETHNORACISM, AND DISCRIMINATION

Research has found that race shapes the ways in which immigrants are incorporated into U.S. society. Immigrants who are white by U.S. standards experience a different mode of incorporation in comparison to black immigrants in different realms of society such as education, the workforce, housing, and social interactions.[14] This does not mean, however, that all immigrants who are considered white are automatically accepted into mainstream society. As I have indicated, the mechanisms of racial formation that factor into experiences with ethnoracism suggest that skin color is just one factor (albeit a significant one) that interacts with other markers of a minority status. To illustrate, it is appropriate to examine the experiences of both light and dark-complexioned Puerto Ricans.

Carmen, discussed in chapter 2, is a state legislator in the United States. She was visiting one of the towns in her state, a town that is predominantly white. Other local government officials were at the event, and one of them was introducing Carmen to his wife. Carmen, who could pass for white, was standing next to her assistant, Mirella, whom Carmen described as "trigueña." The politician's wife thought that Mirella was the "Latina legislator:"

The woman is thinking that my assistant is the legislator and the man continues to tell her, "No, it's not this one, it's that one" [pointing at Carmen]. And she [says], "But it can't be, she is white. No, it's her." [pointing at Mirella]. . . . *A tal extremo que la mujer no salía de su asombro* . . . To such an extent that the woman could not escape her amazement and she'd say, "She's white, she's white, she's white!" The woman touched my face and with her finger she did this [ran her thumb across her cheek] and she told me, "But you're white, you're white!"

Carmen discussed her reaction to the woman who simply refused to believe that Carmen was Puerto Rican, in spite of her light skin:

I had to laugh and tell her, "Look, the blond hair is dyed, so yes." *Y le dije: "Pero los ojos son míos y el color es mío, mamita. Eso no me va a salir . . ."* And I said, "But the eyes are mine and the color is mine, deary. That won't go a way." I had to tell her because I thought it was interesting. I took it as an act of ignorance on her behalf. And she also said, "You are whiter than I am, how can that be?" That is an act of ignorance. . . . *tienen una imagen de que el latino tiene que ser oscuro, que es inconcebible que un latino sea blanco* . . . They have an image that a Latino has to be dark, that it is inconceivable that a Latino would be white.

This example illustrates individual racism toward a Puerto Rican who was preconceptualized as racially different because of her ethnic background. This is because Puerto Ricans are juxtaposed to Americans—that is, white Americans and African Americans, as an "in-between" group. For the wife of the politician, it was out of her realm of possibility that the Puerto Rican legislator she was about to meet could be fair-skinned. As seen with previous examples, when a group is conceptualized as different yet appears to look the same (as the dominant group), then the accents and other traces of otherness will serve as proxies for race. In short, skin color confounds expressions of ethnoracism given that those on the "outside" may physically resemble those on the "inside." Racial ambiguities appear to be unsettling to dominant group members who rely on appearances to identify minorities.

Eliud's experiences of racialization are important to examine in evaluating to what extent skin color, in contrast to other markers of racial otherness, affect experiences of discrimination. A medical doctor in his forties and a return migrant to Puerto Rico, Eliud originally moved to the United States in 1992 with his family. The move was precipitated by the birth of his daughter who had a congenital disease. Eliud and his wife were in search of better medical options than those available on the island. Because there were no pediatric neurosurgeons in Puerto Rico at that time, one year after their daughter was born, with the help of friends who lived in the United States, Eliud's wife took their daughter to receive treatment in Florida. Upon experiencing the positive conditions in which their daughter was being treated, they made the decision to relocate permanently. Eliud secured a job in the United States, in which he would further his own medical training, allowing him to join his family.

Eliud, however, struggled during the time he lived in the mainland. He constantly felt like an outsider. As a result, his desire to return to the island grew over the years. He explained,

> I didn't feel like I was from there [United States], I didn't feel comfortable . . . the five, six years that I was there, I came every year to Puerto Rico for a vacation and once I landed here [P.R.], I entered the airport and I felt at home. And it wasn't the same there. Over there [United States] I felt uncomfortable.

In spite of his dislike toward mainland living, Eliud was professionally fulfilled because the hospital where he worked had state-of-the-art facilities. Eliud experienced the rewards of structural incorporation into the receiving society regarding occupational mobility and greater income in comparison to Puerto Rico. Once he left the workplace, however, Eliud felt these feelings of discomfort again. In essence, Eliud felt like an outsider in every context except at work, where he felt most comfortable.

One experience in particular brought his feelings of discomfort from an emotional level of perception to a cognitive level of interpretation, reinforcing his desire to leave the United States. Interestingly, this experience occurred at work.

> Well, I had this guy, I admit him [to the hospital] . . . and was treating him. Then his son calls me and the first thing he says on the phone, *porque yo tengo mi acento en inglés* . . . because I have my accent in English, [he said] that "No 'third [world] country doctor,'" he doesn't want treating his father. *Yo le contesté que: 'Yo no era ningun* third [world] country doctor' . . . I answered that, "I was no third [world] country doctor." *Que venía de una escuela acreditada por su gran nación* . . . That I came from a school accredited by his grand nation. *Que soy ciudadano americano* . . . That I'm an American citizen, "in case you don't know that Puerto Ricans are American citizens" (he laughs). *Y le tengo los "boards" de su gran nación* . . . And I passed the "boards" from his grand nation. I told him all of that.

Eliud's sarcastic use of the term "grand nation" represented the paradox of his situation. He was living in one of the "grandest" nations of the world, but it was a nation built on racism; a legacy that continues to have a direct impact on Eliud's well-being. In short, Eliud's emotional quality of life deteriorated. In spite of structural incorporation, white racism and American nativism prevented him from *feeling* integrated. Moreover, this experience, in fact, did not end there. The patient's son would call Eliud and say things such as,

> *"Que me cuidara . . .* That I watch myself." *Que él no iba a permitir que ningun "Hispanic, Jewish," católico ni protestante tratara a su papá . . .* That he wasn't going to permit . . . a Hispanic, Jewish, Catholic, or Protestant [to] treat his father and that if I touched his father he was going to fracture both of my hands. . . . He would call me (sic), and he wanted information about his dad but he was always threatening me. And one day he was drunk and called and when I answer the call he [said], "Your time is up."

Eliud never met his aggressor face to face. The harassment occurred over the phone because this man only visited his father after Eliud's shift ended. Even though Eliud had a brown complexion, it was his Spanish accent that elicited this manifestation of racism. The character of Eliud's struggles as they related to mainland life, however, went beyond this isolated incident. At a broader level, Eliud tried to decipher how his background, culture, language, and identity could invoke such treatment. This incident casts light on why Eliud never felt like he belonged in the United States.

This is not to say that there are no benefits afforded to a particular skin color in a particular society. Paula Rothenberg has called this "white privilege."[15] Whiteness allows one to blend in, or integrate; what we know as exercising the privileges of whiteness. This is particularly poignant when one considers issues related to racial profiling. As such, skin color remains a fundamental aspect of ethnoracist structures. Carmen, discussed earlier in this chapter, illustrates these privileges while recounting some of her experiences. Despite her encounters with prejudice and discrimination, her white skin insulated her from discrimination that visible markers expose one to; forms of discrimination that blacks and other dark-skinned racial subjects face constantly, whether they be Puerto Rican, African American, Dominican, and so forth. Carmen tells of the time when she was shopping with a black Dominican friend and they were being followed by security around the store. Carmen's white privilege vis-à-vis her black Dominican friend's became evident. The fact that they were speaking Spanish to each other as they were being followed, however, relegated both of them to the status of outsiders. The same can be said for Antonio, whose dark skin color led to several experiences in which he was profiled and harassed by the police. He recounted one of them in the following quote regarding U.S. racism:

> A: *De que hay racismo, sí hay racismo . . .* Whether there is racism, yes there is racism. People simply [see] that you are not white, Anglo-Saxon, *no quieren saber de uno*, they don't want anything to do with you. Because (sic). Like one

day you are sitting on a patio, and the police come because someone called them that there was a, a, disorder. That you are sitting with a few friends, talking.

L: Did that happen to you?

A: Yes it happened, and they called the police. Three or four of us were sitting in chairs, talking, and a whole bunch of police cars came.

L: Were you outside of your house?

A: I was at someone else's house. We were sitting outside. And they called. And a whole bunch came (*sic*) *porque creían que había un "riot"* . . . Because they thought there was a riot. On another occasion, some friends of mine were here, they were from Puerto Rico. We were waiting in front of a church to go to church, to go in. And it was closed; we arrived too early. . . . And we were there waiting, because we knew the minister. And it was early, [we said] *"Pues vamos a quedarnos aquí en el carro en lo que abren* . . . Well, let's stay here in the car until they open." And the police arrived. [They said] *"¿Qué hacen ustedes aquí?* . . . What are you guys doing here?" "Well we're here waiting for them to open the church (*sic*)." And (*sic*) they left.

Experiences such as these reveal that light-skinned Puerto Ricans have an advantage over dark-skinned Puerto Ricans: they are less likely to be labeled and discriminated against. This is not to say that other factors do not serve to identify them as nonwhite people. Whiteness, among other factors, will mediate their experiences with racism; at the microlevel, it is a mechanism of situational privilege that can be invoked, and allows for Puerto Ricans to "pass" for white. In the case of darker skinned Puerto Ricans, this course of action is not an option, leaving them more vulnerable to blatant forms of racism such as racial profiling.

Puerto Ricans' white privilege is forfeited to some extent, however, when considering other factors such as accents, and in Marta's and Ricardo's case, Puerto Rican identities. When a light- or dark-skinned Puerto Rican speaks with an accent or otherwise reveals his or her Puerto Ricanness, any possible confusion that may have enveloped that person's racial/ethnic identity is clarified and racial difference is solidified. As Raquel, who is phenotypically white, states: "Well, the accent, I have a brutal accent. I mean, I've been here eleven years, I speak English very well, but I speak it with an accent. So when I open my mouth people know I'm not white."

One of my respondent's experiences indicate that when these linguistic signs are absent as well, the mere knowledge that one is Puerto Rican is enough to alter someone's behavior toward them. This was Ricardo's experience. Ricardo settled in the mainland and resettled on the island twice. He looks white, and has blue eyes and light brown hair. He related some of his experiences when working in Florida, and how employees reacted to him once they learned of his Puerto Rican background:

The time I worked [in the United States] . . . one of the most noticeable things during that time that was very negative, because it was a very negative experience, was prejudice. When I worked there, *la mayoría de la gente no sabía que yo era puertorriqueño, hasta que me preguntaban, y yo le decía* . . . The majority of people did not know that I was Puerto Rican, until they would ask me, and I would tell them. On many occasions, as soon as they would realize or know . . . *punto. Los empleados cambiaban* . . . Period. The employees changed. . . . Before, I mean, instead of now treating you and reciprocating friendship, well they change, and it occurred on various occasions.

While Ricardo noticed this change in how the employees interacted with him, one experience in particular left an imprint in his mind. Ricardo discussed one afternoon in which he, a colleague, and his boss (the owner of the company where he worked) went to lunch. He described what transpired:

One time he made a comment in the car. I was with him. We went out to eat. It shocked and bothered me but I realized what I was dealing with. We were talking about women and pregnant women and children, etc. And he told someone else who was in the car, "I had the best sensation in the 'mall,' because I saw quite a number, a large number of white women who were pregnant."

Ricardo discussed how this comment, not necessarily directed toward him, but racist and offensive nevertheless, resulted in his decision to leave the company where he worked. He continued:

Hizo un comentario extremadamente racista . . . He made an extremely racist comment. And from then on I realized a bit more of the things that he would do and I realized he was a completely racist man and that my opportunities were limited. *De ahí no iba a llegar a ningun otro sitio* . . . From there I would not go anywhere else. . . . And that's why I made the decision to leave. He was a pretty prejudiced person against blacks, Hispanics, whites, whatever, as long as they weren't a [white] person.

For both light- and dark-skinned Puerto Ricans, color is not the only marker of "otherness." Even though Puerto Ricans are U.S. citizens, the stigmas associated with being a "dressed-up colony"[16] means that they are often looked upon negatively as a people, regardless of color. Marta alluded to these images earlier when she discussed the popular conception of Puerto Ricans as those depicted in the movie, *West Side Story*. Even though traditional understandings of racism imply that white Puerto Ricans, in theory, should be able to pass for white and thus experience lesser amounts of racism than black Puerto Ricans, the stigma attached to being Puerto Rican is nevertheless present, as Ricardo indicated, and can offset the benefits of individual white privilege. Moreover, as Joe Feagin has argued in his work on systemic racism,

> How whites view a group's identity usually shapes what happens to them in public institutions, especially in regard to access to key white-controlled resources and opportunities. The white racial mindset looks at racial identities from a distinctive perspective honed over centuries of racial oppression.[17]

Within this system of racial oppression, Feagin argues that people of color are limited in their responses to the racial identities imposed by whites in "everyday worlds outside your home and local community."[18] From this perspective, the everyday worlds of Puerto Rican migrants are all-encompassing. On many occasions, experiences with ethnoracism and racist individuals often proved to be baffling to Puerto Ricans because they stood in stark opposition to institutionalized racial understandings in Puerto Rico, and in Latin America generally. I discuss this in the following section.

TRANSNATIONAL RACIAL MEANINGS

Many of the Puerto Ricans I spoke to believed that racism was a U.S. problem. Indeed, the U.S. color-coded system of racial classification differs from island conceptions of race. Some of the participants of this study discussed the shock they experienced when they arrived in the mainland and faced discrimination, as if island society was the antithesis to U.S. racism. Puerto Rico is, in fact, a multiracial society. As Carmen explained to the woman who could not believe she was Puerto Rican,

> "You can find a Puerto Rican to be white, *trigueño*, black, and he's Puerto Rican. . . . In reality, it is unpredictable what color Puerto Ricans are going to be because of the rich mixture that we have, thank God. *Por eso el mismo puertorriqueño puede ser en la misma familia blanco, negro y amarillo y como quiera es puertorriqueño y hermano* . . . That's why the same Puerto Rican can be in the same family, white, black, and yellow, and still Puerto Rican and brother. *El problema lo tienen ustedes aquí* . . . You here are the ones with the problem."

In Puerto Rico, as in other Latin American countries, race is popularly depicted as a continuum of multiple gradations between black and white.[19] These categories are fluid; movement between them is influenced by other factors aside from skin color, including social class, facial features, and hair texture, among others. This is in opposition to the traditional U.S. racial hierarchy in which membership to a particular racial group is ascribed and static. Within the U.S. framework, Puerto Ricans share the lower rung with other racial minorities, yet on an individual basis, their positioning in this two-tiered framework is contextual and, at best, ambiguous. Moreover, in spite of the fluidity of Puerto Rico's racial classification system (e.g., one can achieve a higher racial status through the acquisition of wealth), Carmen's suggestion that island society is colorblind is misleading, and probably a conclusion to which she arrived at that is rooted in her own whiteness and her position of racial privilege.

Migration is, indeed, the conduit through which Puerto Ricans formally enter into the mainland racial hierarchy. While for some it means experiencing racism for the first time, for others, racism is nothing new—discrimination may have always been present in their lives, even on the island, indicating the persisting significance of skin color. The U.S. system of race relations and racial discourse, however, triggers an evolution of their own racial consciousness that is sharper in comparison to its level of development on the island. Antonio, discussed earlier, illustrates how this racial consciousness is refined as a result of U.S. racism. Antonio is black and was often mistaken for being African American. The realities of U.S. racism initially shocked him. In the following quote he described his initial reactions to racism:

> Sometimes . . . [racism] shocks you in the beginning, but since you're not accustomed to that in that way, then, you don't know, you don't understand what it is. You don't know how to react! . . . *Es una cosa totalmente nueva . . .* It's something that's totally new. Well, with time, you begin to understand, and you learn how you will deal with that. . . . *Entonces uno empieza como a, a crear una conciencia . . .* Then you begin to, to develop a consciousness, of what you can do and what you cannot do. . . . At the same time, I mean, you can identify what is supposedly being done to us, and what is really being done. . . . Then, you begin to identify racism.

Mainland settlement and U.S. white racism have enabled Antonio to see the covert Puerto Rican racism on the island he had experienced prior to migrating. He discussed the evolution of this racial consciousness:

> *Y es bien interesante porque entonces, al tú hacer eso, entonces tú empiezas a identificar el racismo en tu propio país también . . .* And it's very interesting because then, when you do that, then you begin to identify racism in your own country too. . . . You begin to see, "*No, ésto lo conoces . . .* no, I'm familiar with this." And you see how it works. And you say, "*Coño, pero en Puerto Rico, también pasaba esto . . .* Shit, but in Puerto Rico this happened too." And that's what you didn't realize, but it was there, but you didn't realize. Because you weren't, you weren't sensitized. When you become sensitized to it, then you begin to say, "*Espérate, pero allá también hacían tal cosa. Allá también discriminaban a la gente por ésto . . .* Wait, but over there [Puerto Rico] they did this. Over there they also discriminated against people because of this." And it's very,

it's different, obviously; it's another country, but, the effect is the same, and the purpose is the same. You become sensitized to racism as a person. You can identify it, you can understand it.

It was not until Antonio moved to the mainland and confronted racism and racial profiling that he began to interpret his experiences on the island through a racial perspective. Mainland society gave him the tools to interpret his own experiences. Island racism was so ingrained in the culture that it was not typically identified as something that occurred among Puerto Ricans themselves, even if it did.

Marisol discussed the covert nature of racism in Puerto Rico and within her own family. Having light brown skin and identifying as mulatto, she explained that even though adapting to U.S. racism was a difficult process, she recalled similar dynamics when she lived in Puerto Rico:

Yo recuerdo que en mi propia casa mis tías me decían que no cogiera mucho sol para que no me pusiera muy prieta . . . I remember that in my own home my aunts would tell me not to get a lot of sun so that I would not get dark. *El apodo que me tenía mi tía era chorizo prieto* . . . My aunt had a nickname for me which was dark pepperoni for example. And they wanted to straighten my hair. I don't just have curly hair, I have a lot of hair so that it is torture to comb it. So they wanted to take out hair to thin it out, I mean [make it] less bulky.

On an interpersonal level, racism is prevalent in both societies. The privileges afforded to whiteness is not a phenomenon exclusive to the United States. While many dark-skinned Puerto Ricans recognized racism while living in Puerto Rico, it is on the mainland that both dark- and light-skinned Puerto Ricans come to recognize what being a minority entails. Vilma, for example, has light skin and green eyes. She did not come to understand racial marginalization until she moved to the mainland to get her graduate degree. In spite of her whiteness, she saw herself as a racial minority. She recounted her earliest recollection of this status:

I encountered those color differences when I got to [college]. *Porque antes de eso yo no tenía conciencia, te lo juro que no tenía conciencia de los colores* . . . Because before that I had no awareness, I swear that I was not color conscious. . . . I mean [it was] a very difficult experience in the sense that *tú encontrarte por primera vez en tu vida, con un prejuicio por solamente de donde tú eres y quien eres* . . . you find yourself for the first time in your life, with prejudice only because of where you're from and who you are. The first time, because I don't know, I wasn't conscious of that, *pero sí lo viví* . . . but I lived it.

Vilma moved into a dormitory with a roommate from the Northeast. She explained that her roommate seemed put off when she found out Vilma was Puerto Rican. Vilma noticed that her roommate seemed overly guarded with her belongings. Within a few months, they developed a friendship and her roommate confessed that she indeed was disappointed and worried when she found out Vilma was Puerto Rican. Thus, in spite of her whiteness, Vilma interpreted this experience as a racial one, lending support to the notion that racial formation is based on factors besides skin color, in this case national origin.

As Feagin contends, racial oppression against non-Europeans is systemic across all major institutions in the United States. He argues that the United States is unique in that it is the only major Western country explicitly founded upon racial oppression. While many believe racism to be a relic of the past, only about 10 percent of U.S. history has been free of slavery and legal segregation.[20] It is this social structure that Puerto Ricans incorporate to. Moreover, their experiences of marginalization often resulted in the development of bonds with other U.S. minorities. I discuss this in the next section.

PAN-MINORITY IDENTIFICATIONS AND RACE RELATIONS

Thus far, I have documented Puerto Ricans' experiences with U.S. racialization. These experiences, however, are not always obvious to those going through them or those studying them. In fact, to some, Latinos are generally not a racialized group at all.

In his book *Two Nations: Black and White, Separate, Hostile, and Unequal*, Andrew Hacker explains his title by stating, "In many respects, other groups find themselves sitting as spectators, while the two prominent players try to work out how or whether they can coexist with one another."[21] He based this on the assertion that "other" identities are more culturally or nationally oriented than those of blacks and whites.[22] Recent scholarship has debated the appropriateness of this "black-white paradigm" by arguing that the invisibility of other groups in the dominant racial discourse discourages the perception of common interests, impedes solidarity, and diminishes the "others'" subordination.[23]

Earlier in this chapter I discussed the case of Marta, who was racialized both for her accentless English and on behalf of her students for her global social location as a colonial racial subject. In the course of interpreting her own experiences with U.S. racism, she saw parallels between her experiences and that of Puerto Ricans generally, with those of other minority groups, particularly African Americans. The following quote illustrates this parallel:

> I think that the Hispanic community in the States is in a struggle very similar to the black people in the 1960s. It is a struggle for respect, validation, for

recognition. And, I think that is why I had that struggle because they have such a poor opinion of Puerto Rico. They know nothing about Puerto Rico.

Widening the lens through which to interpret racism to include ethnic, cultural, and global-colonial dimensions is indeed conducive to pan-minority identities and bonds of intergroup solidarity. Cuqui represents another case in which such interracial bonds developed. Recall that Cuqui felt out of place in her social circle of friends and acquaintances in the United States. Settled in a wealthy suburban area, she knew very few Puerto Ricans and felt like she did not quite fit in. It took Cuqui a long time to decipher the roots of her feelings of marginalization. In the course of doing so, she reached out to her fellow African American neighbor. She related to me the story of how this came about.

Within one year of moving to this suburb, Cuqui's son developed a friendship with a neighboring boy. Cuqui's neighbors were having a birthday party for their son, and even though they invited Cuqui and her family, they did not invite their black neighbors and their son. Cuqui explained the reason why she thought that the black family was not invited. She also discussed what transpired at that children's party:

> *El esposo no quería gente negra en la casa* . . . The husband did not want black people in the house. And they, they invited us and we arrived . . . and, they started to tell a bunch of jokes about blacks, that I could not believe. *O sea, yo nunca había oído cosa semejante, y que todo el mundo riéndose* . . . I mean, I had never heard anything like that, and everyone was laughing. You know, stuff like, really, really, a lot of prejudice among that whole group. And I got out of there. That I could not believe it. *Claro, que yo no dije nada* . . . Of course, I did not say anything. I mean, I didn't say anything to anyone or anything. Simply, my husband and I looked at each other, and we said good-bye, and we left. *Porque, él es judío, y yo soy puertorriqueña (risas). Imagínate* . . . Because, he is Jewish and I am Puerto Rican (laughs). Imagine. . . . *Yo digo: "En el momento que nos vayamos, pues van a empezar los chistes de este otro lado"* . . . I said, "Well, the jokes from this side will start the moment we leave."

That night Cuqui's African American neighbor called her to ask her if she knew why she was not invited to the party. Cuqui was blunt in her explanation:

> [Cuqui said], *"Mira, tú perdona, pero eso es un chorro de racistas ahí* . . . Look, pardon me, but those are a bunch of racists." And I had to tell her, . . . "Look, I'm sorry to tell you this, but I don't, you know, I feel like I have a responsibility to tell you, because your son goes to play there. And you don't know what, what, the comments that they make. . . . " *Yo me sentí horrible, porque yo pensaba que yo estaba arruinando una, una relación de vecinos* . . . I felt horrible, because I felt like I was ruining a neighborhood relationship. But at the same time, I felt responsible for, that she know. And then, *eso abrió una conversación*

entre ella y yo, entre mi vecina negra y yo. Y ella pues, me pudo decir y, y educar un poco de, de, como es, del "struggle," de la lucha de los negros y todas esas cosas que yo pensaba que era antigua . . . That opened up a conversation between her and I, between my black neighbor and myself. And she, well, was able to tell me, and educate me a bit about, the, how, the struggle, the struggles of blacks and all those things that I thought were in the past. I did not think those occurred today. And, *en esta área es bien prevalente* . . . it is very prevalent in this area.

Like many others, Cuqui believed that racism was a thing of the past. These experiences opened her eyes to the prevalence of bigotry and how members of certain U.S. groups continue to struggle with racism and prejudice. She reflected back on the meaning of this experience as an "eye opener":

Yo pensaba que el racismo era cosa del, de los años sesentas, y que éso ya no existía . . . I thought that racism was a thing of, of the sixties, that it no longer existed. And that is when I started to think about the social changes of the black race in the United States since slavery. And with all that, and to see the "struggle" of what they have been through. And, *empecé a identificarme un poco con eso* . . . I began to identify a bit with that. But of course not so much, because I have not had, I have not been a victim of any of that. *Pero, empecé a pensar que a lo mejor yo estaba viviendo algo que socialmente yo no me había dado cuenta de los cambios que me habían pasado* . . . But, I started to think that maybe I was living something that socially I had not realized the changes that had happened to me.

Cuqui began to see commonalities between her feelings of marginalization and African Americans' experiences with racism. She did not attempt to equate the two, careful to not compare her own history to that of blacks' history of incorporation by way of slavery. But her last statement in this quote suggests that both the Puerto Rican and black experiences are rooted in the dynamics of systemic racism in the United States. She continued:

Me empecé a identificar con la raza negra . . . I started to identify with the black race. That blacks often have these things happen to them too here [referring to neighborhood dynamics]. . . . *Y entonces yo dije: "A lo mejor, el 'struggle' de ellos es el 'struggle' mío"* . . . And then I said, "maybe their 'struggle' is my 'struggle.'" Except mine is much more, um, *no se ve* . . . you can't see it. It's something so, so superficial, and so subtle, *que yo no me doy cuenta* . . . that I don't realize. That I lived, like I never realized these things. I'm not black, so those things are, well, *está ahí todo mezclado en el mismo plato* . . . It's all there mixed together on the same plate.

Cuqui confided to me that she went into therapy, and that this helped her sort through all of these issues. This is what she meant with her last comment regarding everything being "mixed up on the same plate."

Unfortunately, racial solidarity was not always the outcome of Puerto Rican marginalization. Patterns of segregation are embedded in American culture, as many of the Puerto Ricans in this study realized. Pablo, for example, a return migrant to Puerto Rico, discussed how bad he felt one Sunday when he was living in the mainland. He was looking for a church to go to and ended up finding an African American church. In the following quote, he describes what happened:

> We went to a church and without knowing, it was a black church. . . . And when we got out of church a woman came to us and in a very amiable way, I don't know, told us, "*Yo creo que es mejor que ustedes sigan buscando otra iglesia con gente que sean más como ustedes* . . . I think that it might be better if you keep looking for another church with people who are similar to yourselves."

Pedro retold that story when I asked him if he had ever experienced U.S. racism. He had a very negative reaction to this incident, one that speaks toward the levels of racial segregation in the United States and the possible results when others attempt to cross the color line. Other Puerto Ricans also spoke of how deeply rooted segregation was. Carmen discussed with me her perceptions of segregation in the United States, and her interpretation of where Puerto Ricans fit into this racial schema. In her opinion, solidarity with either group (blacks or whites) was impossible given how entrenched patterns of racism and segregation were:

> The only problem I've seen . . . here is the racial problem, where the black [person] does not accept the Puerto Rican because he's Puerto Rican, because supposedly he's white and . . . the white [person] doesn't accept the Puerto Rican because he's black. *Nosotros somos el jamón del sandwich* . . . We are the ham of the sandwich. And . . . the basic problem I've found here [in the United States] has been racism. That if you look a bit darker or if you have an accent, that rejection is automatically there. Now, even though people say times have changed and that it's not so much, it exists.

According to Carmen, Puerto Ricans are "sandwiched" in between the white and black racial categories, unable to garner acceptance from either of the two groups, each shunning them for being too much like the other. In essence, her discourse suggests that the particular shade of skin color does not really matter; the overarching problem is of invisibility, of a severe lack of recognition. According to her, while Puerto Ricans come in all shades of color, not one of those shades fits within the U.S. racial structure. It seems as if the U.S. obsession with an imagined sense of racial purity, where the presence of blackness automatically eliminates the possibility of whiteness (the one-drop rule), posits Puerto Ricans against their own cultural myths and traditions, which are based on the much too-often romanticized fusion of the black, white, and Taíno (Native Indian) races.[24] This, in turn, leads Puerto Ricans to buy into color-blind myths, sometimes even romanticizing island society for its seemingly colorblind structure.

The tendency to contrast the island with those negative factors experienced in U.S. society can sometimes affect settlement decisions as Puerto Ricans assess in which location they *feel* most comfortable. One factor that affects these subjective interpretations and how Puerto Ricans see their placement within U.S. racial landscapes involves the types of neighborhoods in which they settle. I turn to this in the next section.

RESIDENTIAL INCORPORATION AND EMOTIONAL EMBEDDEDNESS

Part of Puerto Ricans' subjective interpretations of incorporation into mainland society involved assessments of well-being and comfort—one's own and one's family. When moving to the mainland meant greater economic and/or professional opportunities, they usually assumed that these opportunities would benefit all who migrated. As seen in Natalia's case in chapter 2, however, the benefits of migration are sometimes met with costs. In some cases, these costs were associated with the kinds of neighborhoods in which Puerto Ricans settled. Given patterns of racial segregation in the United States, the mode of incorporation of each Puerto Rican influenced the kind of neighborhood they could afford to live in. As such, in spite of social mobility, it was still common for Puerto Ricans to integrate into mainland segregated communities.[25]

Settling in suburban versus urban areas, particularly in affluent neighborhoods vis-à-vis working-class ethnic communities, had its advantages, as well as its disadvantages. Public schools in suburban middle-class communities, for example, are generally better than those located in economically disadvantaged communities.[26] The respondents who lived in the suburbs were quite happy with the quality of life they experienced regarding housing, access to services, and satisfaction with the opportunities available to them, particularly when compared to those who resided in working-class and poorer communities, who were worried about how their neighborhoods (and exposure to the problems in poor urban communities) would affect their children's well-being. Previous studies have confirmed that living in poor and racially segregated communities increases one's exposure to drugs and violence.[27] Suburban settlement, however, also had its disadvantages that were not necessarily experienced in ethnic communities. In this section, I illustrate some of the costs and benefits of each particular pattern of residential incorporation in terms of how ethnic community versus suburban settlement contributed or detracted from subjective assessments of well-being on the mainland.

Ethnic Community Settlement

Alejandro was forty-eight years old at the time of our interview. He was one of the respondents in this study who had circulated several times. Born and raised on the island, he moved to the United States for the first time in 1979 to pursue his medical degree. Having left his wife and two children on the island, he abandoned his educational pursuit within a year and returned to Puerto Rico because of the difficulties of this household arrangement. Several years later, his marriage ended, resulting in migration to the United States in 1986. This was Alejandro's second mainland settlement experience, and he remained there for five years.

It was in this period that Alejandro met his current wife, who is also Puerto Rican. She was born and raised in the United States, immigrated to the island to pursue her education, and had settled in the Northeast when they met. She had a small child whom Alejandro has helped to raise. Together, they moved to the island in 1991 and tried to establish themselves there. Within a few years they had two children of their own. Alejandro was working two jobs to support his wife, her child, their two children, and his two older children from his first marriage. Given the economic difficulties and the stresses of maintaining two households, they decided to move back to the mainland in 1996 in search of better economic opportunities.

At the time of our interview, Alejandro lived with his family in a working-class community in New Jersey. He worked as a housing counselor at a nonprofit agency during the day, and sold real estate part-time at night. The first piece of information Alejandro disclosed to me (on the phone when we were setting up our interview) was that he did not like living in the United States, and missed Puerto Rico. During our interview, Alejandro explained that he feared that the social environment in which he lived was hampering his efforts to raise and educate his children. His current struggles involved his sixteen-year-old step-daughter—he felt like she was increasingly "out of control." As the following quote indicates, he was afraid of "losing her":

> Once I lose her, she won't. . . . It's a battle, I'm telling you, incredible [battle]. Those who have children here. Don't you see she goes to school, she talks to the other girl, and the other girl, the previous night slept with some guy and tells her, and those hormones are . . . and then she starts to become distant and when you look, pa pa pa pa. She is wasting time. . . . And then she sees

the other girl who went to school with a baby, and [says], "Oh your baby looks so pretty." That's one of the difficulties; it's the fact that, how do you deal with an adolescent in this environment?

Similar to the Puerto Rican migrants who relocated from Chicago to Puerto Rico in Gina Pérez's study on Puerto Rican transnational communities,[28] Alejandro believed that the environment of urban poverty surrounding his family, with its weak mechanisms of social control as compared to the island (he cites extended family, religion, and community as examples of social control on the island) were not conducive to raising children. He believed that this environment "killed the spirit" of many Puerto Ricans who lived there. He reflected on his two younger children, who were ages nine and eleven:

> They exist; the world is today, and here. Tomorrow, I mean, there isn't anything like, "I want to prepare myself, I want to be this when I'm older," like when I was young. "When I'm older, I want to do this. . . . " It's a sea of frustration, because kids here don't have the hori . . . they don't have a horizon. There's no place where they can say, "I want to go in this direction." They exist, they don't live.

In all, those who did live in or close to Puerto Rican urban communities experienced a mix of advantages and disadvantages. For some it afforded them advantages in that they were connected to an ethnic community and its social networks of support[29]; however, for others like Alejandro, the disadvantages associated with urban poverty and the weak mechanisms of social control affected their families' life chances and, subsequently, their own well-being.[30] In Alejandro's case, he longed to return to Puerto Rico but financial constraints kept him from doing this.

Guillermo was also born and raised in the island, and at the time of our interview lived in a Puerto Rican community in Pennsylvania. Guillermo, however, did not struggle with the issues Alejandro faced because his children remained with his ex-wife in Puerto Rico. A divorced businessman in his late thirties, Guillermo moved to New Jersey in 1991 searching for greater professional opportunities in the area of finance. He chose New Jersey because he had a sister living there, and worked in a bank for two years. He then relocated to Pennsylvania and was doing very well financially as a business manager in the city's Puerto Rican community. In spite of being single and living alone, in contrast to Alejandro, Guillermo indicated that he felt a sense of community on the mainland that compensated for the absence of his children:

> I'm invited here to so many places. Look, on Thanksgiving Day I can eat at six homes . . . and I won't get to two or three, [and they'll say] "Oh, you

didn't come!" So I have here, you could call it, I call it family because they take care of me more than anything.

Guillermo was quite happy with his life in the mainland, particularly because he was able to grow professionally and achieve a social status that he perceived was not available on the island given his own experiences there regarding the lack of occupational mobility. He believed that nepotism in island society kept people like himself out of lucrative financial and real estate markets:

> *Lamento de que yo me tuve que salir de Puerto Rico para hacer ese progreso . . .* I regret that I had to leave Puerto Rico to make progress. I would have preferred to stay there and make progress, but there, imagine that to buy a house is highly difficult. *Si tú no eres hijo del doctor, del fulano de tal, mengano de tal, que tenga conexiones, eso se basa así en conexiones . . .* If you are not the son of a doctor, or so and so, or such and such, that you have connections, that's what it is based on, connections. Not here [United States]. . . . [They say] "Approve me." " I'll approve you." "Okay." [This in reference to how financial transactions unfold.]

Guillermo did express that his children wanted to spend summers with him on the mainland. He was reluctant, however, to allow them to do this. He did not think they were prepared to deal with some of the elements of mainland society to which Guillermo himself had trouble adjusting:

> G: My boy is dying to come here, but I tell him, "*Mira, todo a su tiempo . . .* Look, everything in time."
>
> E: Have they visited you here?
>
> G: For now, no. I still don't want them to. When I came here, when I didn't know about much in this area, *yo no quería que ellos vinieran para acá, para que no se frustraran . . .* I didn't want them to come here, so they wouldn't get frustrated.
>
> I: Why?
>
> G: It's a big change. I mean, you see, in my [Puerto Rican] town you don't see grafitti, you don't see. . . . *Tú no ves grafitis; tú no ves basura; tú no ves rincones lleno de gomas . . .* You don't see grafitti, you don't see trash, you don't see corners full of tires.
>
> I: Was it a big change for you too?
>
> G: For me, I, will sincerely tell you, I am sincere. If I had arrived here to the United States to Philadelphia or New York, I would be back in Puerto Rico the next day. There is no question about it. *Mi pueblo no es así . . .* My town is not like that. . . . The grafitti, the trash, the schools; when I saw that there were not uniforms, it's not like that in my town. Do you understand me? It's not that we're better, but when you have good habits, you have to stick with

the good habits, don't you think? . . . But since I landed in New Jersey, New Jersey is very clean, very, in a way I liked it.

Ella, who migrated when she was thirteen years old with her mother and siblings, felt firsthand the frustration Guillermo was discussing. Ella was twenty-three years old at the time of our interview, and a single mother of a two-year-old. She lived with her mother, her daughter, her older sister, and her younger brother in a home in the same neighborhood where Guillermo resided. Ella completed her associate's degree and was finishing up her bachelor's degree at a local university. She worked two jobs—one as a classroom assistant and one in a nonprofit organization—that added up to an annual income of $30,000. She pooled her income with her brother to support the family.

Ella longed to live in Puerto Rico again because she, too, had worries about raising her daughter in the inner city. Ella particularly was concerned about the effects of the social ecology of the neighborhood in which she lived on her daughter's upbringing:

> I love if my girl could be in a place where she could play. That is another problem and there is a huge difference that I find between Puerto Rico and here which is the system of [recreation] . . . . *Los niños sufren mucho* . . . Children suffer a lot, and so I think that this greatly affects the interactions. . . . Because they have no place to play, you understand? *Los parques por aquí en el norte . . . son horribles; grafiti; están rotos. Este, el ambiente es malísimo* . . . The parks around here in the north . . . they are horrible; graffiti; they are broken. Um, it's a very bad environment. . . . Sometimes you see a (*sic*) sleeping there, so it's very uncomfortable to take a child to a park. So if you want to go to a decent place you have to travel. . . . The recreation system here, it's awful, and, the children obviously have no place where they can play. They have to play in the street, where there are sometimes shootouts, where sometimes there are discussions and nasty things that they often see. It's not something that is relaxing. *Tú vives en tensión. Aquí hay mucha tension* . . . You live in tension. There is a lot of tension here.

Since Ella's migration experience occurred when she was a teenager, she had some insights into the experience of adolesence in the inner city. Many of the issues that concerned her were the ones she herself faced as a teen. As such, she wanted to avoid the "tension" that characterized life in her community. Moreover, she wanted to shield her own daughter from these stressors. Even though Ella had not been to the island to visit in years, she still aspired to one day return to recapture a lifestyle that she perceived was less stressful.

Carmen and Pedro lived in another ethnic community of Puerto Ricans and Latinos in the Northeast. They echoed similar sentiments regarding the low quality of life. From Carmen's point of view, however, it was an issue of racial segregation and poverty. She explained how she believed neighborhoods became segregated, and what she perceived happened to Latinos and African Americans when they tried to move out of disadvantaged areas:

> *Los pueblos limítrofes, los suburbios son de blancos* . . . The towns outside of the city limits, the suburbs belong to whites. As they begin to move, and you see it, as they begin to move, for example . . . let's take as an example Mid-town, a town adjacent to ours. As African Americans and Hispanics start moving to Mid-town, it starts. *Tú pasas y ves los "signs" de ventas, para las ventas de las áreas blancas moviéndose a otros sectores porque se están moviendo negros e hispanos* . . . You go by and you see the for sale "signs," white areas for sale moving to other sectors because blacks and Hispanics are moving in. . . . Because these people still cannot conceive to live with other people who might be of another race and you see it. And that is, whoever tells me that there is no racism, what they have to do is get in a vehicle and go around and you will notice. You get in the car, and you see that they are all like crabs walking backwards, backwards when they see that blacks and Hispanics are moving into the area. . . . *Si eso no es racismo, tú dime lo que es* . . . If that is not racism, then you tell me what is.
>
> E: Yes, yes. So, they try to move away?
>
> C: As we would say, they, *te mastican pero no te tragan* . . . they chew you but they won't swallow you.

The disadvantages bestowed upon racially segregated communities did not mean Puerto Ricans could never get out. Many in my sample had either moved further out to the suburbs or integrated straight into the outlying suburbs once they moved to the mainland. This has contributed to what some scholars have called a class-based bifurcation in the mainland Puerto Rican community.[31]

In their study on the status of mainland Puerto Ricans, Francisco Rivera-Batiz and Carlos E. Santiago conclude that while a segment of Puerto Ricans in the United States shows significant occupational and economic gains, the other segment remains concentrated in deteriorating neighborhoods of older, Rustbelt cities. Their argument is that the mainland Puerto Rican community "has polarized into two groups."[32] Many of my respondents fell into the wealthier of the two groups. A few, like those I have discussed in this section, fell somewhere in between these two groups—their occupational and educational backgrounds reflected those of the middle class; however, financial constraints and racial segregation relegated them to areas that were not as stable as white, suburban, middle-class neighborhoods.[33]

In his interview, Alejandro demonstrated that he was aware of this bifurcation, and he felt caught in the middle and resentful toward those who did move away from the *barrio*. Alejandro talked about this in the following quote; however, he used the language of race to get his point across:

> Unfortunately, the Puerto Rican who comes here . . . *piensa que es blanco* . . . thinks he is white (laughs). I'm telling you, because it's, I see them. And I talk to them. And, I don't have that problem because I don't. But they speak of. . . . *Los puertorriqueños hablan de los puertorriqueños, como si ellos no fueran* . . . Puerto Ricans speak of Puerto Ricans, as if they weren't.

Even though Alejandro wanted to exit this system and return to the island, he was aware that these class divisions are transnational. He felt that part of achieving a certain status in Puerto Rico is the ability to display symbols of material success attained in the United States. These societal pressures contributed to his own feelings of inadequacy, and his reluctance to return until he achieved these things himself. Despite his modest gains in the United States, he feels that he is not ready to face these pressures, given that he still lacks the kind of capital required to live up to these constructed social standards:

> We've copied many patterns [from the United States]. One of those patterns is that in North American society, *tú vales lo que aparentas, no lo que eres* . . . you are worth what you appear to be worth, not what you are. I mean you live out of appearances, Puerto Ricans live from appearance. That's why you have to have three cars at home, although you use one. And society dictates that you have to have a 4Runner, and everyone has to have a 4Runner. And you go to urbanizations in Bayamón or in Río Piedras, and everyone has a 4Runner in their garage. *Y tú dices: "Pero, ¿dónde está la finca de esta gente?"* . . . *Y es que se vive con unas presiones* . . . And you say, "But where are these people's farms?" . . . And you live with these pressures.

Alejandro believes these same pressures can be found in mainland suburban communities where some Puerto Ricans move. He believes that, for someone like him, these social standards carry more meaning because he must also contend with racial barriers to entering these neighborhoods—the barriers that Carmen alluded to in her quote. Alejandro explained:

> If you go and move to the northwest [of the city], *usted tiene que llevar unos estándares de vida* . . . you have to take with you a certain standard of living. In the northwest up there, you can't go with your old car, (*sic*) and the kid with no [good] clothes, (*sic*) you can't go as you are accustomed to.

While many of these issues are class-based, their importance becomes greater when Puerto Ricans perceived they had to improve their racialized images by displaying these symbols of success. As such, Alejandro perceived these suburban neighborhoods to be closed to him.

In sum, incorporation into ethnic communities comes with its set of advantages and disadvantages. The disadvantages are rooted in racial segregation and poverty. For those who did incorporate into predominantly white suburbs, the issues to contend with were different. In other words, "making it" economically did not mean that settlement in suburban communities was without struggles.

Suburban Settlement

When it comes to the impact of suburban settlement on Puerto Ricans' assessments of incorporation, those from more affluent backgrounds did contend with issues related to being an ethnoracial minority in predominantly white areas given persisting patterns of residential segregation. As a result, some reported feeling socially isolated and culturally alienated. Diana, a lawyer who lived in a predominantly white neighborhood in the Northeast, is an example:

> [I haven't established friendships] in the immediate community. I've established friendship ties that I've gotten to know through work, or at church because I know that those people, if something were to happen to me, I can call them and say, "Could you pick up my son in x place?" . . . Here I barely talk with my neighbors; everyone does their own thing. . . . In that community sense that you knew, or you have the tranquility of knowing that the children could go play, and if something would happen someone would intervene, I don't feel that here.

Diana was also a single mother. She dealt with this sense of isolation by building a network of friendships with other Puerto Rican professionals who were dispersed throughout that area. As I discussed in chapter 3, Puerto Ricans like Diana recognized the significance of cultivating social ties in order to feel connected to the society in which they lived. Not all Puerto Ricans, however, were able to connect with other coethnics simply because they could not find them. Cuqui, discussed earlier in this chapter, is one such example:

> This is very difficult for a person who is not from here. . . . Because, people aren't that open; life in the suburbs, at least in this area . . . it's people who have lived here many years, and it's very difficult for one to enter in these circles, and it's a different way of relating. . . . It's not like I feel like I've gotten to know people like me, and that, even though they accept how I am, but I'm the only [Puerto Rican]. And it's like, you are always looking for a part of yourself in other people. And that part, I don't find very often, if ever.

Although a middle-class background increased the likelihood of successful incorporation along socio-economic lines, it had the potential of exacerbating feelings of isolation from sources of cultural familiarity among professionals, who lived in suburban areas. In Cuqui's case, not knowing any other Puerto Ricans in the area with whom she could identify, she began to compare herself to those around her, and felt like she did not fit in. As she stated in her interview, "I am an island. . . . I'm still an outsider." Cuqui's geographic metaphor reveals her own conception of herself as apart from the others, almost adrift. She simply felt different. Cuqui's search to understand her feelings turned into a process of self-discovery in which she began to better conceptualize her place in mainland, upper middle-class, white American society. Not only did she begin to understand that she had internalized the ethnocentric views she perceived herself to be judged by, but she also realized the importance of having cultural sources of support—which she did not. In short, Cuqui did not feel up to the task of being on the front lines of racial integration:

> In this area there are white-only clubs. My neighbor belongs to one of those clubs. And she called me one day and told me, "You should apply to join that club." And I said to her, "Yes, for what? *Si ahí no hay ni un latino* . . . If there is not even one Latino there." And she told me, "*No, es que ellos están tratando de cambiar, y, este, a ellos les gustaría tener una pareja coma la tuya* . . . No, it's just that they are trying to change, and, um, they would like to have a couple like yours." And I told her, [gasp] "*Pero, ¡ yo no quiero ser la única persona en [ese] sitio (sic) de blancos!* . . . But, I don't want to be the only person in that place (sic) of whites!" And so, they are all, what I told you, WASPS, and everyone acts a certain way that, that, is not for me. And so I would tell her that, that no. *Que yo no quiero ser la cuota de un hispano y un judío en el club de 500 personas* . . . That I don't want to be the quota of the one Hispanic and one Jew in a club of 500 persons.

One of the ways in which Cuqui attempted to compensate for this and nurture her cultural identity while at the same time influencing her children's evolving identities, was by taking them to a cultural center located in the heart of the Puerto Rican barrio, a thirty-five-minute drive from her house in the suburbs. In spite of this effort, she felt like she did not fit in there either. Class segregation within the Puerto Rican diaspora reinforced her isolation:

> I've taken the kids [to the Puerto Rican cultural center], but even there, I'm still an *outsider*. I am, I haven't gotten to know, I am not part of that community. . . . I feel a barrier (pause). Maybe it's that, a social barrier (*sic*). No, I haven't found any other professional people that are here. . . . I don't know where they are . . . we are not united.

As discussed earlier, while some Puerto Ricans managed to construct social networks involving coethnics through church and work, being disconnected from areas with established Latino or Puerto Rican communities made this difficult. They felt marginalized because they were not only on the cultural fringes of American society, they also felt segregated—perhaps a self-imposed segregation—from mainland sources of cultural nourishment found in Puerto Rican urban communities. As such, they missed out on the communal support systems afforded to those living in ethnic, albeit in many cases, more disadvantaged communities. In short, the lack of diversity in many of these neighborhoods and the scarcity of ethnic social networks exacerbated the loss of their own kinship networks left on the island. As I illustrated in the previous chapter, engaging in transnational activities that reconnected them to these networks helped to fill these voids created by settlement in mainland communities.

In sum, the geographic dispersion of Puerto Ricans given their class-based modes of incorporation impeded the development of a collective identity; for some, not being able to connect with other Puerto Ricans who were going through similar struggles, and feeling marginalized from other race-ethnic groups meant that they nurtured their ethnic identities individually while searching for a sense of emotional embeddedness in other spheres of their lives. Their collective identities were thus rooted in island culture and families rather than diasporic or mainland communities. In this sense, continued contact with kin on the island, including frequent visits to the island, became mechanisms by which these identities were nurtured. Moreover, settlement decisions made previously came under scrutiny and were up for renegotiation when Puerto Ricans faced obstacles due to their ethnoracial backgrounds, whether by virtue of individual acts of discrimination or through patterns of institutional discrimination (e.g., residential segregation).

ETHNORACISM, EMOTIONAL EMBEDDEDNESS, AND SETTLEMENT PATTERNS

The experiences of Puerto Ricans with U.S. settlement discussed thus far had the effect of compromising feelings of emotional embeddedness into mainland society. Even when Puerto Ricans could not identify blatant acts of discrimination toward them, they were aware of racism in the Untied States. Ethnoracism and its embeddedness into patterns of social relations and societal arrangements resulted in covertly hostile living environments for minorities, eroding sentiments of group membership. These feelings of weak acceptance into the dominant society required work to manage, particularly among Puerto Ricans who, having enjoyed privileges on the island, were faced with reconciling their former majority-group status in Puerto Rico with their minority-group experiences in the mainland. These emotional negotiations are complicated by their middle-class backgrounds, as they realized over time that contrary to the ideological basis of the American dream, hard work does not always result in merit in societies in which racial and ethnic inequalities are still rampant. I return to Noel's case discussed in the introduction to this chapter to illustrate this point.

Over the years, Noel exerted much mental and emotional energy into making sense of the barriers to his own professional success. In order to continue at his job and be happy, he had to overcome his feelings of cultural alienation that resulted from marginalization at work. He described these struggles in the following quote:

> I had reached a point of frustration, where I was thinking, "Here, I'm not. . . . " *Ya yo he entendido, que yo no voy a poder llegar a los lugares más altos en la jerarquía de los Estados Unidos. Eso para mí está prohibido, porque soy puertorriqueño* . . . I have come to understand that I will not be able to reach the top positions in the hierarchy of the United States. That for me is prohibited, because I'm Puerto Rican. *No lo digo con resentimiento* . . . I don't say this out of resentment, nor do I say it for any other reason. That is my experience. Maybe someone else has another experience. But I will reach a certain point and from there on, everybody feels threatened with my presence. So instead of things progressing, *llega un momento donde se estancan* . . . there comes a moment when they stagnate. And basically the way I decide to resolve it, *yo hago mi propio camino, yo tengo mis propias maletas y las hago y me voy para donde yo quiera* . . . I make my own path, I have my own bags and I'll pack them and I'll go wherever I want.

In this quote, Noel acknowledges reaching the glass ceiling. Yet, the neutral tone in which he expressed his frustration suggests that he is attempting to normalize this inequity by dissociating himself from this social system, revealed in his statement, "I make my own path, I have my own bags and I'll pack them and I'll go wherever I want." Thus, while Noel is not deciding to return to Puerto Rico, he is not necessarily emotionally invested in mainland society either. The last part of this quote suggests that returning to Puerto Rico is not out of the realm of possibility in Noel's future. In the end, Noel did not stay in this job. He moved to another department within the institution in which he was working. Although this did not necessarily amount to a promotion, Noel found a renewed sense of personal satisfaction in his new position and in the opportunities of professional fulfillment it afforded.

Unlike Noel, in Ricardo's case return migration was an indirect out-
come of his experiences with the head of his company. As discussed earlier, Ricardo's boss commented on the positive feelings he had when he
saw pregnant white women. Even though that experience was not directed at Ricardo, he nevertheless realized the racial dynamics surrounding him. This experience chipped away at his feelings of belonging. He
discussed with me how this incident made him feel:

> *Bueno, me sentí como que no era parte del grupo* . . . Well, I felt like I wasn't part
> of the group. Even though I was there with them, I wasn't part of what he
> [boss] understood to be accepted as normal, in his own vision of (sic). But
> that's all, I mean I didn't give it much thought after that, it didn't haunt me.
> . . . *Uno sigue para adelante* . . . You move on.

Ricardo's feelings of belonging in his work environment weakened. Although he appeared to shrug off this incident, as he stated earlier, this experience made him realize that he had probably gone as far as he could in
terms of mobility within this company. Having proof of his superior's
racist outlook, he began searching for another job.

Feelings of belonging, whether toward the society in which they lived,
their community, or to their social group eroded as a consequence of ethnoracial prejudice. This is seen in most of the cases documented in this
chapter. When comparing Ricardo's and Cuqui's reactions to prejudice,
however, the observable difference is in the gendered expression of frustration when confronted with these experiences. Cuqui's expressions of
nonbelonging were articulated in the discourse of feelings and emotional
well-being. She felt depressed and isolated, and she internalized racist assumptions and attacked her own way of being. Ricardo, on the other
hand, minimized the situation, as the last part of his quote indicated. He
"moved on." And he literally did; his experience with the racial glass ceiling led him on a job search that resulted in his resettlement on the island
for a second time. This decision was not a direct result of his racial experiences. In fact, Ricardo felt connected to U.S. society where he enjoyed a
higher quality of life than on the island. He made an explicit attempt to
explain to me that he did not return to the island because of this experience with his boss. It just so happened that the job opportunity he received was from an American company based on the island that offered
to pay him much more money than he was making on the mainland. Important to note is that the experience with prejudice led him to go on the
job market in the first place. As such, experiencing the effects of being a
race/ethnic minority led to a shift in Ricardo's sense of belonging to his
reference group, a feeling that, in combination with the economic effects
of discrimination, led to a job search that opened the door to return mi-

gration, and brought him back to Puerto Rico for the second time. Like Noel and Ricardo, many other Puerto Ricans discussed how feeling like outsiders eroded their feelings of belonging.

In sum, ethnoracial marginalization affects levels of emotional embeddedness. The shock of prejudice and ethnoracism strengthened Puerto Rican "immigrant" ties. Lacking solid networks of support and middle-class Puerto Rican communities to which they could identify, migrants tended to play up their ties to island society. This had the inadvertent effect of enhancing emotional embeddedness to the island context, not necessarily the mainland communities where they lived. This in turn, strengthened transnational "ways of belonging."[34] As these ways of belonging within transnational social fields fluctuate over time, persistent barriers to emotional embeddedness can result in decisions to migrate again. In Marta's case discussed earlier, she felt like her work environment in Florida was a hostile one; in addition, she was missing her family of origin in Puerto Rico. These two factors—racism and loneliness—ultimately culminated in her decision to return to the island. When asked to rank in order of importance the reasons for why she returned, she said:

> I would say . . . loneliness, and . . . professional dissatisfaction. . . . I would have to change jobs in order for me to see some progress [in how she was treated and in her career]. . . . And I realized that if I stayed in that boarding school I would be doing the same thing again, again, and again. And even if I did get a raise, still that wasn't enough because I needed a, something that [was] more satisfying. It is more than just money. . . . I was so dissatisfied, I was so disgusted that it only took one phrase from my mother, "Why don't you come back?" One question. And I said "Yes!" But if I had been fulfilled in the States I don't think that my mother saying "Why don't you come back" would have brought me back here. . . . So I ended up coming back, 'cause I knew that here [Puerto Rico] I could get a good job; here I didn't have to prove myself. And here I would have, more respect.

For Marta, loneliness was a factor; but also, her own marginalization tipped the balance toward resettlement. Her words at the end of this quote, noting that in Puerto Rico she would not have to "prove" herself, and that she would have more respect, is in reference to the humiliation she experienced from her colleagues and her own students in the United States. Moving back to Puerto Rico was an act of self-preservation.

Issues of well-being are embedded with work-related reasons, so that prejudice is often an obstacle to job satisfaction. For professional migrants whose identities are often entangled with their careers, prejudice is not something they are willing to tolerate, particularly when comparing it to a formerly privileged status in island society. This class privilege may also make them more reluctant to acknowledge discrimination and racism, because acknowledging prejudice implies that Puerto Ricans need to come to terms with being on the fringes of mainland society.

Even though Puerto Ricans like Antonio sharpened their racial consciousness in the mainland, for some, marginalization and discrimination were not articulated in the traditional discourse of racism but within the context of migration and settlement. Diana, discussed earlier, has dark skin and was living in the United States with her son. After completing her law degree in the mainland, she began practicing her profession in a Pennsylvania suburb. Yet, she explains:

> I have not been a victim of discrimination here [United States], but this is not my home. And well, you feel like you're a stranger. Obviously I speak differently, I speak with an accent and I look different. Wherever I go, I know that people are going to look at me. When they see me they'll know that I'm not from here and well sometimes I really miss that, to be in a place where I look how everyone else looks and that's my home. This will never be my home. It doesn't matter how long I'm here. And it hasn't been bad and I haven't been treated badly, but this is not my home. And it will never be my home.

Diana's discussions of home indicate a lack of emotional embeddedness—feeling incompatible with her surroundings. Not being able to feel like one is home after more than a decade of mainland living suggests that Puerto Ricans may feel like they do not have a place. Though Diana does not interpret this as racism, the quote, "Wherever I go, I know that people are going to look at me, when they see me they'll know that I'm not from here," illustrates the presence and perception of a dividing line, or an ethnoracial "color" line. There should be no mistaking her discourse as an indication of a privileged racial position; Diana, in fact, has been subject to racism. When she bought a house, she was steered away from the neighborhoods in which she wanted to live. As a lawyer in the courtroom, she feels like she constantly has to prove herself. She feels that she has to overcome biases related to having an accent. Perhaps because many Puerto Ricans do not fit neatly into binary racial categories, they have trouble conceptualizing these experiences as racism.

This suggests that U.S. binary notions of race affect the way "the others" themselves interpret racism. If not considered a racial group, how do "the others" make sense of their racial experiences? One of the outcomes of this ambiguous framework is that Puerto Ricans have trouble conceptualizing racism as such, and making sense of their marginalized, contradictory positions as Spanish-speaking colonial racial subjects who happen to be U.S. citizens. In short, Puerto Ricans are sandwiched between the intersecting points of this ethnoracial matrix of domination, rendering it difficult to assign meaning to their experiences, especially within the con-

text of the black-white dichotomy. Consequently, the dynamics of race relations and how Puerto Ricans fit into this come through in discussions of
adaptation and settlement, as this chapter has shown. As a result of these
structural dynamics, growing emotional connections to island society can
be interpreted as a strategy to combat the struggles and alienation rooted
in ethnoracism that erode emotional embeddedness to mainland society.
In the next chapter I discuss this as well as the conditions under which
Puerto Ricans move back and forth between the island and the mainland.

NOTES

1. This chapter contains excepts from a previously published article with
Guillermo Rebollo-Gil, "Ethnoracism and the Sandwiched Minorities." *American
Behavioral Scientist* 47(7) (March 2004): 910–27.

2. Rodríguez 2000.

3. Bonilla-Silva 2000; Grosfoguel and Georas 2000.

4. Andersen and Collins quoted in West and Fenstermaker 1996, 362.

5. Waters 1999; Levitt 2001.

6. Urciuoli 1996.

7. Nazli Kibria uses this phrase to characterize the placement of second-generation Chinese and Korean immigrants within the U.S. social fabric. As members
of the second generation, the respondents in her study were U.S. citizens—a part
of the United States. But, due to racialization, they were still considered outsiders,
or "apart" from the mainstream (Kibria 2002).

8. Grosfoguel and Georas 2000.

9. Grosfoguel and Georas 2000.

10. González 2000, 264.

11. González 2000.

12. Grosfoguel 1999.

13. González 2000, 265.

14. Waters 1999; Stepick et al. 2003.

15. Rothenberg 2004.

16. González 2000.

17. Feagin 2006, 291–92.

18. Fegain 2006, 290.

19. Rodríguez 1991.

20. Feagin 2006.

21. Hacker 1995, xii–xiii.

22. Hacker 1995, 6–7.

23. Martínez 1998; Perea 1998.

24. Diaz-Quiñones 1993.

25. Patillo-McCoy 2000.

26. According to a study of public elementary schools by William Yancey and
Salvatore Saporito (1995), the quality of schools is affected by the character of the

communities in which they are embedded. Just as urban and suburban schools differ in this regard, socioeconomic, race, and ethnic boundaries differentiate inner city schools according to the neighborhoods from which they draw their students.

27. Anderson 1999; Dohan 2003; Krivo and Peterson 1996; Logan and Stults 1999.

28. Pérez 2004.

29. Pérez 2004.

30. See Edin and Kafalas (2005) for an in-depth discussion of these issues.

31. Rivera-Batiz and Santiago 1994.

32. Rivera-Batiz and Santiago 1994, iii.

33. Mary Patillo-McCoy (2000) has documented the trend in which, in spite of social mobility, residents of African-American middle-class neighborhoods confront many of the issues afflicting poor urban neighborhoods given their proximity to these areas.

34. Levitt and Glick Schiller 2003.

5

⟋⟍

Emotional Embeddedness and Professional Migrations

Patterns of Settlement within Transnational Social Fields

The opening chapter of this book discussed the experiences of Rosana, a Puerto Rican woman who had moved to the United States and back to the island several times. Her most recent experience of U.S. settlement involved periods of time in three different states. After going through a divorce and several difficult experiences finding work, Rosana decided to move back to Puerto Rico.

Rosana's decision to return "home" is not unlike the decisions that most return migrants in my sample made. In fact, nineteen out of the twenty Puerto Ricans in my study who resettled on the island expressed that family was an important factor in their decision making. For several of these, taking care of immediate relatives, such as parents, was the precipitating factor in returning. For others, being with family members and having them involved in their daily lives drew them back to the island. In all, family and kinship, as well as the issues discussed in the preceding chapters were significant factors that again pulled Puerto Ricans into the migratory flow within the transnational fields that link island and mainland communities and networks. In this chapter, I examine the patterns of decision making that differentiated those who remained settled and those who engaged in subsequent migrations. I also examine how life course events factored into settlement decisions. I elaborate on the notion of emotional embeddedness and the circumstances that enhanced or eroded attachments to each place. I conclude with a discussion of the implications of my data for our current understandings of circular migration among Puerto Ricans.

DUAL REFERENCING AND EMOTIONAL EMBEDDEDNESS

Part of life within a transnational social field is being able to identify which context or society one feels most embedded in. Dual referencing—which often entailed comparing one's level of well-being in each location considered to be home—resulted in constructing this context in opposition to the other. Puerto Ricans' constructions of the nurturing capacities of each context are gauges of emotional embeddedness. Although a highly subjective assessment of incorporation, the emotions it represents are real: one's level of emotional embeddedness is an expression of affect toward one's surroundings, reflecting an assessment of where someone feels she or he belongs. It is also an expression of cultural citizenship, and feeling the freedom to live as one is without being looked upon suspiciously. These feelings encompass levels of attachment or detachment that develop over time to a particular place, often in reaction to life experiences, particularly experiences with inequalities and/or opportunities. The affective foundations and subjective interpretations of one's own experiences of incorporation to a place are powerful enough to alter the course of settlement.

There are cases, however, in which there is no clear attachment to any one society, which may result in several different scenarios. For example, an immigrant might feel attached to both places and believe that she or he could be happy in either one. While this expands settlement options, it could also lead to a situation in which a person feels split and unable to fully determine where she or he should be. While a person may not be a "transnational" because she or he is not moving back and forth, the transnational condition each person faces entails "trying to decide where home is," as the title of the newspaper article discussed in chapter 1 suggests.

A second scenario involves someone who might feel marginalized in both contexts, and in which there is no attachment to either society within a particular transnational social field. In this case, settlement decisions may be confounded by the fact that neither option will result in a sense of well-being. As such, the transnational condition may involve managing feelings related to dislocations, and trying to reconcile these issues that lead to feeling displaced regardless of where one settles within a transnational social field.

Although the emergence of each of these scenarios differed among samples, four patterns of emotional embeddedness, migration, and settlement emerged (see table 5.1). In the following sections, I present examples that illustrate each of the observed patterns of transnational emotional embeddedness and the conditions under which dislocations are resolved (or attempted to be resolved) and remigration occurs.

Strong Emotional Attachments to the Island; Weak Attachments to the Mainland

For those loosely attached to U.S. society, social constructions of homeland culture defined it as a nurturing social context vis-à-vis American culture. Eliud, discussed earlier, is an example of this first pattern of emotional embeddedness. Eliud moved with his family to the United States in search of health care for his daughter. He found a good job that facilitated this move. However, in spite of years of mainland living, he did not feel

Table 5.1. Emotional Embeddedness and Migration*

	United States Society	
Puerto Rican Society	*Strong Feelings of Emotional Embeddedness to U.S. Society*	*Weak Feelings of Emotional Embeddedness to U.S. Society*
Strong feelings of emotional embeddedness to P.R. society	*Desire*: Equal desire to return to P.R. or remain in U.S. *Mobility*: Equally likely to return or remain, perhaps circulate; Structural constraints or life cycle events more likely to shift desires	*Desire*: High desire to return to P.R.; low desire to remain in U.S. *Mobility*: Most likely to return to P.R.
Weak feelings of emotional embeddedness to P.R. society	*Desire*: Low desire to return to P.R.; High desire to remain in U.S. *Mobility*: Not likely to return to P.R.	*Desire*: Equal desire to return to P.R. or remain in U.S. *Mobility*: Equally likely to return or remain, perhaps circulate; structural constraints or life-cycle events more likely to shift desires

*Structures of inequalities (e.g., race, class, gender) affect levels of emotional attachment to each society.

as though he belonged. Structural integration did not translate into successful incorporation, nor did it facilitate the United States becoming his "home." As indicated in the previous chapter, Eliud was the object of discrimination during the time he lived in the United States. He expressed a constant sensation of feeling like an outsider.

> *No me sentía de allá, no me sentía cómodo . . .* I didn't feel like I was from there [United States], I didn't feel comfortable . . . the five, six years that I was there, I came every year to Puerto Rico for a vacation and once I landed here [P.R.], I entered the airport and I felt at home. And it wasn't the same there. Over there [United States] I felt uncomfortable.

As his affect toward U.S. society eroded, his longing to be in Puerto Rico and his emotional attachment to the island intensified. As such, his desire to return permanently to the island grew over the years. Eliud tried to make sense of his ambivalence; he recognized that he should have been excited about the quality of life he was experiencing. His interpretations of incorporation are captured in the following quote:

> It wasn't that it was bad; to be realistic, the quality of life over there is very good. Everything is accessible; everything is comfortable. But I didn't feel like myself, as a person. I mean, I didn't like it personally. But in reality looking at it like that, it was a good place. *Pero no sé, qué era lo que había aquí [P.R.] que una vez llegaba aquí, tocaba el aeropuerto, me sentía tranquilo, "relax" como yo digo. Allá me sentía como que no era de ahí; como que no pertenecía . . .* But I don't know, what it was here [P.R.] that once I'd arrive, I'd touch the airport and I felt calm, "relax" as I say. Over there I felt like I wasn't from there; like I didn't belong.

Although Eliud's "quality of life" was good in terms of economic conditions, professional development, and the medical opportunities for his daughter, his emotional state deteriorated, as evidenced in his constant feelings of discomfort in the mainland society. Interestingly, he stated that this feeling of discomfort dissipated a bit when he traveled to cities with greater proportions of Latinos:

> I don't know if it is that after being here [P.R.] for thirty-two years and I've lived all of my life among Hispanics, that encounter over there, in reality it was the first time I lived with persons that were different from me. It could be that. And I would seek out that [Latino] area . . . *que era más compatible con donde yo me crié . . .* that was more compatible with where I was raised.

Even though Eliud expressed in this quote a preference to be around people more like himself, the following quote indicates that what he liked about being in such a context was that his presence was not the object of question. As I illustrated in chapter 4, Eliud had ample experiences with being singled out because he looked, sounded, and was considered to be "different"; he was frustrated at the assumption people had that he was not from the United States: "Where are you from?" was a question he was constantly asked. This question was problematic because it served to reinforce his feelings of nonbelonging. It was this perception of difference to which he attributed his discrimination. His discourse suggested that he interpreted his experiences on the mainland within a dual frame of reference, cognizant that he never experienced such treatment in Puerto Rico:

> *Y siempre estaba esa parte de que si uno, miraban [y preguntaban]: "Where are you from?"* And there was always that aspect that one, they look "Where are you from?" And that's what they always asked. Here [Puerto Rico] nobody is ever asking, "Where are you from?" And, "What are you?" That struck me; that part of always finding out what you are and where you come from. It's like here [Puerto Rico] you are not accustomed to that, at least I'm not.

Eliud's reactions to these questions illustrate that they reinforced his detachment from, and weak sense of emotional embeddedness to, U.S. society. This lack of social integration increased the value Eliud placed on the meaning of belonging. He could feel the stark contrast in his own well-being when he compared his feelings toward visiting the island to when he would return to the United States:

> When I would get on that airplane, once I arrived in Puerto Rico, *me sentía como que estaba en mi casa* . . . I felt as if I was home. Over there [United States] I would arrive to the house, and [say], "Okay." I don't know, "It has a pool; that's nice." *Pero no me sentía de allí* . . . but I didn't feel like I was from there.

Eliud's notion of home was grounded in Puerto Rico. Although he lived in the United States with his family, he had a good job, and was occupationally successful, socio-economic incorporation did not translate into successful incorporation if measured through his own assessment of this process. Eliud's experiences embody the barriers to incorporation that immigrants and other minorities often perceive. Racism and American nativism prevented him from *feeling* incorporated or like he belonged, confounding his own interpretations of his migration, especially considering that U.S. settlement had tangibly benefited his daughter. These conflicting feelings and his emotional attachment to the island eventually led him to reassess his settlement decisions, opening the door to return migration.

Even though Eliud eventually returned to the island, for six years he experienced the dislocating effects of migration. Eliud's greatest burden was to manage the conflicting feelings of wanting to return to Puerto Rico for his own emotional health, and needing to stay in the United States for his daughter's physical health. This is not unlike other Puerto Ricans who, faced with barriers to return migration, had to find ways of negotiating their alienation from U.S. society and their strong attachments toward Puerto Rican society. Eliud reflected on his own life as a Puerto Rican and searched for information and cultural artifacts to nurture his longing for the island and, more important, what the island represented to him. Nurturing his ethnic identity allowed him to survive while he remained where he did not want to be. It also was his way of reconnecting with his home; "*Yo, individualmente lo sentía así. Yo, como dije, nací aquí, me crié aquí* . . . I personally felt that way. Like I said, I was born here [P.R.], I grew up here . . . "

> . . . but once I left it's like my thinking changed, not toward nationalism, but of searching. Every time I came to Puerto Rico, I'd try to find things, native things of Puerto Rico to take with me, be it music, or books. . . . When I lived here [P.R.] I never did that. . . . Truthfully when I was here I wasn't interested, but once I was there [United States] the principal thing was trying to find that type of music, and that's what I listened to when I was there and books about the history of Puerto Rico, I have tons that I bought and I read when I was there. That maybe here they might make me read them in high school and I'd throw them aside. (Laughs). And that's how it was. *Cuando yo venía de viaje aquí [P.R.], siempre llegaba a [EE.UU.] con dos o tres [libros de Puerto Rico], eso no fallaba* . . . When I'd travel here [P.R.], I always arrived to [U.S.] with two or three [books about P.R.], it never failed.

Nurturing his interest in his background and his homeland was a way in which Eliud could reconnect with what he felt he had lost, almost substituting his longing to be on the island with his newfound identity:

> *No sé si es que quería sentirme más de, o que me siento que soy de Puerto Rico* . . . I don't know if I just wanted to feel more from, or that I felt that I was from Puerto Rico. It's like they say sociologically it is a nation, but not politically, and that's what I felt. Maybe it's like someone from another country goes to the United States and tries to seek out the things from his country, at least for me it was like that.

Individuals are bound in solidarity through shared emotional energy.[1] Given the low levels of solidarity among middle-class Puerto Ricans and the individualistic lives that middle-class settlement fosters, the "adhesive" function of emotions in this context is for migrants to feel united in island culture, not necessarily among themselves. This means that not being privy to the communal sources of cultural support and the social networks that tend to aid immigrants in the process of adaptation and integration documented in studies of immigrant modes of incorporation, investing in material culture is akin to reconstructing one's identity to feeling part of a collective identity, in part to ease the emotional dislocations of migration.

While this strategy was helpful to some, it was not always completely successful. Certain levels of cultural alienation persisted, as was the case with Eliud. He did, however, eventually resettle in Puerto Rico once he located a doctor who could treat his daughter, and subsequently found a job in his field. Regarding the latter, his educational and occupational experiences in the United States aided in securing a well-paying job on the island, thereby facilitating his reentry into Puerto Rico's professional labor market.

Both Puerto Ricans who lived in the mainland and those who resettled on the island recognized that achieving a position in which they could reconnect with island networks and maintain a middle-class lifestyle would require high levels of education and money. The ability to travel, the ability to support families on the island, the ability to pay for daily long distance calls, or the ability to relocate all hinged on financial resources and, indirectly, on educational attainment. As such, being attached to island society was not sufficient to result in return migration. Moreover, return migration was not sufficient to resolve the dislocations experienced in the mainland, particularly when island structures of inequality did not allow Puerto Ricans to take care of their financial needs.

Regarding Eliud, he and his wife reconnected with their families upon return migration. As one of six children, Eliud had been the only one living outside of Puerto Rico, which meant that he was separated from kin and the lifestyle he was accustomed to (which involved regular face-to-face contact with family). Returning to the island symbolized recapturing the positive feelings that came with reentry into kinship networks, as this quote indicates:

> Sometimes you would call and they'd all be together. Or sometimes we would visit, which was almost always on special occasions. Once on vacation, on "Thanksgiving" one of my brothers got married and we shared "Thanksgiving" with my wife's whole family and then at night with mine. And after my brother's wedding, you leave and you always have that [feeling of]: *Caramba, allá [Puerto Rico] está todo el mundo y acá no hay nadie . . .* Gosh, everyone is over there [Puerto Rico] and there is nobody here. *Pues, amistades, que es lo que uno consigue allá [EE.UU.]. Amistades puertorriqueñas que es lo que uno busca, pero por más que digan no es lo mismo. La familia de uno por lo menos . . .* Well, friends, which is what you find over there [U.S.]. Puerto Rican friends which is what you look for. But for all they say, it's not the same, [as] one's own family at least. I understand that it is, it is better to be over here [P.R.] with family.

Eliud says that now in Puerto Rico, they spend much more time with
both families. As he discussed the meaning of family and of feeling happier, his discourse was strikingly different from his discourse describing
his experiences in the United States:

> *Bueno, el sentir de que son las personas con la que tú creciste . . .* Well, to feel that
> those are the people you grew up with and with whom you, at least my
> brothers, we are the oldest three. We are more or less the same age and we
> share and we know more or less what each one thinks and sometimes we
> don't even have to speak.

The familiarity, comfort, and emotional satisfaction that came from a renewed sense of belonging emerged from Eliud's reinstatement within his
family; this is what return migration meant to him. His chief complaint
throughout the interview was that he felt like an outsider abroad. This
was clearly not the case on the island. He valued these relationships and
longed to get them back, no matter the costs:

> *Inicialmente [la mudanza] nos puso bien atrás [económicamente] . . .* Initially [the
> move] set us back [economically]. Because . . . the value of the house did not in-
> crease a lot and when I sold it, we lost money. We lost almost eight thousand
> dollars that we had to find to be able to. . . . Aside from the move. Because they
> [employer in Puerto Rico] did not move us. . . . And that is costly to move. And
> the tax on cars . . . when you bring them here [P.R.] you have to pay taxes, which
> was an additional two thousand in taxes. Plus the eight thousand that I lost in
> the sale of the house. Initially we reached negative. . . . *Que fueron cosas que yo
> acepté . . .* They were things that I accepted.

In addition to kinship ties, other factors endemic to island society
strengthen attachments among those who have left. The following quote by
Juan, who had settled in the United States on three different occasions, illustrates the conceptualization of Puerto Rico as "home":

> *[La añoranza] yo la asocio con un grado de tranquilidad . . .* I associate [the long-
> ing] with a level of tranquility. That my senses are saturated with beautiful
> things: an agreeable temperature; cool air; greenery; of the flowers; the wa-
> ters; the rivers; the power of the sea; *de estar junto con la gente que uno quiere
> mucho, que uno se lleva bien. La familia sobre todo, que vale mucho, algo que es muy
> importante . . .* Of being with the people you very much love and with whom
> you get along. Family above all, that is valuable, something that's very im-
> portant. That is with what I associate that longing.

In many cases, mainland struggles strengthened ties to place and the social and emotional connections to the island, even if home society constructions downplay the negative aspects that originally cause people to enter the

migratory flow. Although some might have over idealized the island, they wanted to feel like they belonged; they wanted to feel emotionally embedded by existing in a socio-cultural context that nurtured their identities.

Even though many of those in the sample of return migrants made this decision because of strong attachments to island society and to kin who remained there, some in this study had weak attachments to both island and mainland societies. This constitutes the second pattern of emotional embeddedness observed in my data.

Weak Emotional Attachments to the Island and Mainland

Emotional embeddedness manifested itself in a second pattern. Return migration was not always the desired outcome when emotional attachments to island society were weak at the outset. The perceived sense of emotional connection to Puerto Rican society is partly a function of its structures of inequality. Marginalization along race, class, gender, and/or cultural lines on the island meant that return migration was not always a practical option, regardless of the desire to reconnect with certain aspects of island culture. In these cases, mainland struggles consisted of dealing with feelings of dislocation and alienation while attempting to establish a greater emotional connection to mainland society. When these emotional connections were unattainable and home society emotional embeddedness was still low, Puerto Ricans dealt with persistent attempts to define where home was and where they belonged. As I demonstrated in chapter 3, this was the case for some women who perceived island opportunities and gender roles to be restrictive; it also was the case among those who had struggled in the past to find well-remunerated work on the island. In such situations, life cycle events (e.g., an illness in the family) or certain experiences (e.g., discrimination) would sometimes act as deciding factors regarding future migration decisions.

Recall Raquel's case discussed in chapter 3 in which she felt an intense desire to reconnect with her island networks, but was apprehensive about returning because of her perceptions that Puerto Rican societal gender norms were restrictive. These perceptions erected a barrier that kept her from fully embracing her attachments to the island. At the same time, even though her professional experiences in the mainland were going well (she recently had earned a promotion), she battled feelings of cultural alienation that she had experienced since the time she moved to the mainland as a college student:

> At Cornell was the first time I got used to spelling my name every time I mentioned it. It wasn't "Raquel González." Ah, do you know what it is [to always have to spell your name]? G-O-N-Z-A-L-E-Z? [she spells out last name].

There was no way that it. . . . I had to "spell my name" even at the grocery store. I mean, everywhere . . . and it has changed but they are not accustomed to Latinos. . . . Truthfully, during those moments at first, it was new, so I [would say], "Well, poor things, they just don't understand." But throughout the four years it was the same, and the same. I had to show my passport because they wouldn't believe my license was real. And I [would say], "Do you know Puerto Rico is part of the United States?" I mean, people didn't. . . . I'd take my passport everywhere. . . . Because people didn't understand.

These feelings amounted to cultural alienation throughout the time Raquel lived in the United States. They kept her from feeling embedded into mainland society. At a broader level, migration and U.S. settlement transformed her identity. For those unable to fully feel connected to island or mainland societies, they molded their identities to better fit their perceived "in between" global positions. Raquel expressed her perception of her in between status through her metaphor of a "bridge":

Yes, that is part of who I am. . . . I think that I, like many Puerto Ricans, to be metaphoric, we live on a bridge. I mean we don't live in one place, or the other, we live on an imaginary bridge. And every time there are more and more people on the bridge. And they are not just Puerto Rican; they are Mexican; they are people from, many people—immigrants to this country. They can be migrants—because Puerto Rico is part of the United States—or they can be immigrants—especially the Puerto Ricans. . . . I think we, and I definitely feel that I live like on a bridge. And that sometimes I'm more on this side, and sometimes I'm on the other side of the bridge. But I'm not alone on the bridge. There are more and more people on it.

While this quote indicates Raquel's solidarity with groups that find themselves on that "bridge," a sense of ambiguity comes through as well. Raquel feels solidarity with the idea of other transnational (or in-between) populations, but she is not necessarily emotionally connected to any members of these groups. This bridge is obviously imaginary; it is an in-between condition—a transnational condition—even though her daily activities may not adhere to dominant definitions of what makes a transnational actor (e.g., sustained, cross-border activities).[2] While Raquel's construction of her own identity and her place on this bridge reflects her perception of not quite fitting into island or mainland societies, it also reflects a level of doubt regarding how a Puerto Rican such as herself would fit in with the other groups on this bridge because of her citizenship status: [Those on the bridge] "can be migrants, because Puerto Rico is part of the United States, or they can be immigrants, especially the Puerto Ricans." Raquel certainly feels like her experience is parallel to members of other immigrant groups, even though it may not be recognized as such. In short, it is evident that Raquel has thought a lot about where home is, and the implications of this question for her own future migration path:

> *Ahora estoy pensando seriamente en regresar [a P.R.]* . . . *Es que es un sentimiento* . . . Now I'm seriously thinking of returning [to P.R.] . . . It is a feeling. I mean (silence). For example, I go roller-blading through *Central Park* and I'm moving along and I look at the city [skyline]. And it's like I still see it as a "foreign city." I mean, there are few times, there are times that I have felt that yes, that sometimes *es mi ciudad,* it is my city. But . . . I go to Puerto Rico and I sit on the beach to read a book *y estoy en mi ambiente* . . . and I'm in my environment. So *es diferente* . . . it is different.

This quote is suggestive of attachments to the social ecology of Puerto Rico, and how much more comfortable Raquel feels in this context; however, it is more than just Puerto Rico's nice beaches. It is the sensation of belonging, of familiarity. A longing for place represents desires for emotional embeddedness and the positive feelings and comfort that living in a familiar cultural context engenders. Raquel's emotional dislocation was also a manifestation of cultural displacement and how the social ecology of place captures these emotions. In Raquel's view, the U.S. city in which she lived for several years still felt like a "foreign city." Regardless of her many years in the United States, she cannot claim ownership to this society—it is not hers; and in spite of her U.S. citizenship, she does not feel like she belongs to it.

Alejandro also experienced this sense of detachment from his environment, but he was also struggling with issues related to his socio-economic status at the lower boundary of the mainland middle class. As discussed in chapter 4, Alejandro was struggling with issues related to raising his children and stepchild in a disadvantaged urban environment with its weak mechanisms of social control. He himself, however, did not feel integrated to mainland society, nor did he feel comfortable with the idea of return migration given that he did not feel like his placement in the middle class was solid or stable. Even though Alejandro made a decent living, he believed that his current income would only be attainable on the island if he had a graduate degree, which he did not. For this reason, even though he longed to return to the island, he realized that the level of pay he would receive would not be conducive to family stability. Recall that Alejandro had tried to establish himself in Puerto Rico prior to his most recent experience of U.S. settlement. Supporting two households, however, proved to be too difficult, even though he was holding down two jobs at that time. Given this experience, which led him to move to the United States again, he

will not resettle in Puerto Rico until he has greater financial security
and a higher degree of education:

> *Puerto Rico es mi patria. Es muy lindo. Yo lo añoro 24 horas al día. Lo extraño . . .*
> Puerto Rico is my country. It is very pretty. I long for it 24 hours a day. I miss
> it. But the possibilities for work are, I won't say rare, because I, in the field in
> which I have training I can work anywhere. But it doesn't pay well. . . . *No
> hay cosa que de-estabilice más a un hogar, que la cuestión económica . . .* There is
> nothing that destabilizes a home more than economic matters. Forget about
> everything else, the economic situation destabilized.

By "destabilization," Alejandro was referring to the effects of his own
economic instability (when he used to live in Puerto Rico) on his family
life, specifically his first marriage. As such, a lifetime of economic marginalization has led to feelings of deep-rooted resentment toward the island's class structure and his inability to break through into the island's
professional class. As such, even though he feels attached to the idea of his
homeland, he does not feel like he could integrate into Puerto Rican society, given his past experiences that led him to enter and reenter the migratory flow. Alejandro's migration to the mainland is a means to an end.
The end is the accumulation of education and capital. Until this end is accomplished, he is bound to the United States. As Alejandro straddles the
social demarcations of class within and between Puerto Rican society and
its diaspora, he grapples with class divisions in which he always envisioned himself on the other side of where he currently is. In this sense, his
discontent is not just with the lack of community he feels in the United
States, but his inability to be part of the community he was once a part of
in Puerto Rico. The result is a lack of emotional embeddedness to either,
seen in his perception that he does not fit into the community he lives in,
a community that like him, is economically struggling: "I'm here, but I
feel like a foreigner every day . . . *Estoy aquí, y me siento un extranjero todos
los días."*

Alejandro exists between two societies and is caught in a holding pattern. His self-imposed, class-based expectations did not permit him to
consider returning to the island, even if the reason was to remove his children from the environment that he perceived to be so dangerous. Interestingly, his wife did want to return. Similar to the women discussed in
chapter 3, she longed to reconnect with her own family and to experience
greater communal sources of support:

> *Ella quiere regresar a Puerto Rico . . .* She wants to return to Puerto Rico. Be-
> cause there she sees more security for the children. . . . Me, it's not that I
> don't want to. At this moment I cannot do that. . . . I still have some things

to accomplish. I mean, I'm not old, but I'm also not a kid and I have to establish certain things, you know? I can't keep jumping from here, from there. . . . Just because of how things look, or how (*sic*) keep running. Because I'll be running to all parts of the world. Problems should be confronted. . . . *De que regreso, regreso. Pero no puedo ahora* . . . That I'll return, I will return. But I can't now.

Scholars have argued that notions of femininity and masculinity mediate migration and settlement decisions among immigrants. As Pierrette Hondagneu-Sotelo argued in 1994, the consequences of returning to the home country without having accomplished "success" according to economic and material standards are dramatically different for women and men. She argues that since not much is expected economically of women who leave Mexico for the United States, there is no stigma to returning empty-handed. Returning, however, with "nothing" undermines notions of masculinity as linked to economic success and being a good provider.[3] This is the case with Alejandro. The contradictory class mobility he has undergone, however, adds another dimension to a gendered pattern of settlement. Therefore, even if it's what he believed was best for his children, and in spite of his wife's wishes, Alejandro will not return until he has achieved a greater social status that he can then rely on for self-worth when one day, he returns as a "return of success."[4] His sense of self and feelings of emotional embeddedness to the island are predicated upon upward social mobility. Without this, he believes he is worthless:

> That I cannot do things when I want to, is frustrating. *Me hace sentir a mí, como honestamente yo no valgo* . . . It makes me feel, like I honestly am worthless. But what can I do? And then, I don't sell drugs, nor am I involved in illegal dealings. . . . And many times, the fact, it tears you up the fact that you've been unable to do certain things, that if you had a weak spirit, you would honestly believe that you're worth, that you're worthless (laughs). It kills your spirit. It's a terrible thing (*sic*). I struggle with it every day. I know what I am; I know what I can achieve; my spirit. . . . And I thank God, I got this from my father. I have an untamable spirit in that sense. I know what my goals are. . . . *Actualmente, yo tengo unas metas que cumplir, cuando yo cumpla esas metas, yo regreso a Puerto Rico* . . . Currently, I have some goals to achieve. When I achieve these goals, I'll go back to Puerto Rico. I mean, I want to return to Puerto Rico because, I feel Puerto Rican; I carry that inside. But, I want to be happy in Puerto Rico. I want to bring something; I can't arrive so my homeland receives me with . . . empty hands and a hollow mind. I can't arrive to Puerto Rico like that.

For Alejandro, emotional embeddedness to the society that he longs for hinges on overcoming the economic marginalization he has lived through in the past. The way he intends to do this is by securing more education and greater economic stability.

One other issue to consider when examining these patterns of embeddedness, particularly detachment from multiple homes, is that depending on the area of the island Puerto Ricans left (e.g., rural versus urban), the level of change that had enveloped that particular area could contribute to Puerto Ricans feeling detached from island society generally, and/or their home communities specifically. This is more likely seen when those settled in the United States had been there for a long period of time. Ella, who was discussed in chapter 4, mentioned that she was apprehensive about the prospects of returning to a society that was no longer familiar to her. Having lived in the mainland for ten years, she dreamed of one day returning to Puerto Rico to raise her daughter. She acknowledged this fear, however, when she discussed those factors that pulled her toward the island:

> What attracts me is the food (laughs); the environment. But in reality I'm talking about ten years ago. I have been told that it has changed a lot. Maybe I'll go and find there [P.R.] many of the things from here [United States] that I don't like, you understand? But I hope not. And I still think that there are still some virgin areas left, that's how I refer to them (laughs).

The infusion of American culture into Puerto Rican society throughout the twentieth century magnified debates regarding Puerto Rican culture and identity in and outside of the island.[5] Different cultural ideologies intersect on the island as Puerto Ricans are often faced with reconciling the impact of values and customs from their parents' generation with the influences of new values and ideas that have resulted from American cultural penetration into the island from above (through U.S. capital and policies), and from below (through migration).[6] Consequently, island culture has become a "moving target."[7] As transnational migrants individually constructed culture in the mainland, the definition of home society culture varied according to their own social and economic backgrounds, and the length of time away from the island. In this regard, cultural alienation that resulted in weak emotional embeddedness to mainland society took on a transnational character. Even though Puerto Ricans from urban areas had different constructions of Puerto Rican culture as compared to those who came from rural island communities, overall, when Puerto Ricans visited the island, they were surprised to encounter vast changes (e.g., new construction and infrastructure developments) in relatively short periods of time although this varied by generations. As the home society culture was in flux, migrants' perceptions of these changes reinforced the question of "Where is home?" This question reflected that search for familiarity, comfort, and belonging that the idea of island culture typically embodied, but that perhaps, it ceased to embody upon the realization that their understandings of Puerto Rican culture were caught in a time warp. This realization potentially could result in alienation from island culture and society as well, leading to situations in which Puerto Ricans felt these weak attachments to both societies.

For some Puerto Ricans, however, these changes did not necessarily compromise feelings of island embeddedness. In fact, for some, feeling attached to both societies meant that unless they could physically live in both places simultaneously, they had to decide in which one to settle. I turn to these examples in the next section.

Strong Attachments to Island and Mainland Societies

The third pattern of emotional embeddedness that emerged from my data involved Puerto Ricans who felt attached to both home *and* host societies. For this group, migration decisions were still difficult to make, because both societies pulled them in opposite directions and multiple attachments left open the option to live in either place. Similar to those Puerto Ricans who felt alienated in both societies, certain life cycle events, economic opportunities, or negative experiences carried the potential to alter the course of settlement, as if tipping the balance toward future migrations. This is what happened with Ana.

Ana, discussed in chapter 2, had been living in Georgia for about seven years. Her father had a heart attack that he survived. This event introduced a new phase in the course of Ana's mainland settlement that would extend itself over approximately two years. The event itself resulted in a stronger desire to be in Puerto Rico with her family. Ana was pulled between two places she considered "home"; she kept moving up in her career working as an engineer in the mainland, but she felt drawn to Puerto Rico to be with her parents. This phase involved balancing work and family as a daughter in a transnational family. She even admitted that after her father's heart attack, although she continued to reside in the United States, her mind was in Puerto Rico. She felt like she wanted to be in both places at the same time. To ease the burden of these conflicting emotions, she began to visit Puerto Rico more frequently:

> Because of that I started to travel more often. . . . At least every two months. And since in my work I travel so much, I had to add another trip. And a moment came in which I was worn out. I couldn't do this anymore. Dragging a suitcase from here to there, from there to here. I'd go to Miami; from Miami then I'd come down for the *weekend* to Puerto Rico; then I'd go up to Charlotte, just to travel somewhere else. And well, that added another trip to my

schedule. I was exhausted. Exhausted from running around. From here to there; wanting to be in two places at the same time.

Ana felt that she was needed in Puerto Rico and she wanted to be in Puerto Rico to help her parents. Her father's brush with death changed the way she viewed her migration and U.S. lifestyle. As such, she felt more pull toward the island, a pull that weakened her attachment to Georgia. After years of living in the United States, Ana now felt compelled to return "home." Ana's account of her grandmother's death is important in understanding the change that occurred in her during this time:

> My grandfather was very sick; my grandmother after that, she passed away during Christmas, when I was here in Puerto Rico. That I said, *"Pues, es increíble como todos sus nietos ya habían llegado a Puerto Rico . . .* Well, it's incredible how all of her grandchildren had already arrived here in Puerto Rico." She died on the twenty-fourth, but it's a coincidence that you were here because you came for Christmas. *Otra época del año ya te enteras tarde . . .* Another time of the year and you find out too late; after the fact.

These events and Ana's interpretation of these events led her to realize that:

> This time I was lucky that it [grandmother's death] coincided with one of my visits to Puerto Rico. *Pero son cosas, que uno dice: "¿Eso es lo que yo quiero para mí? ¿Siempre llegar tarde?" . . .* But they are things, that you say, "Is this what I want for myself? To always arrive late?"

There was a profound sense of loss in Ana's words. Her father's condition triggered a process of introspection in which she questioned how she really wanted her life to be. The juncture that she arrived at in the course of U.S. settlement placed her at a crossroads. Realizing the duality of her situation, Ana felt compelled to resolve it: *"Y ahí es que uno decide si quiere aceptar que las cosas sucedan así. O tomar cartas en el asunto . . .* And that's when you decide if you want to accept that things happen this way. Or take matters into your own hands."

After two years of shuttling between the island and mainland, Ana decided to resettle in Puerto Rico. As she put it, "In the 'win and lose' on my scale, well, my career weighs less . . . and being close to family weighs more." Even though she was attached to both places, her father's illness, as she put it, "tipped the balance." Interestingly, Ana was well adjusted to mainland living. She had no problems with the language. She felt integrated (although her group of friends consisted mainly of Latinos). She was structurally incorporated as she experienced upward mobility in her career, economic stability, and high levels of job satisfaction. She traveled with her job and was happy. She even bought a house, a step toward consolidating settlement by establishing roots and ties to a place.

In short, Ana was fully incorporated into mainstream U.S. society. Or at least, like Eliud, she appeared to be so. At one point in our interview, Ana admitted to me that she still felt strange, like the United States wasn't her home: "*A lo mejor es que a mí aunque me fascina [la ciudad] yo siempre me sentí extraña; me sentí que ése no era mi hogar*. . . Maybe it is that although I love [the city] I always felt strange; I felt like it wasn't my home." Ana eventually made the decision to return to Puerto Rico. Reflecting on this decision, she stated the following:

> You win and you lose. *Si lo que te estás ganando por estar allá es más importante, pues tú decides quedarte allá* . . . If what you are gaining by being over there [United States] is more important, then you decide to stay. The moment in which I left [P.R.], my career was more important. I left what I had to leave here [engagement, family]. *Ahora, que la vida te da ese cantazo* . . . Now, life gives you a blow. I mean, my father was lucky to tell [survive]. . . . And you say, "Dear God, I wasn't thinking about this, and I don't want to get a call and tell myself, 'I would've liked to spend more time and get to know my father,' for example." *Y pues, por eso es que las prioridades cambian* . . . So, that's why your priorities change. And it is not right or wrong. *Simplemente que en el "win and lose" en mi balanza, pues, ahora la profesión pesa menos* . . . Simply that in the "win and lose" on my scale, well, now my career weighs less . . . because of the fact that I am in more control of working where I want to work. *Y estar más cerca de mi familia, pues tiene más peso* . . . And being close to my family weighs more.

As Ana's case illustrates, life cycle events affect feelings of emotional embeddedness by either enhancing or quelling attachments to a particular place. These events and their effects were often tied to families and households. They included changes in family structure such as marriage or divorce; the birth of a child; the death of a family member; or an illness in one's family. Ana's experience with her father's illness illustrates how these kinds of events change perceptions of settlement. As I have illustrated throughout this book, this was also the case with Vilma.

After a couple of cycles of U.S. migration, island resettlement, and remigration to the mainland, Vilma had returned to Puerto Rico and was working for an American company. She had been involved in a relationship in which she had a baby. The relationship, however, dissolved, leaving her a single parent. A year after the birth of Vilma's baby, her company was in the process of merging with another transnational company. It was in this context that Vilma met her second husband, a Greek American. His home base was in the northeastern United States, and once they married, Vilma moved to the United States for the fourth time with her second husband and son.

Even though Vilma had resettled in Puerto Rico to be closer to her family, the circumstances of her fourth migration were different: she was moving to the United States to consolidate her new family unit. She explained these different circumstances:

> *Ahora es bien diferente* . . . Now it is very different. First because there's another maturity. Now I'm with my family; this is my family nucleus. *Antes siempre que yo me moví yo me sentía que mi familia se quedaba en algun sitio* . . . Before every time I'd move I felt like my family would remain in a certain place. First because I didn't have children; now that I have a child, well, he moves with me and he is my family and my husband obviously. That's the major difference. *Ahora yo no me siento "homesick"* . . . Now I don't feel "homesick."

At the time this interview was conducted, it seemed unlikely that Vilma would move back to Puerto Rico again. She established herself in her new home with her husband and son. When she does get homesick, she has the economic flexibility to travel to the island to visit. On other occasions, she arranges for her family to visit her. Like others in this study, she has developed transnational strategies to reformulate the meaning of distance in her relationships: "I send for my mother and tell her 'come.' And she'll come for up to two weeks. So that helps; that it's not that you said farewell forever. *Siempre mantienes tus lazos* . . . You always maintain your ties."

The maintenance of transnational ties facilitates life on either side of the border. Family settlement, however, facilitates living "locally" within a transnational social field. The contour and character of one's household can enhance or detract from levels of emotional embeddedness. In Vilma's case, having her own nuclear family unit in the mainland made adaptation to U.S. society more tolerable than on previous settlement experiences. What remains to be seen is whether or not in the course of raising her son, she finds herself again at a crossroads within this transnational social field. Will the events in her life reshape her attachments to her social group, local community, and more broadly, her placement in mainland society? That she now feels comfortable on either side of this social field means that she might be likely to move again. This, however, remains to be seen.

One important consideration when understanding patterns of embeddedness across transnational social fields, particularly among those who feel strong attachments to both societies, is that given the rapid pace of industrialization and urbanization in the post–World War II era, widespread social change has engulfed the island within a matter of decades. In a material sense, returning to Puerto Rico is not like returning to an undeveloped country. The influx of American corporations and products into the island's economy and socio-cultural landscapes means that in many areas of the island (mostly urban and sub-urban), although aspects of daily life and culture might vary, they are not drastically different from the United States—many of the comforts of daily life that characterize life in the United States can be found on the island. Therefore, regarding return migration, the emotional nego-tiations that might be necessary to reconcile different material realities in home and host societies are not nearly as drastic as they might be for migrants returning to developing countries. These factors may influ-ence the likelihood of Puerto Ricans developing strong attachments to both societies.

Weak Attachments to the Island; Strong Attachments to the Mainland

Although not as prevalent among those in my samples, the pattern did emerge in which strong attachments to mainland society developed alongside loose attachments to island society. Among respondents in the return migration sample, Ricardo, discussed in the last chapter, was the only one for whom family did not encapsulate the main underlying rea-son for island resettlement. Ricardo was married and had four children. A self-employed businessman in his late thirties, Ricardo preferred life in the mainland. He had moved to the United States and returned to Puerto Rico twice—the first time to earn his undergraduate and graduate degrees in two different northeastern states, and the second time to take a job in Florida. In spite of island resettlement, he enjoyed the quality of life he ex-perienced in the mainland when he lived there:

> The quality of life that I experienced during my college years was pretty . . .
> more than positive. . . . Everything related to the infrastructure of govern-ment; the quality of life for children; education and crime; everything that is related to lifestyle and quality of life. And that stayed with me. And when I began working [in P.R.] . . . I always had in my mind that when I started to raise a family, I was going to return to the United States and stay there.

Ricardo would have remained in Florida if he had not been offered a lu-crative job in Puerto Rico. Recall from chapter 4 that Ricardo's job search began when he realized that his boss was a prejudicial man. After he re-located to the island to take that job, even though he was settled there, as I discussed in chapter 2, he appeared to want to move back to the main-land. When asked if the metaphor of "one foot in the mainland and one foot in the island" described him, he answered:

> I am strictly here [P.R] for money. I have no other love, except for money. If I do not manage to reach where I want to be, then I'll leave. So, I don't have, I don't know if it's one foot [here] or my pocket here, and the rest there [United

States]. . . . I'm telling you, not even family pulls me. I'm not a person to become attached to things or my surroundings. . . . And it would not be fair to say I have a foot here and a foot there, my heart is there [United States]. The problem is that the money is here [P.R.]

For Ricardo, the option of someday moving to the United States again was not out of the realm of possibility. He liked mainland living, more so than any of the other study participants. Even though he stated in this quote that he "does not become attached to things or my surroundings," he interestingly chose to correct the metaphor of "one foot here and one foot there" by stating that his heart was in the United States. These feelings outweighed other links to the island (except for money). Regarding family, as I discussed in chapter 3, he preferred to have more distance separating him and his extended family because he valued the independence of the nuclear family (particularly the conjugal unit) from the extended family.

Living in Puerto Rico was also a source of tension for him given the issues discussed in chapter 2 regarding readapting to island living. As the following quote illustrates, Ricardo also was deeply dissatisfied with Puerto Rican politics. This was one of the major reasons he felt alienated from Puerto Rican society.

I am someone who understands that politics here, and people here. . . . People here have deteriorated too much. It's not that over there [United States] there is no politics . . . the system filters it well. *Aquí el sistema no filtra, el sistema te deja caer encima todo* . . . Here the system does not filter, the system lets everything fall on you and it's the people who suffer. . . . I don't see a solution and I don't see the light at the end of the tunnel. On the contrary, I see it worsening, worsening.

Ricardo felt alienated from island society and attached to the idea of some day returning to the United States. Moreover, he seemed to have acculturated significantly as the following statement indicates: *"Porque es que yo entiendo que yo puedo vivir mejor mi vida allá* . . . Because my understanding is that I can live a better life over there. *Y yo soy bastante americano* . . . And I'm pretty American, I'm very Americanized."

Although Ricardo and his wife would like to leave the island, their situation reveals the complexity of settlement decisions when the desires of other household members are weighed into the decision-making process. Ricardo would probably be more proactive about resettling in the mainland were it not for his children who, as teenagers, wanted to remain on the island with their friends and extended family. In spite of being "Americanized" too, Ricardo's children wanted to stay in Puerto Rico:

Ya están acostumbrados y ya hablarle a ellos de irnos, no es aceptado . . . They are already adjusted, and to speak of leaving is not acceptable. They already got used to having family around. One of them has a girlfriend; the other one has her friends here; the other one, they are adjusted. One of them, if I say, "*Vámonos mañana . . .* Let's go tomorrow," will go. *Pero también se quedarían aquí . . .* But they would also stay here.

When they initially returned to the island, Ricardo's children were unhappy about this transition and wanted to go back to the United States. This was particularly the case with the youngest child, who had experienced life on the mainland for a longer period of time than island life before their migration. Return migration, however, has allowed them to have a set of different experiences from what they had in U.S. society. Even though the youngest child is the only one that would be enthusiastic about returning to the mainland, overall these experiences now bind them all to Puerto Rico:

En términos de la experiencia que han tenido aquí, yo creo que el aspecto familiar, la familia. . . . Que ese aspecto como no tenían allá y tienen mucho aquí ahora, le da a ellos una experiencia diferente, a lo que tenían . . . In terms of the experience they've had here, I think that the family aspect, family. . . . Since they did not have that aspect over there [United States] and they have it a lot here, it gives them a different experience from what they had. They also have more freedom here too. In the United States my wife was a bit more, you know, she was a bit more, fearful. She wasn't in her world, in her environment. She was always watching where they went. Not here. Here they have more freedom. They have had a lot of freedom here. And they like that. Aside from that, they are grown, I mean they are basically teenagers. *O sea que ésta es la mejor parte de su vida . . .* So this is the best part of their lives.

Ricardo is not as satisfied as his children are with Puerto Rican settlement. Having experienced life in two different social, cultural, and political contexts, he continually interprets his day-to-day experiences through this dual frame of reference—constantly comparing life in U.S. society vis-à-vis life in Puerto Rico. Ricardo's children are second-generation migrants, but also second-generation return/circular migrants. Upon returning to the island, they experienced a reconnection with familial ties that engendered positive feelings, much like it did for those return migrants discussed in chapter 3. These experiences outweighed for them the costs of returning. Reentering kinship networks also served as new mechanisms for social control. Ricardo and his wife's strategies for dealing with their children were more relaxed in Puerto Rico because they were in a culture that was more familiar to them. They gave their children more freedom in their activities given the reliance on informal networks to monitor their well-being. These were among the tangible benefits of reintegrating into families and island networks:

> *Bien positivo* . . . It's quite positive. I mean, we get together every weekend with her [wife's] family, with mine, and our kids with our nieces and nephews and with everyone, uncles. But we still maintain that closed nucleus and that has helped us deal with many situations that otherwise we would not have done.

The reconstitution of extended family networks and collective patterns of living typically associated with Puerto Rican culture, in addition to their own emphasis on the nuclear family unit, suggest that Ricardo and his children are culturally hybrid. They illustrate patterns of selective acculturation typically associated with the children of immigrants when they combine home and host society ideologies into hybrid identities. As such, in spite of their Americanization, it is understandable how Ricardo's children have also developed attachments to island patterns of living.

For now, Ricardo and his family will remain in Puerto Rico. He believes that his children eventually will want to go to college in the United States; this expectation reveals that alternating periods of settlement in the mainland and island are intergenerationally transmitted. Rather than displaying patterns of circular migration which suggests multiple back and forth movements in a short period of time without the multitude of experiences that are part of the settlement process, Ricardo and his family's experiences of migration and settlement more likely resemble patterns of circular settlement. Following this pattern suggests that when Ricardo's children do go to college abroad, he intends to move with his wife back to the mainland.

ALTERNATING PATTERNS OF SETTLEMENT
AND DIFFERENTIAL EXPERIENCES WITHIN FAMILIES

Immigration researchers have argued that immigration is a family experience.[8] Although this study has focused on individuals, the findings support previous research confirming that settlement and migration decisions involve household considerations. My findings also reveal that migration and settlement, regardless of place, takes on different meanings even for members of the same family.

In the case of Ricardo's children, for example, the experience of return migration for each individual child varied based on whether they were: born in Puerto Rico prior to their U.S. migration; born in the mainland; their level of exposure to American culture before they returned to the island; and, the particular stage of childhood they were at when their family settled on the mainland or resettled in Puerto Rico. Based on the timing of each of these migration experiences, it is unrealistic to expect uniformity among children regarding their desires to resettle in the mainland or remain in Puerto Rico. Each member of the household had different experiences; as a result, each child will have a different disposition toward migration and future settlement decisions. This complicates our understanding of emotional embeddedness because one's level of emotional embeddedness is possibly influenced by other family members' feelings and experiences as well.

Eliud and his family are examples of these different patterns of embeddedness within the same family. Eliud was not the only one who experienced the emotional benefits of being in proximity to his extended family upon island resettlement. This was an aspect of social life on the island that Eliud's children, ages eleven and thirteen, enjoyed as well:

> *A ella [hija] le encanta de estar visitando a lo abuelos* . . . She [daughter] loves visiting her grandparents, my wife's, her maternal ones and mine. More the ones here because we visit them more often, my in-laws. They are the ones she has most contact with. But she likes that aspect, to see her cousins and her grandparents. *Le encanta* . . . She loves it.

Even though Eliud and his children were elated to reestablish themselves in Puerto Rico, Eliud explain that his wife, Gabriela, was not. Gabriela was happy in the United States and was reluctant to return. She was well connected to a group of friends, and adjusted more than he did to their new lives in the mainland. Important to consider is that Gabriela herself is the daughter of return migrants to Puerto Rico. As such, she had spent some of her own childhood in the United States. In addition, although she used to work outside of the home on the island, in the United States she remained at home with their children. Eliud believed that because of this arrangement, she was not as vulnerable to some of the experiences Eliud had with discrimination in public spaces in his capacity as a physician. She was more likely to be able to choose who to spend her time with. Having access to a network of Puerto Rican female friends, she was less likely to experience being viewed as an outsider. This may have impacted their differential views toward mainland settlement and return migration. Thus, although Gabriela was adjusting to island living, there were times when she regretted leaving the United States. Eliud explained:

> *A veces ella trae que si "allá la vida era mejor"* . . . Sometimes she brings up that, "Over there [United States] life was better." Sometimes she gets kind of

melancholic, as we say. Because of some situation that might occur here, she says that there [United States] "this, this, and this." But then she always ends up saying, "no, because. . . ." *Ve lo positivo que ha ocurrido acá y se queda tranquilita . . .* She sees all the positives that have occurred here and she remains calm.

In sum, although the process of readjustment to island society had its ups and downs, reconnecting with their relatives eased this process for the members of Eliud's family. His daughters enjoyed the time they spent with their extended family. His oldest daughter, in particular, has made it clear that she does not want to go back to the mainland, while his youngest daughter often misses it (similar to Ricardo's children). Among the other Puerto Ricans in this study, some also expressed that depending on the age of their children during migration and settlement, children developed particular preferences and affiliations to each society they were exposed to. Like Gabriela, many Puerto Ricans themselves were children of return migrants, suggesting that the enduring socializing effects of migration can result in remigration in adulthood.

Moreover, Eliud and his family were transformed migrants: they interpreted their experiences through a dual frame of reference. While Eliud had no intentions of returning to the mainland, because of the lack of legal restrictions to migration, as well as the transnational links that bind cross-border friendships, families, and communities, it is difficult to predict whether their decision to remain in Puerto Rico is, indeed, final, particularly considering the constraints that their daughter's medical condition poses.

Questions remain regarding the effects of having members of different generations spend parts of their lives in multiple socio-cultural contexts. In the course of experiencing alternating patterns of settlement across borders over time, the acculturation patterns of children and adults sometimes varied, as each subsequent generation could be more or less acculturated than the previous one (depending on the stage of childhood in which they experienced mainland or island settlement), or, more bicultural and hybrid than the previous generation. This can pose struggles similar to those documented in the research on the children of immigrants,[9] except that the children of Puerto Rican migrants often become return migrants, and later in life, circular migrants themselves. These findings suggest that emotional embeddedness is likely to be a product of more than just the context of settlement, but also social statuses such as gender, race, class, and *generation*. Given the histories of migration present in some of my participants' own families of origin, further research is needed on the effects of circular, episodic settlement on children's levels of emotional embeddedness and how identity changes regarding migration are integrated into their developmental stages. This may help us further understand family dynamics among Puerto Rican households whose members have spent their lives living transnationally.

In sum, for populations who have no legal restrictions to crossing borders, the option of migration is always available. Even when migration decisions appear to be final, in reality, they may not be. Levels of emotional embeddedness shift throughout the life cycle. Particularly in the case of middle-class Puerto Ricans, their educational backgrounds and financial resources facilitate episodic settlement patterns. Given each individual's subjective assessments of incorporation, these resources and the occupational opportunities they encounter structure further migration options. Rather than circular migration, which implies a continual back and forth flow of people, at the household level these processes result in alternating periods of settlement in the United States and Puerto Rico, or patterns of circular settlement within transnational social fields. While circular settlement is seemingly a paradox, the comings and goings of professional immigrants and their families often involve more than several years in either location. Even though their lives are lived locally in whichever society they are in, their emotional, intellectual, and family lives are lived transnationally. Over longer periods of time, these episodes of migration and settlement amount to forms of transnational settlement.

NOTES

1. Collins 1990, cited in Jasper 2003, 154.
2. Guarnizo, Portes and Haller 2003.
3. Hondagneu-Sotelo 1994.
4. The return of professionals who migrate to "accumulate assets" and then return has been referred to as "returns of success" (Enchautegui, 1991).
5. Dávila 1997; Duany 2002; Pérez 2004.
6. Smith and Guarnizo 1998.
7. Waters 1999.
8. Grasmuck and Pessar 1991; Hondagneu-Sotelo 1994.
9. Portes and Rumbaut 2001.

6

⌒

Conclusion
Weighing Hearts and Minds

Throughout this book, I have discussed the case of Rosana who had spent time living in the Northeast, the Southwest, the Southeast, and the mid-Atlantic regions of the United States. As I discussed in the previous chapter, a few years after the birth of her son and her subsequent divorce, she moved back to the island to live closer to her family.

When I interviewed Rosana in Puerto Rico, she was living with her mother and her son and was working out of their home as a freelance translator. Additionally, for the last six months she had been working part-time, from Puerto Rico, for a mainland university. They carry out large-scale research studies in which they offer part-time and full-time employment opportunities. While the part-time work was more flexible and could be accomplished from the island, the full-time work needed to be done from the mainland. When I arrived at Rosana's home to conduct this interview, I found that most of her belongings were packed; having taken the full-time job offer, Rosana decided to move to the U.S. mainland for the third time.

Recall that Rosana returned to the island to have more help raising her child. Although Rosana's economic well-being and her professional life in Puerto Rico left much to be desired, she believed that in terms of family life, it was well worth it. She used her grandmother's illness as an example. Her grandmother had a stroke at ninety-two, and died at ninety-eight. But for those six years, both Rosana and her son were a big part of her care:

[Abuela] era loca con David . . . [Grandmother] was crazy about David. The only person she responded to or talked to was with him. *Ellos tuvieron una relación preciosa* . . . They had a beautiful relationship. *Tú ves, esas cosas son difí-cil de borrar* . . . You see, these are things that are difficult to erase.

Although return migration did not increase her financial capital, the emotional rewards she and her son gained by returning were invaluable. Taking an active part in family life, which included living with them, off-set her financial difficulties. More importantly, Rosana believed that the decision to return really made a difference in her son's upbringing and their relationship:

> *En ese sentido me siento bien de haber regresado porque él ha tenido una vida de familia bien bonita* . . . In that sense I feel good about returning because he has had a beautiful family life. He has had a lot of experiences that will mark him for life, that alone in the United States he wouldn't have had those experiences. He helped take care of his great-grandmother; we have been "home schooling" for six-and-a-half years; we have had a lot of experiences thanks to that; we have traveled to Europe. *Que tal vez yo sola allá, no hubiera podido* . . . That perhaps with me alone over there [United States], we would not have been able. *Seríamos dos extraños* . . . We'd be two strangers.

Rosana's son was now a teenager. Moreover, the death of her grand-mother one year ago removed some of the family obligations she had in Puerto Rico that kept her from leaving earlier. At this juncture in her life, financial considerations were more important than what they were many years ago. Rosana had reached a point at which living in Puerto Rico became too costly in terms of the energy she expended trying to make ends meet:

> *Va llegando el momento que tu dices: "¿Por qué?" ¿Por que estoy pasando tanto trabajo?* . . . There comes a time when you ask, "Why?" Why am I working so hard? I'm going to be forty-five years old in March and I think [that] I need something more stable. I need to have something to count on and not be so broke. And I live well because I live with my family, but this can't, *esto no puede seguir así* . . . this can't go on this way. So that is why I'm going to make this change. *Sabiendo que en Estados Unidos hay sus limitaciones en cuanto a eso, de que tal vez hay prejuicio, pero tengo que sopesar que es más importante* . . . Knowing that in the United States there are limitations in terms of that, that there may be prejudice, but I have to weigh what is more important.

While Rosana's emotional livelihood was at the heart of her return to Puerto Rico, now her economic well-being was at stake. Taking this main-land job opportunity, nevertheless, was conflictive for her:

> I feel bad. I feel like I have a duality. I feel bad leaving Mami, and my aunt. I am a natural "care taker." But at the same time I realize that I have to find something more stable.

The transnational context for Rosana's decision making is important. For those who have no legal restrictions in crossing borders, the option of migration has been always available. Even when migration decisions appear to be final, such as Rosana's decision to return to Puerto Rico, in reality they may not be. For Rosana, return migration proved to be a paradox. On the positive side, she received ample emotional support from her family of origin, and cherished the family reconstitution that return migration facilitated. A negative aspect, however, was readapting to island society and reentering the labor market. Rosana did not believe that Puerto Rico was an optimal location to thrive economically given its low salaries and the experiences of gender inequality she had faced in previous years. As such, Rosana felt torn between two places—she felt caught in between two cultural and ideological points of reference. Her family as a source of emotional and cultural satisfaction was in one, and the possibility of economic stability and independence was in the other. In short, Rosana's economic *and* professional goals were not attainable on the island; like many Puerto Ricans and other immigrants, to achieve economic stability and professional growth, Rosana had to sacrifice those aspects of her life that were emotionally rewarding. The duality of her situation made her angry:

> *En cierto modo me da coraje que me tenga que ir otra vez porque no gano bien* . . . In some ways I get angry that I have to leave again because I don't make much. I don't make enough. You know, that I have to find more income, abroad. The jobs that have paid me well have been those abroad. They have never been the ones here [in Puerto Rico]. The ones here have been problematic. The ones abroad have been there, "steady income." *Eso es lo que yo busco. Tener una vida un poco más aliviada* . . . That is what I'm looking for. To have a more alleviated life.

This book has illustrated how the subjective experiences of migration and settlement impact interpretations of the costs and benefits of life on both sides of the "border." With each migration and settlement period, transformations at the individual level occur. This results in a process of reflexivity that changes the individual as well as the context in which settlement decisions are revisited. This dialectic between experiences structured by Puerto Ricans' social locations in transnational hierarchies, and how they respond to and contest these results in alternating periods of mainland and island settlement within a broader transnational context.

The data presented in this book allow for an examination of the complexities that play into each migration decision. Rosana's case, like others, reveal that dislocations are not always resolved upon migration or return migration. Readapting to Puerto Rican society can be challenging, particularly when considering the original reasons migrants leave. In Rosana's case, the economic motivations behind her previous out-migration decision came into play again; her status as a marginal worker and single mother led her to migrate for a third time to increase her economic standing, and to give her son a broader range of opportunities. At a broader level of analysis, her mobility is a manifestation of historical ties between Puerto Rico and the United States in which the emergence of strong transnational links facilitate migration and alternating, or circular periods of settlement.

The dominant approaches to the study of migration consider a transnational actor to be someone who engages in frequent cross-border activities. According to this approach, very few, if any, of the Puerto Ricans in my samples would be considered transnationals. This is because their everyday lives are lived within the boundaries of their communities of settlement. Their subjective, internal states, however, cross borders on a regular basis. As I have documented in this book, many Puerto Ricans see themselves as living on these emotional bridges that connect island and mainland social spaces. Holidays; family events; stages of life; and experiences that require them to *"recargar baterías . . .* recharge energies," such as experiences with prejudice and discrimination, lead them back to the island. Similarly, U.S. migration is, more often than not, the ultimate safety valve to economic difficulties. While both real and symbolic, these subjective, emotional, and economic links binding both societies can be viewed as indicators of thick transnational social fields.[1] As such, in the realms of their hearts and their minds, patterns of thinking and feeling transcend Puerto Ricans' particular places of settlement. In short, using Peggy Levitt and Nina Glick Schiller's terminology, while their "ways of being" may not be transnational, their "ways of belonging" are.[2]

Transnational ways of belonging can also affect the experiences of those left behind. While this study did not address this group, my findings do indicate that living in a transnational social field, whether one moves within it or not, comes with its own sets of struggles. This has implications for theoretical assumptions guiding immigration research. The emotional fallout of these separations can have a variety of results; among them, the pain of separation from loved ones can result in constant ruminations over one's past migration decisions. In a context of fluid borders, this suggests that settlement decisions are periodically reevaluated and renegotiated. As such, migration decisions that are seemingly final can turn one-way migration streams into international circulation. This has implications regarding contemporary migrants' assimilation patterns.

The classic assimilation theories envisioned most immigrants as the poor and hungry masses entering expanding industrial economies. In an era of globalization in which the workforce has become segmented, assimilation takes on a different course depending on whether we are examining members of unskilled labor migrations or professional migrations. In addition, as this study has indicated, there are those in the middle whose educational backgrounds might have prepared them for middle-class jobs, yet their material realities reflect their social locations (e.g., gender, race) and their class backgrounds. While recent theoretical reformulations of assimilation theories argue that we must pay attention to the human capital immigrants bring with them upon migrating as well as the patterns of assimilation to different groups that vary by class and race statuses, we must also focus on the relationship between assimilation patterns and how the international segmentation of labor and the resulting class dynamics in each society of origin structure patterns of human capital acquisition and the likelihood of social mobility, particularly within the contexts of growing income inequalities within and between nations.

The class selectivity of my samples may contribute to the findings regarding alternating periods of settlement in which Puerto Ricans can afford to relocate in their attempts to contest their dislocating experiences. As such, a stable socio-economic status might be conducive to circular migration (and circular patterns of settlement) given that professional migrants can afford to take pay cuts upon resettlement, while others transfer to jobs within multinational corporations with minimal financial risks. The educational levels of this sample also suggest that return migration options are more available for migrants with advanced degrees, because their specialized knowledge assures them placement in tight labor markets, which also eases the process of resettlement. Considering that studies of Puerto Rican migration have associated poverty with circular patterns of migration,[3] these findings suggest that there are other underlying causes of migration at work for all groups. Similarly, migration may be a consequence of mainland poverty and racism rather than a cause.

As seen with some Puerto Ricans in this study, return migration did not always translate into upward mobility, in spite of their college degrees. This was especially the case for single mothers for whom occupational sex segregation and gender inequality on the island meant that the jobs most available to women paid less, a problem of critical importance to female heads of households. As such, while they had more social support on the island than on the mainland because most were not settled in ethnic communities, their chances for economic survival were better on the mainland. These women often had to choose between their family's economic well-being and their own emotional well-being. While there were divorced fathers in this sample, they were largely noncustodial fathers with more resources to provide for their children, and more freedom to pursue their individual goals. Moreover, although members of both samples had to make difficult choices in terms of how to combine economic considerations with emotional needs, single mothers had the most constraints. As class struggles be-

came more pronounced, and class injuries grew deeper, the process of readjustment to Puerto Rico became more taxing, opening the door to remigration, as seen with Rosana.

For others, Puerto Rico's location in the global segmented labor market
meant that migrants had to transfer to jobs in the United States to move
up professionally. U.S. affirmative action policies facilitate access to these
opportunities, particularly with regard to higher education, a require-
ment in attaining these positions. In all, the expectations of the professional transnational workforce called for mobility.

Those who are subject to mobility in the structure of global capitalism
have varying levels of power afforded to them depending on whether
they are the "servants of globalization," as the title of Rhacel Salazar Parreñas' book suggests, or the executives of globalization, as a few in my
samples were. It is unclear, however, how these power differentials affect
trajectories of assimilation. It is not just the increasing transnational linkages and the changing migration streams that call for the reformulation of
theories to better capture the experiences of contemporary immigrant incorporation; the global segmentation of the labor force, and the extent to
which different groups are subject to mobility and other expectations of
global capitalism calls for theoretical reformulations that take these power
differentials into account as well. Moreover, the race and ethnic backgrounds of these immigrant populations complicate our understandings
of these processes.

Recent reformulations of assimilation theories have taken into account
how racial hierarchies mediate immigrant outcomes, and how the post–
civil rights era in the United States has increased multiculturalism, thus
removing (at least theoretically) the nativist expectations regarding the assimilation of newcomers. In spite of this increasingly multicultural and
multiethnic context, and with the changing social constructions of racial
otherness permeating post–September 11 American society, one can understand how the assessments of Puerto Ricans themselves reveal that
these "declining expectations" are not necessarily the case. In this study,
the experiences of members of the Puerto Rican middle class are documented. This is a group that has U.S. citizenship; they are privileged
economically; and they are fully bilingual; yet many of their settlement
struggles involved experiences with prejudice, ethnocentrism, and xeno-
phobia, all revealing the persistence of racism in the United States. In spite
of structural integration regarding their citizenship status, their professional occupations, their middle-class incomes, their patterns of residential integration, and their acculturation into U.S. society in the form of fluent bilingualism, they still perceived themselves to be outside of the U.S.
mainstream, perceptions that are reinforced through prejudicial interactions with their fellow Americans. If these are the experiences of the
"privileged," then it is not difficult to imagine how populations who are

more vulnerable to inequities and who are not "as integrated" as middle-class Puerto Ricans are experience U.S. settlement. In short, in spite of meeting many of the expectations regarding assimilation and accultura-tion, Puerto Ricans were still marginalized and experienced racially hos-tile environments in the mainland. Given that I collected these data before September 11, 2001, it is unclear how Puerto Ricans' experiences with in-corporation might have changed.

U.S. citizenship, structural integration, and acculturation do not auto-matically translate into membership in a society. Puerto Ricans' feelings of membership into mainland communities are fractured by the ethnoracist contexts that often receive them. While these experiences may not be dra-matically different from immigrants of the past,[4] given the advances in technology, communications, and travel, the patterns of frequent mobility that it engenders is worthy of further exploration. Although we know that some immigrant groups of the early twentieth century repatriated to their countries of origin, we must consider that these repatriations occurred *be-fore* the civil rights era. Given the overwhelming patterns of circulation among Puerto Ricans, and the fact that almost half of the population now resides in the mainland, questions remain regarding how different seg-ments of the Puerto Rican population integrate into the U.S. social fabric. Comparative studies are particularly needed to ascertain whether and to what extent patterns of U.S. incorporation are bimodal and how ethnoracial constructions mediate these patterns. Moreover, within the pattern of mi-nority group mobility documented in this book, will patterns of racial seg-regation envelop the Puerto Rican middle class, as they have the black mid-dle class?[5] Or will integration patterns splice along class and racial lines?

At a broader level, western standards of success for the middle classes are geared toward status attainment; for many, the fulfillment of these goals ingrained in them through western socialization are contingent upon mi-gration. The dominant views on assimilation, however, have argued that acculturation is necessary for assimilation to come about. The success of some immigrants groups, for example, that of Cubans in Miami challenged this assumption, indicating that a group can assimilate without acculturat-ing.[6] Given the modes of entry of professional immigrants, the Puerto Ri-cans documented in this book illustrate patterns of selective acculturation: they embrace U.S. patterns of living and U.S. standards of success, but they also strive to nurture their ethnocultural roots and kinship ties across bor-ders. Given that they do not necessarily have at their disposal ethnic com-munities to nurture ethnic retention, maintaining transnational ties embod-ies how they merge elements of both societies into their identities.

Navigating through the web of global capitalism, Puerto Ricans, like many other immigrants, struggle to resist feelings of alienation in their lives that can result from settling in societies that are deeply entrenched with racism. As such, immigrants and even native minorities cling to their constructed identities and the social groups that they feel a part of (e.g., family and community) in efforts to restore logic to illogical realities. They also desire, however, to be in places that genuinely receive them and in which they feel comfortable. If these places are not available on the mainland, then the bridges leading back to Puerto Rico are crossed again. Thus, Puerto Ricans, like other labor and professional migrants, engage in negotiations in which they not only weigh what their hearts and minds tell them, but try to integrate them into lives that can be lived locally.

Assimilation theories, even the recent reformulations, do not acknowledge the power of emotions in structuring incorporation outcomes, revealing the male-centric approaches that have traditionally guided the formulation of these perspectives. Issues that have traditionally been associated with women, such as families, emotions, and culture, however, are often the basis for migration decisions and strategies of incorporation. By digging into the unperceived realities that are often missed in surface level investigations of motivations, these approaches enhance our understandings of the complexities of the transnational struggles of individuals and families "in motion," and migrants' own creative strategies used to combat these struggles.

In conclusion, employing alternative approaches to the study of international migration has facilitated the recognition that as part of the unperceived realities migrants experience, there are a large number of people who in the course of pursuing goals that will enable their survival and enhance the quality of their lives, have become attached to two places. And there are some who, in the process of navigating through the social and cultural spaces of both societies, have trouble integrating into either. As a result, there are people who are caught between two worlds; in the process of trying to meet their emotional needs, insure their economic survival, and preserve culturally constructed meanings, they experience barriers to full incorporation, and have to negotiate which goals, which priorities, to sacrifice. Given this, migration decisions are constantly open to renegotiation, as the object of mobility is to achieve a balance in those elements of social life that bring about personal fulfillment.

NOTES

1. Levitt 2001.
2. Levitt and Glick Schiller 2003.
3. Falcón and Gurak 1994.
4. Foner 2002.
5. Massey and Denton 1993; Patillo-McCoy 2000.
6. Stepick et al. 2003.

References

Alba, Richard and Victor Nee. "Rethinking Assimilation Theory for a New Era of Immigration." *International Migration Review* 31, 4(120) (Winter 1997): 826–74.

Alicea, Marixsa. "'A Chambered Nautilus': The Contradictory Nature of Puerto Rican Women's Role in the Social Construction of a Transnational Community." *Gender & Society* 11, 5 (1997): 597–626.

———. "Cuandro nosotros vivíamos: Stories of Displacement and Settlement in Puerto Chicago." CENTRO 13, 2 (2001): 167–95.

Anderson, Elijah. *Code of the Street: Decency, Violence, and the Moral Life of the Inner City*. New York: Norton, 1999.

Aranda, Elizabeth. "Global Care Work and Gendered Constraints: The Case of Puerto Rican Transmigrants." *Gender & Society* 17, 4 (August 2003): 609–26.

Aranda, Elizabeth, and Guillermo Rebollo-Gil. "Ethnoracism and the 'Sandwiched' Minorities." *American Behavioral Scientist* 47, 7 (March 2004): 910–27.

Ashton, Guy T. "The Return and Re-Return of Long-Term Puerto Rican Migrants: A Selective Rural-Urban Sample." *Revista/Review Interamericana* 10, 1 (1980): 27–45.

Badgett, M.V. Lee, and Nancy Folbre. "Assigning Care: Gender Norms and Economic Outcomes." *International Labour Review* 138, 3 (1999): 311–26.

Bailey, Adrian J., and Mark Ellis. "Going Home: The Migration of Puerto Rican-Born Women from the United States to Puerto Rico." *Professional Geographer* 45, 2 (1993): 148–58.

Basch, Linda, Nina Glick Schiller, and Cristina Blanc-Szanton. *Nations Unbound: Transnational Projects, Postcolonial Predicaments, and Deterritorialized Nation-States*. Langhorne, PA: Gordon and Breach, 1994.

Bonilla, Frank, and Ricardo Campos. *A Wealth of Poor: Puerto Ricans in the New Economic Order. Daedalus* 110 (1981): 133–76.

Bonilla, Frank, and Héctor Colón Jordan. "'Mamá, borinquen me llama!' Puerto Rican Return Migration in the 70s." *Migration Today* 7, 2 (1979): 1–6.

177

Bonilla-Silva, Eduardo. "This is a White Country": The Racial Ideology of the Western Nations of the World-System." *Sociological Inquiry* 70, 2 (2000): 188–214.

Bourdieu, Pierre, and Loic Wacquant. *An Invitation to Reflexive Sociology*. Chicago: University of Chicago Press, 1992.

Cabán, Pedro. "Redefining Puerto Rico's Political Status." Pp. 19–40 in Edwin Meléndez and Edgardo Meléndez (eds.), *Colonial Dilemma: Critical Perspectives on Contemporary Puerto Rico*. Boston: South End Press, 1993.

Canabal, María E., and Jose A. Quiles. "Acculturation and Socio-economic Factors as Determinants of Depression among Puerto Ricans in the United States." *Social Behavior and Personality* 23, 3 (1995): 235–48.

Cancian, Francesca, and Stacey Oliker. *Caring and Gender*. Thousand Oaks, CA: Pine Forge Press, 2000.

Centro de Estudios Puertorriqueños, Hunter College. *Labor Migration Under Capitalism: The Puerto Rican Experience*. New York: Monthly Review, 1979.

Cervantes, R.C., V. N. Salgado de Snyder, and A. M. Padilla. "Post Traumatic Stress Disorder among Immigrants from Central America and Mexico." *Hospital and Community Psychiatry* 40 (1989): 615–19.

Chavez, Leo R. *Shadowed Lives: Undocumented Immigrants in American Society*. Orlando, FL: Harcourt Brace, 1992.

Chávez, Linda. *Out of the Barrio: Toward a New Politics of Hispanic Assimilation*. New York: Basic Books, 1991.

Collins, Randall. "Social Movements and the Focus of Emotional Attention," in (eds) Jeff Goodwin, James M. Jasper, and Francesca Polleta. *Passionate Politics: Emotions and Social Movements*. Chicago: University of Chicago Press. Pp. 27–44.

Conway, Dennis, Mark Ellis, and Naragandat Shiwdhan. "Caribbean International Circulation: Are Puerto Rican Women Tied-Circulators?" Geoforum 21, 1 (1990): 51–66.

Dávila, Arlene. *Sponsored Identities: Cultural Politics in Puerto Rico*. Philadelphia: Temple University Press, 1997.

———. *Barrio Dreams: Puerto Ricans, Latinos, and the Neoliberal City*. Berkeley: University of California Press, 2004.

Díaz-Quiñones, Arcadio. *La memoria rota: Ensayos sobre cultura y política*. San Juan, P.R.: Ediciones Huracán, 1993.

Dietz, James. *Economic History of Puerto Rico*. New Jersey: Princeton University Press, 1986.

———. "Migration and International Corporations: The Puerto Rican Model of Development." Pp. 153–70 in Carlos Torre, Hugo Rodríguez-Vecchini, and William Burgos (eds.), *The Commuter Nation: Perspectives on Puerto Rican Migration*. Río Piedras, P.R.: Editorial de la Universidad de Puerto Rico, 1994.

Dohan, Daniel. *The Price of Poverty: Money, Work, and Culture in the Mexican-American Barrio*. Berkeley: University of California Press, 2003.

Duany, Jorge. "Common Threads or Disparate Agendas? Research Trends on Migration from and to Puerto Rico." *Centro* 7, 1 (1994–1995): 60–77.

———. *The Puerto Rican Nation on the Move: Identities on the Island and in the United States*. Durham: University of North Carolina Press, 2002.

———. "Nation, Migration, Identity: The Case of Puerto Ricans." *Latino Studies* 1 (2003): 424–44.

————. "Puerto Rico: Between the Nation and the Diaspora—Migration to and from Puerto Rico." Pp. 177–96 in Maura Toro-Morn and Marixsa Alicea (eds.), *Migration and Immigration: A Global View*. Westport, CT: Greenwood, 2004.

Edin, Kathryn and Maria Kefala. *Promises I can Keep: Why Poor Women put Motherhood before Marriage*. Berkeley: California University Press, 2005.

Ellis, Carolyn, and Michael G. Flaherty. "An Agenda for the Interpretation of Lived Experience." Pp. 1–16 in Carolyn Ellis and Michael Flaherty (eds.), *Investigating Subjectivity: Research on Lived Experience*. Newbury Park: Sage Publications, 1992.

Ellis, Mark, Dennis Conway, and Adrian J. Bailey. "The Circular Migration of Puerto Rican Women: Towards a Gendered Explanation." *International Migration* 34, 1 (1996): 31–64.

Enchautegui, María E. *Subsequent Moves and the Dynamics of the Migration Decision: The Case of Return Migration to Puerto Rico*. Ann Arbor: Population Studies Center, University of Michigan, 1991.

Faist, Thomas. *The Volume and Dynamics of International Migration and Transnational Social Spaces*. Oxford University Press: U.S.A, 2000.

Falcón, Luis, and Douglas Gurak. "Poverty, Migration, and the Underclass." *Latino Studies Journal* 5, 2 (1994): 77–95.

Foner, Nancy. *From Ellis Island to JFK: New York's Two Great Waves of Immigration*. New Haven, CT: Yale University Press, 2002.

Gans, Herbert J. "Filling in Some Holes: Six Areas of Needed Immigration Research." *American Behavioral Scientist* 42, 9 (1999): 1302–13.

Georas, Chloé S. *Rediviva: Lost in Trance.lations*. San Juan, P.R.: Isla Negras Editores, 2004.

Glick Schiller, Nina, Linda Basch, and Christina Szanton Blanc. "From Immigrant to Transmigrant: Theorizing Transnational Migration." Pp. 73–105 in Pries, Ludger (ed.), *Migration and Transnational Social Spaces*. Brookfield: Ashgate, 1999.

González, Juan. *Harvest of Empire: A History of Latinos in America*. New York: Penguin, 2000.

Gould, Deborah B. "Passionate Political Processes: Bringing Emotions Back into the Study of Social Movements." Pp. 155–76 in Jeff Goodwin and James M. Jasper (eds.), *Rethinking Social Movements: Structure, Meaning, and Emotion*. Lanham, MD: Rowman & Littlefield, 2004.

Granovetter, Mark. "Economic Action and Social Structure: The Problem of Embeddedness." *American Journal of Sociology* 91, 2 (November 1985): 481–510.

Grasmuck, Sherri, and Patricia Pessar. *Between Two Islands: Dominican International Migration*. Berkeley: University of California Press, 1991.

Grosfoguel, Ramón. "Colonial Caribbean Migrations to France, the Netherlands, Great Britain, and the United States." *Ethnic and Racial Studies* 20, 3 (1997): 594–612.

————. "Puerto Ricans in the USA: A Comparative Approach." *Journal of Ethnic and Migration Studies* 25, 2 (April 1999): 233–49.

————. *Colonial Subjects: Puerto Ricans in a Global Perspective*. Berkeley: University of California Press, 2003.

Grosfoguel, Ramón, and Chloé S. Georas."'Coloniality of Power' and Racial Dynamics: Notes toward a Reinterpretation of Latino Caribbeans in New York City." *Identities: Global Studies in Culture and Power* 7, 1 (2000): 85–125.

Guarnizo, Luis. "The Economics of Transnational Living." *International Migration Review* 37, 3 (Fall 2003): 666–99.

Guarnizo, Luis Eduardo, Alejandro Portes, and William Haller. "Assimilation and Transnationalism: Determinants of Transnational Political Action among Contemporary Migrants." *American Journal of Sociology* 108, 6 (May 2003): 1211–48.

Gubrium, Jaber F., and James A. Holstein. *The New Language of Qualitative Method.* New York: Oxford University Press, 1997.

Hacker, Andrew. *Two Nations: Black and White, Separate, Hostile, Unequal.* New York: Ballantine Books, 1995.

Hamilton, Nora, and Norma Stoltz Chinchilla. *Seeking Community in a Global City: Guatemalans and Salvadorans in Los Angeles.* Philadelphia, PA: Temple University Press, 2001.

Hernández Álvarez, José. *Return Migration to Puerto Rico.* Berkeley: Institute for International Studies, University of California, 1967.

Hernández Cruz, Juan. "Migración de retorno o circulación de obreros boricuas?" *Revista de Ciencias Sociales* 24, 1–2 (1985): 81–112.

Hidalgo, Nitza M. "A Layering of Family and Friends: Four Puerto Rican Families' Meaning of Community." *Education and Urban Society* 30, 1 (1997): 20–40.

Hochschild, Arlie. "The Nanny Chain: Mothers Minding other Mothers' Children." *American Prospect* 11, 4 (3 January 2000): 32–36.

Hondagneu-Sotelo, Pierrette. *Gendered Transitions: Mexican Experiences of Immigration.* Berkeley: University of California Press, 1994.

Hondagneu-Sotelo, Pierrette. *Doméstica: Immigrant Workers Cleaning and Caring in the Shadows of Affluence.* Berkeley: University of California Press, 2001.

Hondagneu-Sotelo, Pierrette, and Ernestine Avila. "I'm Here, but I'm There: The Meanings of Latina Transnational Motherhood." *Gender & Society* 11 (October 1997): 548–71.

Jasper, James M. "The Emotions of Protest" (from "The Emotions of Protest"). Pp. 153–62 in Jeff Goodwin and James M. Jasper (eds.), *The Social Movements Reader: Cases and Concepts.* Oxford: Blackwell Publishing, 2003.

Kibria, Nazli. "Of Blood, Belonging, and Homeland Trips: Transnationalism and Identity among Second-Generation Chinese and Korean Americans." Pp. 295–311 in Peggy Levitt and Mary Waters (eds.), *The Changing Face of Home: The Transnational Lives of the Second Generation.* New York: Russell Sage Foundation, 2002.

———. *Becoming Asian American: Second-Generation Chinese and Korean American Identities.* Baltimore: The Johns Hopkins University Press, 2003.

Kivisto, Peter. "Theorizing Transnational Immigration: A Critical Review of Current Efforts." *Ethnic and Racial Studies* 24, 4 (July 2001): 549–77.

———. "Social Spaces, Transnational Immigrant Communities, and the Politics of Incorporation." *Ethnicities* 3, 1 (2003): 5–28.

Krivo, Lauren J., and Ruth D. Peterson. "Extremely Disadvantaged Neighborhoods and Urban Crime." *Social Forces* 75, 2 (1996): 619–48.

Levitt, Peggy. *Transnational Villagers.* Berkeley: University of California Press, 2001.

———. "The Ties that Change: Relations to the Ancestral Home over the Life Cycle." Pp. 123–44 in Peggy Levitt and Mary Waters (eds.), *The Changing Face of*

Home: The Transnational Lives of the Second Generation. New York: Russell Sage Foundation, 2002.

———. "Salsa and Ketchup: Transnational Migrants Straddle Two Worlds." *Contexts* 3, 2 (Spring 2004): 20–26.

Levitt, Peggy, and Nina Glick Schiller. "Transnational Perspectives on Migration: Conceptualizing Simultaneity." Princeton University Center for Migration and Development, working paper 3–09J, 2003.

Levitt, Peggy, and Mary Waters. *The Changing Face of Home: The Transnational Lives of the Second Generation.* New York: Russell Sage Foundation, 2002.

Logan, John R., and Brian J. Stults. "Racial Differences in Exposure to Crime: The City and Suburbs of Cleveland in 1990." *Criminology* 37, 2 (1999): 251–76.

Mahler, Sarah J. "Bringing Gender to a Transnational Focus: Theoretical and Empirical Ideas." Unpublished manuscript, University of Vermont, Department of Anthropology, 1996.

———. "Theoretical and Empirical Contributions Toward a Research Agenda for Transnationalism." *Comparative Urban and Community Research* 6 (1998): 64–100.

Martínez, Elizabeth. "Beyond Black/White: The Racisms of Our Time." Pp. 466–77 in Richard Delgado and Jean Stefancic (eds.), The Latino/a Condition: A Critical Reader. New York: New York University Press, 1998.

Massey, Douglas, Joaquin Arango, Graeme Hugo, Ali Kouaouci, Adela Pellegrino, and J. Edward Taylor. "Theories of International Migration: A Review and Appraisal." *Population and Development Review* 20 (1993): 699–752.

———. *Worlds in Motion: Understanding International Migration at the End of the Millennium.* New York: Oxford University Press, 1999.

Massey, Doug, and Nancy Denton. *American Apartheid: Segregation and the Making of the Underclass.* Cambridge, MA: Harvard University Press, 1993.

Massey, Doug, and Kristin Espinosa. "What's Driving Mexico-U.S. Migration? A Theoretical, Empirical, and Policy Analysis." *American Journal of Sociology* 102, 4 (1997): 939–99.

Meléndez, Edwin. "Puerto Rican Migration and Occupational Selectivity, 1982–1988." *International Migration Review* 28, 1 (1994): 49–67.

———. "Changes in the Characteristics of Puerto Rican Migrants to the United States." Pp. 34–57 in Luis Falcón and Edwin Meléndez (eds.), *Recasting Poverty.* Philadelphia: Temple University Press, 2001.

Menjívar, Cecilia. *Fragmented Ties: Salvadoran Immigrant Networks in America.* Berkeley: University of California Press, 2000.

Mulero, Leonor. "Desigual para la mujer la lucha profesional." *El Nuevo Día,* 28 November 1990.

Navarro, Mireya. "Puerto Rican Presence Wanes in New York." *The New York Times,* 28 February 2000.

National Center for Education Statistics, U.S. Department of Education. http://nces.ed.gov/globallocator/.

Nee, Victor, and Jimy Sanders. "Understanding the Diversity of Immigrant Incorporation: A Forms-of-Capital Model." *Ethnic and Racial Studies* 24, 3 (May 2001): 386–411.

Oliver, Melvin L., and Thomas M. Shapiro. *Black Wealth, White Wealth: A New Perspective on Racial Inequality.* New York: Routledge, 1997.

Ortiz, Vilma. "Circular Migration and Employment among Puerto Rican Women." *Latino Studies Journal* 4, 2 (1994): 56–70.

——. "Migration and Marriage among Puerto Rican Women." *International Migration Review* 30, 2 (1996): 460–84.

Parreñas, Rhacel Salazar. *Servants of Globalization: Women, Migration and Domestic Work*. Stanford: Stanford University Press, 2001.

Pattillo-McCoy, Mary. *Black Picket Fences: Privilege and Peril Among the Black Middle Class*. Chicago: The University of Chicago Press, 2000.

Pedraza, Silvia. "Assimilation or Diasporic Citizenship?" *Contemporary Sociology* 28, 4 (July 1999): 377–81.

——. *The Contribution of Latino Studies to Social Science Research on Immigration*. JSRI Occasional Paper No. 36. Latino Studies Series. 1998. http://www.jsri.msu .edu/RandS/research/ops/.

Perea, Juan. "The Black/White Binary Paradigm of Race." Pp. 359–68 in Richard Delgado and Jean Stefancic (eds.), *The Latino/a Condition: A Critical Reader*. New York: New York University Press, 1998.

Pérez, Gina. *The Near Northwest Side Story*. Berkeley: University of California Press, 2004.

Pérez-Herranz, Carmen A. "Our Two Full-Time Jobs: Women Garment Workers Balance Factory and Domestic Demands in Puerto Rico." Pp. 139–60 in Altagracia Ortiz (ed.), *Puerto Rican Women and Work: Bridges in Transnational Labor*. Philadelphia, PA: Temple University Press, 1996.

Portes, Alejandro, Luis E. Guarnizo, and Patricia Landolt. "The Study of Transnationalism: Pitfalls and Promise of an Emergent Research Field." *Ethnic and Racial Studies* 22, 2 (March 1999): 217–37.

Portes, Alejandro, and Leif Jensen. "The Enclave and the Entrants: Patterns of Ethnic Enterprise in Miami before and after Mariel." *American Sociological Review* 54, 6 (December 1989): 929–49.

Portes, Alejandro, and Ruben Rumbaut. *Immigrant America: A Portrait*. Berkeley: University of California Press, 1996.

——. *Legacies: The Story of the Immigrant Second Generation*. Berkeley: University of California Press, 2001.

Portes, Alejandro, and Julia Sensenbrenner. "Embeddedness and Immigration: Notes on the Social Determinants of Economic Action." *American Journal of Sociology* 98 (1993): 1320–50.

Portes, Alejandro, and Alex Stepick. *City on the Edge: The Transformation of Miami*. Berkeley: University of California Press, 1993.

Portes, Alejandro, and Min Zhou. "The New Second Generation: Segmented Assimilation and Its Variants." *The Annals of the American Academy of Political and Social Sciences* 530 (1993): 74–96.

Ríos, Palmira. "Export-Oriented Industrialization and the Demand for Female Labor: Puerto Rican Women in the Manufacturing Sector, 1952–1980." Pp. 89–102 in Edwin Meléndez and Edgardo Meléndez (eds.), *Colonial Dilemma: Critical Perspectives on Contemporary Puerto Rico*. Boston: South End Press, 1993.

Rivera-Batiz, Francisco, and Carlos E. Santiago. *Puerto Ricans in the United States: A Changing Reality*. Washington, D.C.: The National Puerto Rican Coalition, Inc., 1994.

———. *Island Paradox: Puerto Rico in the 1990s.* New York: Russell Sage Foundation, 1996.

Rodríguez, Clara. *Puerto Ricans: Born in the U.S.A.* Boulder, CO: Westview Press, 1991.

———. "Puerto Rican Circular Migration Revisited." *Latino Studies Journal* 4, 2 (1993): 93–113.

———. *Changing Race: Latinos, the Census, and the History of Ethnicity in the United States.* New York: New York University Press, 2000.

Rodríguez Vecchini, Hugo. "Foreword: Back and Forth." Pp. 29–102 in Carlos Torre, Hugo Rodríguez-Vecchini, and William Burgos (eds.), *The Commuter Nation.* Río Piedras: Editorial de la Universidad de Puerto Rico, 1994.

Rothenberg, Paula. *White Privilege: Essential Readings on the Other Side of Racism.* Second ed. New York: Worth Publishers, 2005.

Rumbaut, Rubén. "Assimilation and Its Discontents: Ironies and Paradoxes." Pp. 172–95 in Charles Hirschman, P. Kasinitiz, and Josh DeWind (eds.), *The Handbook of International Migration: The American Experience.* New York: Russell Sage Foundation, 1999.

Sabogal, Elena. "Viviendo en la sombra: The Immigration of Peruvian Professionals to South Florida." *Latino Studies* 3 (2005): 113–31.

Sandoval Sánchez, Alberto. "Puerto Rican Identity Up in the Air: Air Migration, Its Cultural Representations, and Me 'Cruzando el Charco.'" Pp. 189–208 in Frances Negron-Muntaner and Ramon Grosfoguel (eds.), *Puerto Rican Jam: Rethinking Colonialism and Nationalism.* Minnesota: University of Minnesota Press, 1997.

Sassen, Saskia. *Globalization and Its Discontents.* New York: New Press, 1998.

Seccombe, Karen. *"So You Think I Drive a Cadillac?" Welfare Recipients' Perspectives on the System and Its Reform.* Boston: Allyn & Bacon, 1999.

Smith, Robert C. "Life Course, Generation, and Social Location as Factors Shaping Second-Generation Transnational Life." Pp. 145–67 in Peggy Levitt and Mary Waters (eds.), *The Changing Face of Home: The Transnational Lives of the Second Generation.* New York: Russell Sage Foundation, 2002.

———. *Mexican New York: Transnational Lives of New Immigrants.* Berkeley: University of California Press, 2005.

Smith, Michael Peter, and Luis Guarnizo. *Transnationalism from Below.* New Brunswick, NJ: Transaction Publishers, 1998.

Sorensen, Nina, and Karen Fog Olwig. *Work and Migration: Life and Livelihoods in a Globalizing World.* New York: Routledge, 2001.

Stepick, Alex, Guillermo Grenier, Max Castro, and Marvin Dunn. *This Land is Our Land: Immigrants and Power in Miami.* Berkeley: University of California Press, 2003.

Tienda, Marta. "Puerto Ricans and the Underclass Debate." *Annals of the American Academy of Political and Social Science* 501 (1989): 105–19.

Toro-Morn, Maura I. and Marixsa Alicea (eds). *Migration and Immigration: A Global View.* Westport, CT: Greenwood Press, 2004.

Torre, Carlos, Hugo Rodríguez-Vecchini, and William Burgos. *The Commuter Nation: Perspectives on Puerto Rican Migration.* Río Piedras, P.R.: Editorial de la Universidad de Puerto Rico, 1994.

Torruellas, Rosa M., Rina Benmayor, and Ana Juarbe. "Negotiating Gender, Work, and Welfare: *Familia* as Productive Labor among Puerto Rican Women in New York City." Pp. 184–208 in Altagracia Ortiz (ed.), *Puerto Rican Women and Work: Bridges in Transnational Labor*. Philadelphia, PA: Temple University Press, 1996.

Trías Monge, José. *Puerto Rico: The Trials of the Oldest Colony in the World*. New Haven, CT: Yale University Press, 1997.

Urciuoli, Bonnie. *Exposing Prejudice: Puerto Ricans Experiences of Language, Race, and Class*. Boulder, CO: Westview Press, 1996.

U.S. Census Bureau. American Community Survey, 2004. American Fact Finder. www.census.gov.

U.S. Census Bureau. Census 2000 Special Tabulation, PHC-T-22. August 6, 2003.

U.S. Census Bureau. Census 2000 Summary File 1(SF 1) 100 Percent Data. American Fact Finder, www.census.gov.

U.S. Census Bureau. Census 2000 Summary File 2 (SF2) 100-Percent Data. American Fact Finder. www.census.gov.

U.S. Census Bureau. Census 2000 Summary File 3 (SF3), Sample Data. American Fact Finder, www.census.gov.

U.S. Census Bureau. Census 2000 Summary File 4 (SF4) Sample Data. American Fact Finder. www.census.gov.

Vega, W. A., G. J. Warheit, and K. Meinhardt. "Mental Health Issues in the Hispanic Community: The Prevalence of Psychological Distress." Pp. 30–47 in W. A. Vega and M. R. Miranda (eds.), *Stress and Hispanic Mental Health: Relating Research to Service Delivery*. Rockville, MD: U.S. Department of Health and Human Services, ADAMHA: 30–47, 1985.

Vélez-Ibáñez, Carlos, and Anna Sampaio. *Transnational Latina/o Communities: Politics, Processes, and Cultures*. Lanham, MD: Rowman & Littlefield, 2002.

Waters, Mary. *Black Identities: West Indian Immigrant Dreams and American Realities*. Cambridge, MA: Harvard University Press, 1999.

West, Candace, and Sarah Fenstermaker. "Power, Inequality, and the Accomplishment of Gender: An Ethnomethodological View." Pp. 151–74 in Paula England (ed.), *Theory on Gender/Feminism on Theory*. New York: Aldine, 1993.

West, Candace, and Sarah Fenstermaker. "Doing Difference." *Race, Class, and Gender: Common Bonds, Different Voices*. Thousand Oaks, CA: Sage Publications, 1996.

Wolf, Diane L. "Family Secrets: "Transnational Struggles among Children of Filipino Immigrants." *Sociological Perspectives* 40, 3 (1997): 457–82.

Wolf, Diane L. "There's No Place Like 'Home': Emotional Transnationalism and the Struggles of Second-Generation Filipinos." Pp. 255–94 in Peggy Levitt and Mary Waters (eds.), *The Changing Face of Home: The Transnational Lives of the Second Generation*. New York: Russell Sage Foundation, 2002.

Yancey, William, and Salvatore Saporito. "Racial and Economic Segregation and Educational Outcomes: One Tale–Two Cities." *Applied Behavioral Science Review* 3, 2 (1995): 105–25.

Zhou, Min. "Segmented Assimilation: Issues, Controversies, and Recent Research on the New Second Generation." Pp. 196–211 in Charles Hirschman, P. Kasinitiz, and Josh DeWind (eds.), *The Handbook of International Migration: The American Experience*. New York: Russell Sage Foundation, 1999.

stranded between Vanishing Islands

floating on an endless sea of receding coasts
my body is my only land
my hands navigate my skin
mapping the currents with my fingers
abysses fields mountains deserts oceans
so many oceans
echoes and cemeteries

trance . cultural orphan
with feet full of memories
of running barefoot along volcanic cliffs
lightning between my breasts
of sitting on hot asphalt in the rain
watching the steam and the fog exchanging masks
of hurting somewhere
deep outside
everywhere

my feet
the corridors to places i lived places i died places i never went places
i can't remember populated by voices of missing people some dead
some i killed some gone some i left behind some i never met
nor did i touch
nor did i caress
people i never traveled

native of nowhere
a ticket to the wind on my back
i swallow hurricanes
my skeleton floats wildly in my body of floods
earthquakes vibrate through my limbs
reconfiguring my desires

my body
a disaster zone of erotic wastes
a white wooden house lies wrecked
my father pulls the curtains

my body is my only land
a land without homes nor hosts
a land of humidity . edges and edges
a land of volcanoes submerged in quicksand
a land of roaming scars

my land
a body from which i remove the earth with each step
i travel that territory called myself
before i become extinct

once again

Chloé S. Georas, 2001

Index

About the Author

Elizabeth M. Aranda is assistant professor in the Department of Sociology at the University of Miami. She earned her Ph.D. in sociology from Temple University in 2001. Dr. Aranda has been published in *Gender & Society* and the *American Behavioral Scientist*. Her career research is on Latin American immigrants to South Florida, their patterns of incorporation, and the nature of race relations in multi-ethnic, global cities.